ONTARIO IN TRANSITION

JEAN-LOUIS ROY

ONTARIO IN TRANSITION
ACHIEVEMENTS AND CHALLENGES

JEAN-LOUIS ROY

Translated by Jonathan Burnham

mosaic press

LIBRARY AND ARCHIVES CANADA CATALOGUING IN PUBLICATION

Roy, Jean-Louis, 1941-
    Ontario in transition / Jean-Louis Roy.

Translation of: Chers voisins.
Includes bibliographical references.
Issued also in electronic format.
ISBN 978-0-88962-983-7

    1. Ontario--Economic conditions--21st century.
2. Ontario--Social conditions--21st century. 3. Ontario--
Politics and government--21st century. 4. Ontario--
Forecasting. I. Title.

FC3077.R69213 2013   971.3'05   C2013-900861-6

Pubished by Mosaic Press, Oakville, Ontario, Canada, 2013.
Published in French as Chers Voisins (Stanké), 2013.

MOSAIC PRESS, Publishers
Copyright © Jean-Louis Roy, 2013
English translation by Jonathan Burnham, © 2013
ISBN 978-0-88962-983-7
eBook 978-0-88962-984-4
Book and cover design by Eric Normann

We acknowledge the financial support of the Ontario Media Development Corporation (OMDC).

MOSAIC PRESS IN CANADA:	MOSAIC PRESS IN USA:
1252 Speers Road, Units 1 & 2	c/o Livingston, 40 Sonwil Dr,
Oakville, Ontario L6L 5N9	Cheektowaga, NY 14225
phone: (905) 825-2130	phone: (905) 825-2130

www.mosaic-press.com

TABLE OF CONTENTS

ACKNOWLEDGEMENTS

I reserve my first thanks to the many Ontarians who have so generously accepted to greet the unknown fact-finders that we were. An email or a short telephone conversation was often all it took for them to open their door to us, their files, their networks, their history and all the range of their fears and hopes for themselves, their community and their society. Herein, you will find them aware, enthusiastic, precise or poetic but always available, responsive and good-willed. Abundantly quoted in the following pages, their words are the backbone of this book, which is their work as much as mine.

Jonathan Burnham, Jérôme Lankoandé and Yves Ngorbo participated to varying degrees in the research, interviews and other tasks required in the exploration of a neighbouring society, one next to us but remote in many ways, similar and different at the same time, one that confirms and contracts what we thought we knew about it. They took part in the intellectual deconstruction and reconstruction of that society; they shared my doubts and unflinchingly dealt with my restlessness. I thank them for it all. Jonathan has been at my sides ever since the beginning of that project, from the first Ontarian trip to the long-lasting writing process. He also translated the original French version of that book. Two or three stars for his substantial contributions. Yves was the goldsmith of the minute last details, often the most critical. Well worth a star or two.

Our work benefitted from the contribution of the Government of Quebec's Secrétariat aux Affaires intergouvernementales canadiennes. We could also count on the hospitality of York University's Glendon College and even better, on the friendship, support and encouragements of its Principal, Kenneth McRoberts, its External Relations Director, Marie-Thérèse Chaput, and its Executive Director, Gilles Fortin. The team at Mosaic Press, and especially Howard Aster, have made this book with a good dose of professionalism and trust. Let them all be warmly thanked here as well.

Lastly, I would dedicate this book to Ben Marc and Bryan; for the unwavering support of the former and as an answer to the latter's questions, those of a curious child, which sometimes lightened long evenings of writing, and that specific one which inhabits me still: "Tell me why you are writing this book".

INTRODUCTION

AS FAR AS WE CAN SEE IN THE FUTURE, Ontario will be the most populated province in Canada. It will also be the most culturally diversified. If
the ongoing reconversion of its economy succeeds, it could regain its economic élan, and if its cultural momentum consolidates, it will be one of
the most attractive. Furthermore, if the forecasted migration flows enrich
Ontario's Asian population and if Toronto maintains its status of international financial centre, the metropolis could well become the Asian hub of
the northeastern part of the continent. China Investment Corp. preferred
it to all other North-American cities when it came to establishing its first
office abroad. The International Indian Film Academy has shown the same
preference when it decided to hold its awards ceremony, celebrating the
world's most important movie industry, in Toronto in 2011. The next years
will be decisive. Ontarians face a constellation of defiant challenges.

Indigenous as far as we can trace in its immemorial past, European
through its contemporary settlement, North American by geography and
economy, Ontario is also Asian by virtue of the origin of a significant
fragment of its population. This multi-headed genealogy makes Ontario
one of the most diverse societies in the world. In these days of identity
withdrawal, in Europe among others, it represents a true laboratory of the
diversity that constitutes the future of the Occident. Finally, the province
is one of Quebec's "most significant vis-à-vis",[1] its political partner for
almost 175 years.

---

1. Expression deemed to have been coined by Léon Dion, esteemed Laval University political scientist,
   as was shared by prof. Guy Laforest, his colleague at the same university.

A central province in the country, Ontario is at the heart of numerous Canadian, continental and transcontinental networks due to its history, economy and diversity. Due also to information and communications technologies, whose significance was figured out by a succession of Ontarian thinkers, a priceless contribution to contemporary civilization: Harold Innis, Eric Havelock, Marshall McLuhan and Derrick de Kerckhove.

All good reasons to be interested by the Ontarian society, by the projects it is undertaking and the aspirations it holds. But there are others, just as significant: the evolution of values in neighbouring societies, the respective weight of the country's regions, the coming components of the Canadian economy and the management of issues and challenges posed by the international community's geo economic and geopolitical mutations.

If the current configuration of wealth production in Canada, which fluctuates from one historical period to the other, presently, favours Western provinces, it would be risky to draw firm conclusions and proclaim that these provinces now control the country's agenda and will continue to do so in the long run. Admittedly, times are good for them, but Ontario's population today is 12.5 times that of Saskatchewan, 10 times that of Manitoba, 4 times that of Alberta and 3 times as important as that of British Columbia. Even when added up, the populations of these Western provinces remain well below that of the large central one. Incidentally, Ontario's 2010 gross domestic product (GDP) reached $641 billion, compared to Alberta's $238.

To discard the economic progress of Western provinces would be just as absurd as to view the country's economy solely on the basis of the exploitation and export of its natural resources. Such a view has to be exposed as what it is: a regression with disastrous economic, social and cultural consequences. All the country's strengths have to be harnessed, upgraded and developed with clout and boldness: its natural resources, including energy; the production of advanced industrial and technological goods; the development of a high quality service sector, including international financial services; the consolidation of an education economy as well as a culture and entertainment economy, whose market on the world scene keeps expanding. Lastly, the country has a host of respected resources at its disposal, dedicated to political, economic and financial governance, the restoration of which promises to be one of the great tasks of this century. These resources constitute a formidable pool for research, employment, global networking and for Canada's reputation. We think of Waterloo's Centre for International Governance Innovation (CIGI), for example.

The different interests of the country's regions have undeniably become more specific and more difficult to see converge. Hence the rise of regionalism or provincialism in Canada, from coast to coast, including in Ontario. Without diminishing their attachment to the country, Ontarians and their recent successive governments have become increasingly critical of the federal system's equity towards them. Critical also of a good number of policies from the central government, especially economic ones, which appear obsolescent in the new world order. From the managing of management dominating current federal politics, they propose to move towards managing innovation, creativity and productivity. Here's another reason to be interested in the province and wish it success.

What will happen to Canada in the foreseeable future will not take place without Ontario. Will not take place against Ontario. Even if no longer an imperial province, it will remain central in national affairs as far as we can see. It may even be that the coming mutations in our federation will be determined by Ontarian events. In that sense, an interest in the future of Ontarians is tantamount to an interest in the future of all Canadians and the political system that gathers them.

Three questions are at the origin of this book.

A DEMOGRAPHIC MUTATION

The first question concerns Ontarians themselves and the demographic mutation which, in just a few decades, has made of their society a condensed version of the world and of their diversity a core value, no longer mere objective data. Many spiritual, cultural and linguistic components of the human family cohabit in Ontario in apparent harmony. That diaspora society is one in which the idea and reality of majority wears off in favour of a singular entity made up of a constellation of other entities that were recently identified as minorities. The Ontarian society seems exempt from the heinous debates, recurring fears and violent crises that feed, in other parts of the world, a profound Occidental malaise towards the diversity that heretofore defines it.

The practice of diversity as it is known in Ontario is of great interest. Here you have a society that embodied multiculturalism during the last decades of the 20th century only to discover, at the dawn of the new millennium, that it somehow drove past it. Indeed, Ontario's diversity has little to do with that which drove Pierre-Elliott Trudeau to enter the policy of multiculturalism in the history and Constitution of Canada. It is of a different nature and density and as a consequence, it calls for a different policy. How it built and what is is it made out of?

AN ECONOMY UNDERGOING TRANSFORMATION

The second interrogation is about the economy of Ontario, that "outpost of a distant empire which became one of the largest sub-national economies of the world".[2] Still until very recently a fragment of the continental economy—the undeniable source of the province's growth, prosperity and its citizens' high living standards—the Ontarian economy must today become a fragment of the world economy. It is also affected by the "shifting wealth", to use OECD's expression.[3]

The new global competition has reached Ontario. It led it to launch a vast transformation of its economy at the turn of the millennium. That operation was enabled at first by many consecutive growth years allowing for significant investments in strategic sectors: human resources, research, innovation, infrastructure that are said "intelligent", green economy and culture. But that momentum was affected by the financial, economic and social crisis that broke out in 2008 and "kept Ontario's manufacturing core in the cold", according to the strong expression of Peter Hall, Chief Economist at Export Development Canada.[4]

That crisis has made the need for a transformation of Ontario's economy more urgent; resources, however, are scarcer. Hence a subtle mutation in Ontarian patriotism. Without severing ties with their old affection for Canada, Ontarians are discovering that the province's interest do not necessarily coincide with those of the Canadian whole. In that regard, Ontario is now joining movements, west and east of the country, without even speaking of Quebec, that try to give contents and sense to regional groupings of another nature.

At issue is the possibility or not to maintain Ontario's good economic fortune. A low level of public and private investment and a slowed growth would certainly have a direct impact on the demographic, economic and cultural momentum of the province. They would also affect the country's

2. GOVERNMENT OF ONTARIO. (2009) ; Ministry of Finance, 2009 *Ontario Budget.* Toronto: Queen's Printer for Ontario, p13.

3. OECD (2010) *Shifting Wealth Perspectives on Global Development,* Development Centre. Paris: OECD.

4. We take advantage of that quote to inform the reader that the occupations of the interviewees in this book are those which they held at the moment of our meeting.

political and fiscal architecture and the range of policies that are at the heart of the Canadian experience: equalization between the provinces and territories that make up the country, resource transfer in support of programmes defined as national, investment levels in infrastructure, research and development (R&D). Thus the interest in examining the stakes brought forth by the transformation of the Ontarian economy and the consequences of its success or failure. Some concern the private sector of the economy, others the public sectors. As it was established by the Commission on the Reform of Ontario's Public Services in 2012, three tasks face the Ontario government: the understanding of Ontario's economic challenges; the establishment of a balanced fiscal position that can be sustained over the long term and the sharpening of the efficiency of literally everything the government does. The commission insists. "Unless policy-makers act swiftly and bodily to prevent such an outcome, Ontario faces a series of deficit that would undermine the province's economic and social future."[5]

AN EFFERVESCENT CULTURE

Finally, our third question concerns culture and the Ontarian society. That issue has occupied a central place in the intellectual history of Ontario since the Second World War. It resulted in considerable initiatives such as the Kingston Conference in 1941. It gave rise to heavy debates such as that which followed the publication of *Survival,* Margaret Atwood's famous essay. In it, she writes about leaving the colonial posture behind, about going beyond the symbolic, cultural and intellectual structuring that comes from a regime that is of another place and time. About replacing it through the search for a space that will leave room for the Ontarians' own cultural expression and, more broadly, that of Anglo-Canadians, in order for their experience and description of the world to be known and shared.

What place does culture occupy in Ontarian society today? Has it become, in a few crucial decades, a major element of its development, cohesion and identity, as one could be led to believe after observing the considerable investments and accomplishments in the domain in the past 20 years? And if so, how are we to understand this shift? Some claim that it is due to the action of minority groups who, around the middle of the

---

5. COMMISSION ON THE REFORM OF ONTARIO'S PUBLIC SERVICES (2012) *Public services for Ontarians: A path to sustainability and excellence.* Department of Finance. Toronto: Government of Ontario. Queens Printer for Ontario.

last century, have vigorously wrestled with the question of the Anglophone society's cultural specificity. Others attribute it to the arrival of a great number of new citizens that bring with them all of the world's cultures. They argue that these arrivals contributed to the extension of the internal borders of Ontarian society, the enrichment of its imagination, the creation of numerous cultural activities as well as the production of far-reaching works of art. Lastly, that shift could be explained by the entrance in the field of the public authorities and the deployment of a significant political arsenal in support of culture. We shall go down all these explanatory avenues and seek to understand the part taken by the said public authorities, the parts as well of the private sector and civil society in what seems to be an important mutation.

ONTARIAN SOCIETY TODAY

This essay is dedicated to today's Ontarian society, to the citizens and communities that make it up, to the systems that structure and define it, to the perspectives that could affect its future in Canada, on the continent and in the world. Let us state what this essay is not.

It is not a history of Ontario, even though we will constantly draw from sequences of the province's long itinerary. Neither is it a comparative history with such or such society, no matter how close that society may be geographically or politically, and how historical partnerships have endured. We have however taken into consideration the influences, complementarities, alliances and other anchoring that link Ontario with its close neighbours as well as those that are a little further away. Finally, this essay does not belong to the literature dedicated to Canadian federalism. Of course, it is impossible to dismiss a century and a half of Ontario's participation in the Canadian federal system, whose capital is also an Ontarian city. It is difficult also to disregard all the theses and propositions that come from Ontario and evoke a different model and political system for Canada in the 21st century.

In these times of apprehension and hope, the Ontarian society has a need, as all Western societies do, to understand the outcome of recent decades: the exulting 1990s, confident in the major changes affecting the international community, as well as the decade that launched the new millennium and came to a close in the greatest of uncertainties.

One can add to the above inquiries the questioning of the Canadian model, a model bearing Pierre-Elliott Trudeau's signature, and its progressive replacement by another vision of the country, that of Stephen Harper.

Fiduciaries of the Canadian heritage and in charge, for a certain time, of its developments, these two princes draw opposite conclusions. The more Canada of Trudeau aimed at tightening the cohesion and unity of the country through so-called national policies and standards that illustrated and consolidated the mission of the central state. It has little to do with Harper's more Canada. Without giving up on the country's unity, the current Prime Minister sees it as an outcome of more autonomous components in a more decentralized federation and as a common space which values autonomous federated states and the sovereign initiative of individuals. This reshaping of the country is asymmetric and federal bureaucrats must consequently review their copy and the provinces, including Ontario, must re-examine their positioning.

Then came the financial and economic crisis of 2008 and its follow-up, as spectacular and dramatic as the melting of the Northern glaciers. There is, in the Western part of the world, like a "before and after" that monumental crisis. Our Ontarian interlocutors continually refer to this moment of rupture as a call for a review of the country's fundamentals, those inventions of the late 19th century, to make them match the realities of the 21st.

What are the interests of Ontarians and of Ontario in these changing Canadian, continental and global conditions? In these uncertain times, how is the province to redeploy and diversify the levers that contributed to the its wealth, guaranteed high living standards to its citizens and participated in the construction of a society that ranks among the freest and most advanced in the world? How can Ontario, as well as other regions in the country, avoid a decline and degradation in living conditions? Such is the main question we retain at the completion of the material and immaterial trip we undertook in the most important province of the Canadian federation.

Ontarians face these questions at a time when nothing they acquired in the past can be taken for granted. Not the international system, in its triple political, economic and security dimension, set up after the Second World War to guarantee international governance; nor the solidity of the American economy, which made their prosperity. Nor the strength of their economy and the historical arrangements in the distribution of public resources between the Canadian federal government and the provinces and territories.

This work tracks the ongoing debates, the hypotheses and propositions of Ontarians regarding these new situations, the outcomes of which will have important consequences on their living conditions and those of all Canadians.

Outcomes that will also impact the present federal political system and its obvious need for reconfiguration due to all the changes in the world.

We called upon a great number of Ontarians to voice their ideas. They were many in the cities and regions of the province to answer positively and agree to meet with us, welcome us warmly and share with us their experiences, their doubts and their hopes. These encounters were privileged moments of formidable dialogue with those dear neighbours and are the main sources of our work. Our sincere thanks to all those that fed that work and gave it its true dimension. Our best wishes as well for the successful accomplishment of their dreams and aspirations.

CHAPTER 1
THE ONTARIANS

MILLIONS OF MEN AND WOMEN FROM every part of the world came to settle in Ontario in the past two centuries. As depicted by the 900 petroglyphs on the teaching rocks discovered in 1954, near Peterborough, indigenous peoples were present on that land for millennia.[1] Diversity has always been a characteristic of the populations that occupied the territory of the province.

Two million in 1900, close to twelve a century later, Ontario's population could reach eighteen million in 2036 and twenty-two in 2050, that is, more than 50 per cent of the Canadian population according to available median projections.[2] That uninterrupted flow of immigrants constitutes the dominating fact of Ontario's history. Their arrivals, to be sure, but also the mutations they engendered. Those which, as of the 16th century, were caused by the import of European realities on a territory up until then owned and managed by the Aboriginal nations; European realities that provoked their descent into hell in Ontario as in the rest of the Americas. Those ongoing mutations, also, which irreversibly erase the preponderance of the descendants of Europeans to the benefit of a multiracial, multicultural and multilingual society made of men and women from all five continents.

That phenomenon is continental. In Canada, it is most intense in the province of Ontario. The argument that pits identity and immigration as antagonists and that is at the basis of restrictive policies in a num-

---

1. The archeological discoveries of the Barry's Bay site in the Madawaska Valley are witnesses of that presence 10,000 years ago. WRIGHT, J.V. (1981) *La préhistoire de l'Ontario,* Musée national de l'Homme. Montréal : Fides.

2. All the Canadian population data in this book, whether for the whole country or per province, as well as minority numbers, are from Statistics Canada.

ber of European countries, an argument so close to racism, is marginal there. People come from the world over—Nordic countries, Southern European ones, China—to understand the phenomenon and get a grasp on the management approach that makes it possible. They probably go back home disappointed with the explanations heard since the Ontarian diversity is so insoluble with the various available paradigms; its specificity so removed, for the moment, from any idea of political and institutional sedimentation.

"Post-multiculturalism, multiregional identity, bursting effervescence, flowering tolerance, normal set of human interaction". Such are the terms used by our first five witnesses to describe the new Ontarian society. They knew it when it was Anglo-Saxon, monolithic and white. What has it become, according to them?

DIVERSITY AS A COMMON LIVING SPACE

RAHUL BHARDWAJ

For a good number of observers, the Ontarian experience represents one of the fulfilled forms of multiculturalism. Highly risky situation and frightening ambush, according to some; superior form of civilization, think others. For Rahul Bhardwaj, first-generation immigrant and respected member of the new Ontarian leadership, diversity has become the foundation of the very identity of Ontarian society.

Brilliant lawyer converted as animator and manager of great public and private projects, the Toronto International Film Festival (TIFF) among them, he greets us at the headquarters of the Toronto Community Foundation, which he presides since 2007. This foundation is one of a great many Ontarian private charity institutions. They invest more than a billion dollars each year in social development, culture and the environment. This significant volume of activity from charitable institutions is testimony to the spirit and wealth of that society and its proximity, in that field, with American practices.[3]

> In the vast Western landscape, says Bhardwaj, Ontario's situation is almost unique insomuch that the diversity here is a component of the province's fabric and that it quickly imposed itself as THE dominant value. Diversity! Either it

---

3. MARTEL, F. (2006) *De la culture en Amérique*. Paris: Gallimard.

is a dominant value or it isn't. That choice is foundational;
every other debate sits at the margin of that one.

If it is a dominant value, diversity cannot be considered as an added piece to a pre-existing set of references. As a new paradigm would, it includes that set and transcends it. Our host's remarks open on a large debate regarding the policy of immigration and multiculturalism.

Must we review the current system? Must we set up a Royal Commission, as suggested by historian J. L. Granatstein, in the light of the "demographic earthquake" that will change the country in the coming decades "even more than it has over the last generation?"[4]

To answer in the affirmative is to open a sweeping debate on the philosophy and the policy of multiculturalism, and maybe discover that in the federation's most populous province, that which welcomes more than 50 per cent of all of the country's immigrants, these philosophy and policy are conceptually obsolete. So what other model could act as a substitute to multiculturalism and manage to guarantee full recognition to pluralism, a much more demanding concept that implies the acknowledgment of a difference in values and beliefs? "That word, multiculturalism, must be kept" Ratna Omidvar, the much-respected president of the Maytree Foundation, told us, "all the while knowing that we're living and building something else". Even though it endures in the discourse and in public policies, and despite the inspiration it fostered in its time, Pierre-Elliott Trudeau's vision of multiculturalism no longer corresponds to Ontarian society and Ontarians' practices with regard to the racial, cultural and linguistic pluralism that is now part of their world.

A new cultural space

In Ontario, diversity is the very essence of common life; it is quantitative and substantive. In that sense, it is not a fulfilled form of multiculturalism. It goes beyond it and reveals something else, a post-multiculturalism which does not accept the majority's will as the source of the various communities' status.

Diversity thus transcends this conception of a society composed of a majority and minorities. It opens on a new concentration of joint social practices, interethnic relations, intercultural experiences and ongoing shar-

---

4. GRANATSTEIN, J.L "How Do We Make Newcomers Into Canadians?" *Globe and Mail*, December 21, 2009

ing of the public space by fellow citizens that bear values and references that do not necessarily converge. The expression *reciprocal benevolence* came to me spontaneously during my conversations with representatives of various Ontarian communities. Hence the low level of tension stirred by the diversity in the province, a stark contrast with the debates, crises and regressive policies that can be observed in many countries today. Hence also the affirmation of pluralism from Ontarians that came from abroad. But belonging to diverse communities neither quells these new Ontarians' allegiances nor the networks to which they belong, including those which they share with fellow citizens from other parts of the world. We have gotten used to qualify that pluralism as Canada's *ethnocultural mosaic*. For Bhardwaj, that metaphor, just like the terms *tapestry* and *fruit salad*, are obsolete today.

His thinking is close to that of Alden E. Habacon, who suggests another vision of what's coming:[5]

> In the same way that the Internet has evolved into what is called Web 2.0 and now 3.0, Canadians have moved past the rigid paradigm of the ethno-cultural mosaic. Today's Canadians have an incredible level of cultural mobility; with a fluid and multiplied sense of identity, Canadians are able to navigate between a rich variety of cultural spaces. Replacing the mosaic model is the "schema." A schema, as in the root word for "schematic," is defined as "an internal representation of the world; an organization of concepts and actions that can be revised by new information about the world." It is a term conventionally used to describe the complex architecture of a circuit, and it is equally useful as a conceptual tool for understanding the complexity of today's Canadian identity.

Overwhelmed by such mutation, some see in it the failure of common citizenship and the necessity to restore the "values of the country", as shown by a 1993 Decima Research survey. Neil Bissoondath opens the essay which granted him so much opprobrium by reminding us of this wish for such impossible restoration.[6]

---

5. HABACON, A. E. (2009) "Vision de la dualité linguistique et de la diversité culturelle au Canada", in *Discours inaugural, Rapport final, Forum de discussion sur la dualité linguistique tenue à Vancouver le 24 novembre 2008*. Ottawa : Commissariat aux langues officielles du Canada. P.10.

6. BISSOONDATH, N. (1995) *Le marché aux illusions : la méprise du multiculturalisme*. Montréal: Boréal, p. 15.

Rahul Bhardwaj refers to the high level and continued growth of inter-marriage as an illustration of these joint social practices. Other evolutions uphold his conviction. The fact, for example, that a growing number of people from visible minorities hold leadership positions in the public sector of the Greater Toronto Area (GTA) and elsewhere in the province. These people account for close to a quarter of the workforce in public agencies, boards and commissions, according to a study led by the Diversity Institute of Ryerson University, compared to 4.1 per cent in private corporations.[7] In the private sector, 76.9 per cent of companies surveyed did not count even one visible minority on their board and 69.2 per cent of them saw an absence of minorities in high management functions.

The multiplication of festive events displaying that Ontarian diversity, the variety of works that are inspired by it—especially in literature, history and cinema—the need to adapt to it, as evidenced by the Stratford Festival's U-turn in that regard, tend to prove that the memory and presence of immigrants are no longer hidden or obscured, but that they emerge as integral components of Ontarian togetherness. Even if painful, that memory is part of what former Ontarian Premier John Robarts identified, in another context, as "a world made from a high number of worlds from the past". In what is probably an imprudent extrapolation, I scribble: "Toronto, crossbred city; Ontario, crossbred society".

The Ontarian society's DNA

For Rahul Bhardwaj, diversity is the "very DNA of the Ontarian society". It challenges all the "metanarratives" that explain now obsolete legitimacies; that of an Anglo-Saxon world, in the case of Ontario, and that, still dominant, of Canadian multiculturalism. This diversity brought about the dismissal of a certain romanticism, of an apologetic look that identified tolerance and mansuetude as fundamental categories of the Canadian experience, where the worst discriminations have nevertheless ravaged Indigenous Peoples and where more of that discrimination, in the first half of the 20th century, afflicted Black, Asian and Jewish and their communities. This diversity could also scramble, with time, some legal and constitutional rights that emerged in a cultural context that is now out-of-date. For the time being, many unknowns remain; some acquired positions, rules of the political game and constitutional standards being in the way of

---

7. RYERSON UNIVERSITY'S DIVERSITY INSTITUTE. (2010) *DiverseCity Counts: A Snapshot of Diverse Leadership in the GTA*. Toronto: Ryerson University's Diversity Institute.

the country's adjustment to what its most populated and diverse province has become.

Could Ontario's diversity eventually serve as a lever to introduce reviews that would reflect the country's substantial mutation and the evolution of society's values as it reconstructed after the Second World War. No one can say today what that new synthesis will be, but its necessity seems unquestionable. In his brilliant 1998 chronicles, *Vous m'intéressez*, Graham Frazer was already asking himself "if Ottawa could face the new identity challenge that the new Toronto represents".[8] Would he agree today to broaden his question to the whole of Ontario as it is and as it promises to be in the coming decades?

My interlocutor surprises me with an interrogation of his own: "What do you think of Jean-François Lyotard's report, 'The postmodern condition'?[9] We trade thoughts on the great liberal tradition of the West and its most current framings. Our conversation reminds me of another tradition. In the train bringing me back to Montreal, I read for an umpteenth time the famous September 2005 inaugural lecture by K. Natwar Singh, then India's Foreign Affairs Minister, at Brown University.[10]

> The roots that liberal democracy struck in India find some explanation in our tradition of social and religious pluralism. Unlike the West, where the separation of Church and State was a pre-requisite for secularism, its Indian manifestation appears to draw strength from an ethos of multiplicity and choice. The Indian intellectual tradition is an intensely individualistic one, as indeed are many schools of religious and philosophical thought. ... The advocates of democracy in India ... were careful not to fabricate an artificial majority culture in order to create a national identity. They were acutely conscious that in this vast land, everyone is a minority and the difference is only one of degree. The internal balance of a society composed of minorities is distinctly different from one where a dominant majority sets its terms vis-à-vis its minorities. In such a paradigm,

8. FRAZER, G. (2001) *Vous m'intéressez*. Montréal : Boréal, p. 167.

9. LYOTARD, J.F. (1979) *La condition postmoderne*. Paris : Les Éditions de Minuit.

10. NATWAR, S.K. (2005) "The Argument for India ". *The Inaugural India lecture*, The News Service. Rhode Island: Brown University, September 23, p.3.

tolerance as an attitude is not enough because it appears too grudging and meagre. A stronger embrace of diversity has to be the working principle and its wholehearted acceptance a virtual necessity. ... The truth is that our people, secure in their identities, are ready to accept differences and can be non-conformist in their own ways. Diversity has accentuated rather than diminished our nationhood.

I do not know if Rahul knows of this wonderful text and I impute to him no motives to transpose values and systems from one country to another. But his remarks and those of Natwar Singh definitely converge. Ontario is indeed becoming a society comprised of diverse communities whose equilibrium is and will be structurally different from that of a society comprised of a majority that defines the norms and rules that apply to minorities. The province has entered in a new phase of its history.

The maintenance of the ethnic character of the Ontario population and multiculturalism constitute the two precedent phases. The first of these phases has dominated a great part of the 20th century. In a speech to the House of Commons, Prime Minister Mackenzie King thus identified some of its elements:[11]

> The people of Canada do not wish, as a result of mass immigration, to make a fundamental alteration in the character of our population. Large-scale immigration from the orient would change the fundamental composition of the Canadian population.

The second of these phases, multiculturalism, has emerged in the 1970s and found its political and constitutional shapes in the last part of the previous century.

In Ontario's case, these two phases today appear outdated. The massive immigration "from the East" that was carried out and shows no sign of abetting, added to that from other regions of the world, has indeed altered the composition of Ontarian society. If the current projections translate into facts, diversity will keep on enriching and asserting itself. Between five and six million immigrants will add themselves to the Ontarian population from now until the middle of the century, a majority of them coming from

---

11. MACKENZIE KING, W. L. (1947) *Debates of House of Commons*. Ottawa: Parliament of Canada, May 1st, Session 1947, Vol. III, p.2646.

the *"East"*. It is in that sense that diversity is still up-and-coming and still awaiting its societal, institutional and political forms.

MADELINE ZINIAK

On the shores of the Great Lake that borders Toronto, Madeline Ziniak greets us in a recycled building, at the headquarters of one of the world's most important private, multiethnic and multilingual television stations: OMNI Television. Ziniak has been at work at OMNI for 15 years and is now its first National Vice President. In the Western societies' cultural offering, dominated by screens and supports of all kind, Omni Television remains a unique phenomenon: a private, multiethnic and multilingual television network operating and making profits on a fragmented and relatively limited market.

This statement reflects the marked attachment of Ontarians of different origins to an identity and a language that both predate those offered by their new citizenship. It also translates the little attention that Canadian media, private and public, reserve to the importance of communities, and to their presence, as part of their programming or their staff at any level. As is clearly demonstrated in the above-mentioned Diversity Institute 2010 study, that presence totals 4.8 per cent of big media board membership, 5.9 per cent of publishers and 3.6 per cent of senior executives.

Licensed in 1979, the station has since split in two complementary entities: OMNI.1 and Omni.2. The first, accessible to 90 per cent of the Ontarian population and via cable elsewhere in the country, saw its early viewers come from the European, Latino and Caribbean communities. The second, created in 2002, has developed an offer that aims at the Asian and African communities. Together, they produce more than 3,000 hours of programming each year, in 35 languages, including Cantonese and Mandarin, Hindi, Urdu, Bengali, Punjabi, Afghan, Somali and Swahili. Together, they reach over 40 "culturally diverse communities". Madeline Ziniak is evidently proud of her enterprise, which has nothing to do with these mediocre ethnic stations that abound in many North American cities.

> We are no longer that little lakeshore station. We were the first to opt for digital technologies and our equipment is now the envy of many broadcasters. It is really important to offer, as much as is possible, quality ethnic television ... We can get the best audience numbers in Ontario by showing a Bollywood movie on Saturday afternoon.

Madeline is the daughter of Sierhey Khmara Ziniak, famous immigrant, founder and editor of Toronto's Byelorussian Voice, founder and president of the Canadian Ethnic Journalist's, and Writers, Club which Madeline now chairs. She obviously has an intimate, personal and professional knowledge of diversity. Remaining far from the theoretical jabber, she chooses her words with care and rarely strays from the facts that marked diversity's upward trajectory. Members of the Task Force for Cultural Diversity on Television, which she co-chaired with former Federal Minister Beverley Oda, qualify her contribution as "crucial". They remember her pressing calls for diversity to be visible on the country's television screens, for "coloured TV to be more coloured", to use the formula of the Chinese Canadian Youth Against Racism.[12]

Ziniak describes with precision the transformations of Ontarian society, the difficulties of the journalists coming from abroad, yesterday and today still,[13] the social function of her television station. On a daily basis, OMNI shows to Ontarians of diverse origins, and in their language, professionals and specialists stemming from immigration and having a real knowledge of world events. It also shows creators, artists, filmmakers, writers, architects and researchers from these communities as well as their work. Lastly, it makes room for the apprehensions and successes, the interrogations and debates that mark the life of these diverse Ontarian communities.

> For the great number of people that don't know English
> well, or at all, that are not familiar with the laws of the
> land, including those that enshrine citizens' rights, we are
> a preferred source of information

Of regional identities

Although she doesn't reject it, Madeline is hesitant when it comes to endorsing the thesis of Rahul. She admits that experience of immigration in Ontario is without equivalent in the federation and evokes a "multiregional identity" that her network's productions and broadcasts have shown beyond question.

---

12. CHINESE CANADIAN NATIONAL COUNCIL. (2007) *Upping the Antiracism*. Toronto: Chinese Canadian National Council, p.6.

13. THE CANADIAN ETHNIC JOURNALISTS' AND WRITERS' CLUB. (1986) *Mosaic in Media I, Selected Works of Ethnic Journalists and Writers*. Toronto: The Canadian Ethnic Journalists' and Writers' Club. (2004) *Mosaic in Media II, An ethnic anthology of Writings by Members of the Canadian Ethnic Journalists' and Writers' Club*. Toronto: The Canadian Ethnic Journalists' and Writers' Club.

The clienteles are not the same from one region of the country to another. Our programming has evolved quite a lot in order to reflect that evidence. Ontario's viewers are by far the most significant. It distinguishes itself through its volume and diversity. The ethnic population in the GTA-Hamilton region is continually growing. In 2015, close to two-thirds of the population of that vast region will be of diverse ethnic origin.

It seems the OMNI network has a rosy future. I ask Madeline about the philosophy of that network.

Our clients are loyal due to the subtle balance between the attention to news in the countries of origin plus their impact on the communities here and the important events occurring in these very communities.

She mentions the continuing growth of viewers of different origins for shows such as newscasts dedicated to Chinese and South Asian events. She underscores the fact that her network works with close to 30 private producers, of which a majority come from immigration.

Ziniak tells of the fallouts of the work that goes on in that house of all diversities. She mentions the launch of the 20-part series *Once Upon a Time in Toronto*, co-produced by Western Movie Group in China and Goldspin Production in Toronto. The direction of that ground-breaking series was awarded to the Chinese director of world renown, Yang Yazhou; the main roles were played by Canadian actress Lora Sin and Chinese actors Ni Ping and Liu Wei. The series is available in Mandarin, Cantonese and English and will be viewed by tens of millions of people "here and over there, in Toronto households as well as Shanghai's".

MIHNEA C. MOLDOVEANU

Mihnea Moldoveanu is an immigrant from Romania. He put "hell" behind by leaving the corrupted kingdom of Nicolae and Elena Ceausescu. He greets us in his office at the Desautels Centre for Integrative Thinking, which he heads. The urban noise is there replaced by Mozart's music, dear to this former concert pianist. The theoretical propensities which the academic bubble always teems with is counterbalanced here by an experience of creation and business management in the field of cellular technology; an experience that brought our host wealth, independence and fame. The basic question and answer dialectics is replaced in his presence by a reflexive approach that is more complex when it comes to the sources and shaping of thoughts.

It is not simple to interview Mr. Moldoveanu. "He's a poet, philosopher, and management guru, but, most of all, [he] is an entrepreneur of ideas", according to *The Globe and Mail*'s Gordon Pitts.[14] His last book, *Diaminds*, is an exhumation, or at least a rehabilitation of epistemology applied to the world of business, a formidable investigation with today's great leaders, into the shaping of thoughts.[15] "Bold, provocative and engaging", says Jan Rivkin of the Harvard Business School, the work was praised by national and international critics. The point is to learn how to treat and use information in an integrated way, one inspired by engineers, doctors and designers' thought structures, and transferring these to the business world. It is also to impress upon future managers, the idea that the capacity to think belongs to the resume as much as knowledge or experience in finance, marketing or organisational capacities.

> This is not a book. It is a hook. Its purpose is to hook you into a relationship with your own thinking that is un-ordinary. The ordinary way of thinking about thinking is to ask: What do you think? (The answer is usually some answer about the world.) The un-ordinary way of thinking that we will attempt to sketch rests with asking, rather, How do you think? (The answer is not going to be a belief anymore, but rather a description of some way of forming beliefs.)[16]

Mihnea Moldoveanu first came to Toronto 30 years ago. He knows the world's great cities, the real ones, those that have a spirit, a personality, those that are inspired … and others. He recalls a Toronto of the eighties as "an austere place, a city that died after 6 pm where bureaucratic empty discourse dominated … an Anglo-Saxon city in which you didn't communicate and which left you strangely alone". After a long stay at the Massachusetts Institute of Technology, which made him a mechanical engineer, and at the

---

14. PITTS, G. (2008) "Merging the Academic and Practical", *The Globe & Mail*, August 25th.

15. MOLDOVENU, M. /R. Martin. (2010) *Diaminds: Decoding the Mental Habits of Successful Thinkers*. Toronto: UTP

16. *Ibid., p.ix.*

Harvard Business School, where he got his Ph.D. in business administration, he comes back to Toronto in 1999. He then discovers "a transformed city, more animated, with coffee places, strollers, Chinese families, Indian families and others in the parks and public places, a city that cleaned its shabby neighbourhoods, a city that was losing its Waspy character, a city where communication took place".

For our demanding host, this mutation is still unfinished. Admittedly, this big city is now multiethnic. But some strongholds remain. Furthermore, in his opinion, we have still not fully measured what this exceptional diversity has to offer.

He mentions the alignment of resources and networks, particularly in the field of business, that flow from that diversity. He remembers "the value added brought to [his] business by teams with specific and complementary resources: the technical capacity of Romanians, the financial capacity of Canadians and Americans and the salesmanship capacities of Palestinians." He praises that heterogeneity as a tool and support of growth and development. I ask him about the obvious effervescence that sprouts from all these institutes, task forces and specialized forecasting centres focused on innovation, which multiplied in Ontario in recent years. Moldoveanu hesitates, recognizes the phenomenon and asks another question:

> How are we to make sure this effervescence is not simply an illusion? Or research and production without real effects in terms of solving the problems researched? How are we to mobilize them actually and effectively?

In the field of culture, Toronto's "glow" is beyond question, especially because of major and conspicuous investments that profoundly enriched cultural institutions in the city, and elsewhere in the province. Mihnea ponders about the penetration of culture in the city, in the places where citizens live their lives. He remembers the free concerts offered in Boston's public squares and wishes for the cultural offer to be more present in Toronto's urban space and in the life of Ontario's society; a little less elitist, and more accessible. In his opinion, the idea of integrating culture to life has yet to come, not only as a still unaccomplished phenomenon, but mainly as an advent in people's minds. This may occur if Ontarian cultural creation gets even more important and takes its place here and in the world, if the unique experience of the diversity specific to that society becomes the very object of that cultural creation and if great creators choose to live permanently in that society. It will come if we make use of education, if we prioritize it, value it as the shared habitat of all Ontarians.

For this musician industrial entrepreneur, this mechanical engineer in love with French literature, this Harvard Ph.D. in business administration who also authored poetry collections, the central question of advanced societies, and so of Ontario, is asked. "All these tangible and intangible investments, all this accumulate knowledge, to what end?" Are they likely to contribute to the identification and settlement of the problems of Ontarian society? Those are the real end-purposes of knowledge, and they will be attained if disciplines fertilize one another. That is why it is important to "clear some space" to solve issues and an equivalent space where specialists and practitioners that are inspired by "integrative thinking" that is likely to have real and productive effects. So that is why our friend favours a Copernican revolution in our questioning. Don't ask what you think anymore, but how you think.

LISA ROCHON

Lisa Rochon chose the Bymark, at the heart of Toronto's business district, for our meeting. The place is bare, with great wood panels streaked with delicate light beams; the signature, famous, is that of the interior design firm Yabu Pushelberg. Rochon also came from elsewhere, from the other city in the other Canada, Montreal, Quebec.

I am curious to know that woman, a Science Po graduate in Paris and in urban planning from University of Toronto (U of T). I always read with great pleasure her long and too rare the *Globe and Mail* chronicles dedicated to architecture and I am enchanted by her singular texts. There's the form, a superb style, an odd blend of exactitude and fluctuating horizons. And there's the content, this choice of places of beauty or places that fall short of it, a school, a residential complex, a museum or an Olympic pavilion.

We quickly get into the thick of things. Lisa confesses her joy, "a great joy", when the end of her travels bring her back to Toronto. And why is that? She talks of her Parisian stay, at the time when Jean-Marie Le Pen and his cohorts of the extreme right occupied a real place in French politics, with their heinous injunctions regarding strangers, or anything foreign, the people, the customs, the values and all the rest.

> It's as if our city was protected from such hatred. Diversity
> here is a daily fact of life, in the neighbourhoods, at school
> where my son belongs to the white minority, at work, in

our recreational activities. There is something like lightness here that could be due to the absence of a historic weight. Toronto is not imprisoned by or in its history.

In a complex text published in 2008, she draws *a portrait of Toronto* and reminds us that "fractured and imperfect, the city has opened itself to being whole, the mother of all things, by accepting myriad peoples".[17] Of course, the great city does not correspond to the urban beauty criteria usually agreed upon, especially those that dominate on the European continent. Toronto is something else, a city in which it is impossible to know all the human components and all the parts. "To some, the imperfection of the city is a problem. For me, it provides a gritty stage for the courtship of humanity", she writes. The beauty of the so-called "Queen City" lies not in the extravagant stances it has avoided since its origins, as Charles Dickens was already noting in 1842; nor does it lie in its mediocre apartment blocks and inelegant suburban houses.

The beauty of the city is visible "in its still inhabited city centre", which distinguishes Toronto from great American cities such as Detroit, Philadelphia or Chicago. That beauty resides in the tableaux it offers: a woman dressed in a sari on a park swing; a public gathering of Torontonians of South Asian origin around a bunch of happy kids; crowds of thousands listening to musicians in Nathan Phillips Square; a multitude of people in the streets for the *Nuit Blanche*; soldiers serving vodka at the Polish House. Rochon evokes Queen Street West, this new place of innovation and cultural creation, the little jazz bars that are multiplying and theatres spreading all over the city, the Beaches neighbourhood, that former vacationers' paradise now a vibrant part of the city, demanded and magnificent.

The beauty of the city is also in this vast movement of its citizens within, in these laneway houses that we're starting to build, in the urban agriculture, in these hotels that are designed by architects and that take in the folds of the city. It is, to name a last element among others, in the megaprojects developed downtown that draw the citizens' attention to the possibilities offered by architecture. "Toronto occupies a state of becoming. And therein lies its ecstasy", she writes. In the same spirit, she delved further in the issue when we met:

---

17. ROCHON, L. (2008) "The Ecstasy of Saint Jane: Toronto, in the midst of becoming, learns to embrace risk, variety and complexity", in *Azure Magazine*, September 2008, p.102

Time and space are on our side to help Toronto's new conscience to emanate, along with its capacity to surpass constraints imposed by its street grid. Let's not forget the long road we've travelled already. From a city like New York managed by the Swiss, rather clamped in terms of urbanity in a repressive society—the east-end neighbourhood that saw Glenn Gould grow up was known for its suspicion in front of anything different—to a city marked by a flowering tolerance

Of course, no statistical table can account for that intangible and nevertheless very real category: tolerance. It emerges from the experience of living in a society of immigrants where ideas of tolerance and cohabitation are fundamental, according to Lisa Rochon in her important work *Up North, Where Canada's Architecture Meets the Land*.[18] These ideas stem from another value, which she thus underlines:

Canada stretches from east to west for 7,000 kilometres and is bounded by three oceans. It's an outrageous land mass populated by people who barely recognize each other except through a belief that difference and discord can be negotiated.[19]

A flowering tolerance! Once again, Rochon chiselled out the feelings expressed by many of the people we talked to.

HARGURDEEP SAINI

With 50 per cent of immigrants that chose Canada settling in the Greater Toronto Area, the metropolis naturally keeps expanding. The region south-west of Toronto has 1.5 million inhabitants. Mississauga having filled up fast, people move a little farther, to Milton and then Georgetown. University of Toronto opened a campus on 225 acres of protected greenbelt in Mississauga, along the Credit River. Five thousand students in 2000, 13,000—of more than 125 nationalities—today and an expected 20,000 in 2015-16. Its alumni list includes many personalities: author Dionne Brand, astronaut Roberta Bondar, filmmaker

---

18. ROCHON, L. (2005) *Up North. Where Canada's Architecture Meets the Land.* Toronto: Key Porter Books Limited, p. 37.

19. *Idem*, p. 28.

Richie Mehta, actor Zaib Shaikh and FatLabs' recording studio founder, Vikas Kohli. Some claim that the new Toronto, the one that creates wealth, produces advanced goods and provides services before exporting them throughout the world, that this new Toronto is here; young, vibrant and conquering while in the older city, we simply maintain assets and get invited still for tea at Mmes. Wilson or Smith.

The Principal and Vice-President at U of T's Mississauga campus greet us in his office, filled with the daylight that a generous fenestration is letting in. We're in for a direct conversation over a light and enjoyable lunch. Deep Saini is born in India, obtained his PhD in Australia and settled in Canada in 1982. He has a rare vision of the country, having lived in Alberta, Quebec and Ontario, and maneuvering both languages with ease. This renowned scientist is a straightforward man "qui n'a pas mal à la bouche", as our African friends would say.

We obviously discussed about diversity, which he speaks of as the *"best shared thing in the world"*, on campus and in the province. When I ask him about the apparent harmony between the different communities living in Ontario, his answer is surprising:

> I don't know. But I'm glad it's happening. Maybe it's the fact that there's no expectation for the people who come, from all over the world, to subscribe to any kind of Canadian identity. Somehow, a large majority of people settle in and become Canadians. Possibly because there is no imposing Canadian identity that you are forced to conform to. But the current situation has not always prevailed.
>
> The English Canada that I left in 1987 when I went to Quebec, in the hope of my minority situation being better understood, was not very inclusive. I loved my 18 years in Quebec. I learned French to a point where I could actually teach large classes, head the Institut de recherche en biologie végétale and get very involved in civil society. Despite all that, I did not feel that I was a full member of the society. Part of it was because an identity was imposed on you. Then I came back to English Canada and I discovered a totally different society. I was a second-class citizen when I left it. I was the norm when I got back.

What happened in that 18-year interval, between 1987 and 2005?

With the number of immigrants growing incessantly, our host answers, it is becoming increasingly difficult to discriminate against such an important number of people. Furthermore, as he said earlier, an identity wasn't imposed on them, but the "normal set of human interaction" was left to produce its effects. A lot of newcomers then mastered their field of activity and knew veritable success. Many became examples or models for other members of their community and for society as a whole. Finally, members of large ethnic groups, the Chinese and Indians in particular, have emerged as active and efficient agents in the economic relationship between their country of origin and their country of adoption. That is due in part to their linguistic and cultural ease in dealing with former fellow citizens, to their privileged contacts with institutions and networks which predate their emigration, with business, workshop and research partners, etc. Some pursue the economic activities they were practising before they left for Canada. More recently, the transformation of the global economy has shown that we need India more than India needs us.

Our first witnesses describe Ontarian society as it is unfolding at the outset of this new millennium. The idea and reality of transition dominate their discourse, as well as the constitutive diversity as a central value of what it is becoming. If they readily recognize the existence of problems in terms of economic and social insertion, they share a conviction about the general success of the Ontarian society's ongoing mutation. But, in the background, their remarks also highlight the idea and reality of the old Ontarian society, built over a long period of time. Between these two worlds, they evoke a kind of unfinished transition towards something else, something which doesn't say its name but constitutes an opportunity and, to this day, a successful venture.

After survival?

"Have we survived? If so, what happens after survival?" Asked here in a different context, admittedly, the question formulated by Margaret Atwood in conclusion of *Survival*, dawned on us after our countless meetings with Ontarians from every stripe and horizon. Whether they were asked about it or not, many came up with different forms of that same essential question. Have we survived that unique operation of transition from a society to another and if so, what have we found?

The Ontarian society is an aggregate of the answers given to that common interrogation by millions of immigrants that chose to live in it, by their children and their grandchildren. In less than ten generations, they built a unique society and contributed to its obvious success. In *The Globe and Mail*, John Ibbitson wrote in August 2004 that "immigrants are the vital element of our economy and society". The vital element! That society has become theirs. As can be seen with the first witnesses whose analyses and thoughts open this chapter, their presence and their advancement announce a new configuration of the immaterial territory of the province.

A demographic mutation of such scale never comes alone. It announces wider changes that touch upon the very nature of given consensuses and their enrichment through cross-fertilization of the value systems in place. At first, let's limit that period to the first 75 years of the 20th century, the source of immigration was almost exclusively European partly because of the racist policies of the Canadian government. If the question of integration was thus mooted when it came to Western values then, it sure is no longer the case since the lifting of these policies and the massive arrival of immigrants of Chinese, Indian, South Asian, African and Arab origins. The "reasonable accommodations" technique appears risible here given the volumes involved today. These arrivals altered the historical Ontarian immaterial territory. Consequently, that territory will reconfigure itself with the ancient and the new components that are now its complementary materials.

THE ONTARIAN TERRITORIES

The Ontarian territory is first physical. New Ontarians came, at different times, to a precise land in a specific part of the world. It is also immaterial, bringing together all the cultural, intellectual, and spiritual backgrounds that came with these millions of immigrants from their worlds.

The lakes and the granite shield

The dreams of these millions of immigrants became part of a natural landscape made of vast inland seas, the Great Lakes that separate and link Ontario with the United States of America. Water is an integral part of the province, which holds a significant proportion of the planet's drinkable water. Barely twisted, the term "Ontario" comes from an Iroquois word meaning "beautiful water".

Since the very origins, water fascinated foreign and Ontarian creators. Normally present in the 17th century cartography established by Champlain, Nicolas Sanson, geographer of the King of France and by Louis Hennepin, the first to have shown the Niagara Falls, in 1678, water dominates the first representations of the Ontarian territory. Centuries later, it still dominates such representations, as can be seen in the works of James Peachey, of the Group of Seven and in the exceptional photographs of Jesse Boles, which the Art Gallery of Hamilton showed in 2009 with the *Crude Landscape* exhibit. The Great Lakes represent more than just themselves. The St. Lawrence River, which flows over 1,000 kilometres, finds its source there. The great waterway used by hundreds of thousands of immigrants opens up the Ontarian territory by linking it to the Atlantic Ocean.

On a narrow strip of land following the banks of Lake Ontario, the Golden Horseshoe spreads between the Niagara Peninsula and the city of Oshawa. With Brantford, Kitchener-Waterloo, Barrie and Peterborough bordering its northern edge, the vast region includes the Greater Toronto Area. Close to 80 per cent of the Ontarian population lives in that immense urban corridor that is also one of the continent's most significant industrial zones. That population is growing continually and it is forecasted to continue to do so, substantially, in the next 25 years.

The immigrants' dreams also settled in these unique and mythical northeastern landscapes, as far as the remote Hudson Bay. That internal sea of 820,000 square kilometres opens eastward on the Labrador Sea and the Atlantic Ocean and, in its northwest, on the Beaufort Sea and the Arctic Ocean, one of the planet's most coveted spaces. Could it be that, in the very long run, these waterways contribute to the prosperity of the province, as did the St. Lawrence for more than two centuries? Unanswered for the moment, these questions nevertheless shed some light on a possible future for Ontario, which has direct access to the new routes of the planet that may well become the busiest in the long term.

The mythical dimension of the North, that "true northern melancholy", according to Hugh MacLennan's expression[20] is very present in the Ontarian imagination. Great authors from the province, of whom Harold Innis, John Bartlet Brebner, Donald Creighton, Arthur S. Morton, Peter Berton, Farley Mowat, Andrew Cohen, Pauline Johnson, Joseph Boyden and so many more could not resist the call of that "Canadian obsession", as Bruce Hutchison says. They have visited the ghosts of the great explorers and have set their sights on the infinite distances of the North. Some have explored the cosmologies and the material, cultural and spiritual knowledge of the Indigenous populations that live there, the world of shamans and of men that can take the shapes of beasts… They imagined the cross-

---

20. MACLENNAN, H. (1961) *Seven Rivers of Canada*. Toronto: Macmillan Co., p. 1.

ing of the continent by hunters, the savviest about the nomadic ways of animals that espouse Earth's deep rhythms. Others have found their inspiration in the travels of a great number of workers of all origins towards this *terra incognita* with such unique toponymy: Moose Factory, Long Point, Kashecheane, Mammanattawa, Cochrane, Opasatika, Porcupine, Low Bush River, Blackbear River, Ghost River. Finally, the nature of that region made out of immense bodies of water opening on emptiness, bordering on dense forests, muskeg and lichen inspired Ontarian poets and painters, and especially those of the Group of Seven.

> [The north is] not only a place but a direction ... The north focuses our anxieties. Turning to face the north, face the north, we enter our own unconscious. Always, in retrospect, the journey north has the quality of a dream.

One must read and read again *True North*, that unique chapter in Margaret Atwood's *Moving Targets*.

"Where does the north begin?"[21] asks the famous writer that some qualify an international literary rock star. Is it in that place where the granite shield comes out of the earth? Or that other place where a sign informs you that you are midway between the Equator and the North Pole? Is it in these territories where farms become sparse, where trees grow in fewer numbers until they disappear and where lakes become more abundant? In these remote lands, it is the South that is intriguing. "Tell us about the south"[22] asks the father to his daughter Gloria, who is just back from the megacity of Toronto, the Big Smoke, the city where men live in smog. One must also read and reread the Joseph Boyden's short story *Bearwalker*.

Beyond the myths and symbolic representations, the South heads up North for other reasons, among them the exploration of the abundant resources of that forest and gold zone whose natural riches have spread throughout the world and continue to do so.[23] It is there where Ontario found parts of its wealth and where countless immigrants found work. Between 1901 and 1961, the population of Sudbury, great mining town of Northern Ontario, grows spectacularly from 2,000 to 80,000 inhabitants. That growth is attributable to waves of European immigration of diverse ori-

---

21. ATWOOD, M. (2004) *Moving Targets: Writing with Intent, 1982-2004.* Toronto: Anansi Press, p. 45.

22. Boyden, J. (2009) *Born with a tooth.* Toronto: Cormorant Books, p. 84.

23. BROWN, R. (2007) *Unusual things to see in Ontario.* Erin: The Boston Mills Press.

gins with mining experience: Italians, Ukrainians, Polish, but also Finnish, Greek and Croat. Their communities are still present in Sudbury, with their cultural centres, their choirs, their radios, their own neighbourhoods sometimes, like Copper Cliff, where the Italians settled. They live not too far from Little Britain, separated only by the mine and overshadowed by the giant chimney that coughs up smoke above the streets it towers over. These immigrants have joined the British and the French Canadians who, in even greater numbers, have populated Sudbury.

Today, the province is looking for ways to reinforce its great Nordic region, which contracted because of new competition borne by globalization. Such contraction has had serious demographic consequences. Sudbury, after the spectacular population growth mentioned above, will only grow by 2,000 inhabitants between 1971 and 1991, with very few immigrants among these.

Be that as it may, the South also heads up North for its quietness, its splendour, the abundance of its protected areas. It has always drawn travellers, nature lovers, fauna and flora collectors, ecologists and sports enthusiasts.

The myth of the North takes many forms. Many through a relationship with its remoteness, as if it were a part of the world that resembled no other, anchored in incomparable lands. Others lived it in true proximity as a precious moment of their existence. In his book *Changing Places*,[24] Kerry M. Abel shows the North in a splendid simplicity that is only possible through proximity:

> I lived at one of the mining "properties" just outside Timmins for two years of my childhood. At the age of eleven, I thought "The Porcupine" was the most magical place on earth, with its exotic smells of forest and mine, the haunting remains of foundations that hinted at past dramas and mysteries, and the fascinating array of schoolyard companions, with such names as Di Marco, Sauvé, Heinoven and Boychuk, who brought strange and wonderful things to the lunchroom in their little metal boxes. Now it is all a little less mysterious and a great deal less glamorous, but it still retains its magic for me.

24. ABEL, K.M. (2006) *Changing places, History, Community, and Identity in Northeastern Ontario.* Toronto: McGill-Queen's University Press, p.xxiv.

These dreams are also set in the North West, a vast region where ecosystems have not changed since the ice age, never having been perturbed by human activities. Refusing to give in to special interests, the Ontarian government decided in 2009 to forbid any and all mining activities in that territory of more than 225 square kilometres and to reserve half of the boreal forest in that territory for the traditional activities of Indigenous peoples and for touristic ends. That decision was strongly condemned by speculators of all sorts. But it was appreciated by those who still hope that the announced global environmental catastrophes can be held back through the preservation of significant territories.

These dreams also materialized in the great southwestern farming and wine regions such as the beautiful Niagara Valley. Ontario always found there another part of its wealth.

In terms of space, the sum of these regions, as it stands today, has little to do with the Ontarian territory of 1867, when the Canadian federation was born. Ontario then occupied a narrow strip of land that skirted the Great Lakes, a fraction of its current territory which has, since then, been submitted to a considerable expansion. In 1876, the federal government purchased Rupert's Land and temporarily pushed back Ontario's western frontiers as far as the District of Keewatin and its northern frontiers until they reached the shores of James Bay and what was then called the "Northwest Territory". In 1899, Ottawa granted Ontario the Kenora District, which had been until then disputed by Toronto and Winnipeg, both having installed parallel administrations there. Then finally, in 1912, the Ontarian borders were pushed further until they reached the great northern Hudson Bay. The province's territory is now definite. The Ontarian government will have had to deploy considerable efforts, led epic political battles to finally reach its definitive geographic size, an area larger than France and Spain combined.

In 1867, with the exception of the remote colony of Victoria on the Pacific coast, the immense western territory is mainly inhabited by Aboriginal nations and is free of the structure imposed by the British. Four decades will pass before a change in this situation through the creation of Manitoba in 1870, British-Columbia the following year and Saskatchewan and Alberta in 1905. Ontario loses its status of frontier province but gains a central position in the country. An effect of geography and history, the vast province is also pivotal in the northeastern part of the continent, sharing a border with seven American states that have more than 100 million inhabitants today.

In 2009, that favourable position was subtly used in a Government of Ontario ad campaign. It shows a black backdrop on which the Americas are spread out without any border demarcation. In the vast space thus displayed, the long line separating Canada and the U.S. is absent and at the centre of that open continental space, the profile of Ontario appears scarlet red, in the shape of a heart.

An urban civilization

Ontario's urban character imposed itself early on. In 1905 already, a majority of Ontarians lived in cities, compared to 39 per cent Americans and 35 per cent of other Canadians. Today, more than 90 per cent of Ontarians are urban. In 2006, the province had 445 cities in villages and 42 of Canada's 100 most populated cities. Four of them have more than 500,000 inhabitants; twenty count between 100,000 and 500,000 inhabitants. Between 1996 and 2006, twenty-two of these cities registered a demographic growth above 10 per cent. Remarkably, the distribution of immigrant populations really covers the whole provincial territory, albeit unequally. In its main cities, the proportion of immigrants varies between 20 per cent and 60 per cent.[25] Such diversity is even more striking in Toronto, where visible minorities form a growing majority.

If, in the 18th and 19th centuries, the dreams of immigrants were resting in these natural landscapes that had to be mastered, those of the many new Ontarians that came since then settle in this urban landscape built by their successive cohorts of predecessors. As was stated earlier, the dominant fact of Ontarian history resides in the constant flow of immigrants that elected to come and live here. But it also lies in that secular development of an urban civilization and its undeniable material success.

Landscape of the mind

These immigrants' dreams are also set in the "landscape of the mind", to use Cyril Dabydeen's expression.[26] The habits, values and mores of their motherland were faced with and influenced by those of the Indigenous nations and then dominated the minds and institutions for almost two centuries. They still occupy a true place in the components of Ontarian specificity, but these habits and mores now cohabit with the many spiritual and philosophical systems, the ancient and current cultural heritages, the clear or tortured memories of new Ontarians from every part of the world. The immaterial territory of the great province defies any attempt at catego-

---

25. Markham (60%), Mississauga (52%) Richmond Hill (52%), Brampton (45%), Vaughan (40%), Windsor (28%), Hamilton (25%), London (22%), Kitchener (22%) and Ottawa (18%).

26. DABYDEEN, C. (1988) in *A Shapely Fire: Changing the Literary Landscape*. Oakville: Mosaic Press, 1988, p.10

rization. It is such lively, tragic and happy quintessence of the major events of modern and contemporary history that it provided the researchers and author of this work with a constant source of wonder.

Aboriginals

The first invisible territory of Ontario is that of the Amerindian nations; sufficiently sophisticated to offer ontological explanations of life and cosmological explanations of the universe; sufficiently equipped scientifically and technologically to guarantee life and survival in an natural environment with formidable challenges. It is the one that existed before all others. Theirs is a primary history in the etymological sense of the term. Before being a history of resistance, defeat, humiliation and renaissance, it is that which existed before all others. In *A fair Country,*[27] John Ralston Saul decrypted what we owe to these cosmological and ontological explanations, what we owe to this scientific and technological knowledge. He also showed how these value systems penetrated and enriched those of the newcomers that we are. Barbara Godard has showed the contribution of Aboriginal women to the country's literature.[28] The media, whether in English or French, remain insensitive towards these contributions. And suddenly, in this void, a dissenting and precious voice or text emerges, such as that of Isabel Vincent, in the June 10th edition of *The Globe and Mail,* in 1989, celebrating Aboriginal spirituality.

These nations are still present in Ontario, which counts more Aboriginal people than any other province in the federation.

Europeans

That landscape of the mind is an integral part of the European purpose of searching for routes to the Far East and of its morphing into the discovery and occupation of the Americas and the Caribbean. The conquest of these territories belongs to the European powers' vast enterprise of colonizing and dominating the world and that of spreading Western values posed, and often imposed, as universal values.

In that extraordinary expansion of power, whose global aim ended up happening, Great Britain occupied the very first place. Belonging to the British Empire, a power that dominated the planet, mastered the seas, was

---

27. SAUL, J.R. (2009) *Mon pays métis.* Montréal: Boréal.

28. BARBARA, G. (2008) "Some native Canadian women writers" in *Canadian Literature at the crossroad of language and culture.* Edmonton: Newest Press, p.109.

the first producer of industrial and advanced technological goods, having access to its networks, sharing in its preponderance, prestige and symbols, all of that engenders feelings of pride, security and confidence.

These feelings are largely shared by the high levels of colonial administration, by categories of well-established citizens and doubtlessly by a significant part of more modest immigrants that came from the British Isles. They do define thus a power system but still belong to a position perceived as natural by many. Referring to his grandfather living in Nova Scotia, Charles Ritchie profiled this historical and political conception shared by a good amount of people in that colony and in others:[29]

> My grandfather and his remaining contemporaries belonged to a breed now long extinct. They were Colonials. The word carries a whiff of inferiority, but they were not to know this. They thought of themselves as belonging to the British Empire, than which they could imagine nothing more glorious. They did not think of themselves as English. Certainly everything British was Best, but they viewed the individual Englishman with a critical eye. If the English patronized the Colonials, the Colonials sat in judgement on the English. The Colonial was an ambivalent creature, half in one element, half in another; British, but not English, cantankerously loyal... For many years they and those like them had managed the colony under the rule of British governors whom, in turn, they managed. It was comfortable arrangement as long as it lasted, and not unprofitable. It enjoyed the blessings of the Church—the Church of England, of course. They were men of standing and standards, honourable men within the bounds of their monopoly.

Obsolete today, these feelings have saturated Ontarian society since the end of the 18th century. They explain in part the aversion that prevailed for a long period of time with regard to anything that was outside of that favoured sphere: race, religion, language and other imperial specific characters. They also explain the will of some, after the Second World

---

29. RITCHIE, C., "My Grandfather's House" in *From Ink Lake, Canadian Stories Selected by Michael Ondaatje*. Toronto: Vintage, 1996. P.64.

War, to distance themselves from a world vision that had more to do with the historical, intellectual and aesthetic experiences of London, as well as with the City's own interests, rather than those of Toronto's. In the latter, painters, writers, poets were then searching for a different space, one that would be sufficiently open to contain their own experiences and interests in order to shed light on what had been covered up, concealed and prevented by the colonial situation.

Bringing together Canadian intellectuals and creators for the first time, the 1941 Kingston Conference dared to question the system and suggest alternatives. Pierre-Elliott Trudeau identified such emergence of will as the act of birth of Canadianism.[30] In her controversial essay, *Survival*, Margaret Atwood establishes the movement's credentials by exhuming what constitutes, according to her, specific symbols of the Canadian experience. Then, in 1975, the report of the Commission on Canadian Studies, titled *To Know Ourselves*,[31] pursues that continuity all the while advocating for opening up to the world in research and teaching. This succession of analyses and interventions has definite impacts. Barbara Godard declares that in the 60s and 70s, Canadian literature is *the biggest field* for undergraduate and graduate studies.[32]

These evolutions must not make one forget that the British heritage, its representation of the world, its institutions and essential references create a double movement at the heart of Ontarian society. Complementary history, shared language, common political and judicial systems, desire to be distinguished from the United States, personal and institutional networks, just as many elements that feed the relationship with Great Britain. But for some, that relationship has long prevented the emergence of Ontario's own culture. It expresses a political, cultural and intellectual dependence that they consider archaic and that they blame for slowing down the emergence of a legitimate identity for the Ontarian society. For those recently installed in Ontario, that relationship has little meaning, except as a reminder of their adopted country's past. Unless it brings back memories of how the Ontarian society appeared to them when they arrived. Our witness, Mihnea Moldoveanu, referred to that feeling.

---

30. TRUDEAU, P.E. (1967) *Le fédéralisme et la société canadienne française.* Montréal : Éditions HMH, p.39.

31. SYMONS, T.H.B. (1975) *To know ourselves: the report of the Commission on Canadian Studies.* Ottawa: Association of Universities and Colleges of Canada.

32. BARBARA, G. Op. cit. p. 25.

Americans

That landscape of the mind is also inseparable from the continental reality of North America. Since its origins, Ontario's history is intimately linked to that of its big neighbour. In order to make it to the heart of the continent, and then even further at the Mississippi's mouth, the French needed the Aboriginals of the territory, their know-how about waterways, strategic sites and populations in that land that then belonged to the King of France. Taking the opposite way, Loyalists came up and enriched the colony's population, while developing its territory. They too are real pioneers. Their loyalty, as it happens, has sometimes been questioned, but their attachment to British institutions, including the monarchist system, and their rejection of American republicanism, have marked local culture to this day. Blacks also came from the United States in the 19th century, fleeing slavery. Asians came as well, at the eve of the 20th century, after being brutally rejected from the great republic and before being served the same treatment in Canada.

The rest is well known: integration of the Ontarian and American economies and participation in an increasingly united continental industrial sector; development and deployment by the Americans of a powerful sector of cultural and entertainment industries that rank their work and products at the top of the field, economically, in the world and of course, in their immediate neighbours' backyard, that is, Ontario's. The effects of that proximity on Ontarian society are obvious. They are also at the heart of a constant malaise that was illustrated by the fierce opposition of Ontarians to the free trade project presented by the Mulroney government in 1984. That opposition brought to the fore the question of compatibility between the degree of integration and the sovereignty and identity as well as the question of free trade's eventual consequences on the country's autonomy.

So for Ontarians, as for many societies in the world, but with a particular acuteness in their case, America, a superpower following the war, a hyperpower following the implosion of the Soviet Union, constitutes a sort of magnetized horizon. Geographic proximity, common language, attraction power of a vast creditworthy market, daily access to broadcasts of American pop culture and shared global geopolitical interests: all the planets are aligned to create the double movement at the heart of Ontarian history. On the one hand, a deep agreement with that shared border with one of the planet's most dynamic societies, whose model seduced large parts

of the world.[33] Reserves, on the other hand, with regard to the dispropor-
tionality of the relationship, which only better highlights the fragility of the
republic's northern partner.

In that context, America's attractiveness was and remains unquestion-
able for creators in "English Canada". Already in 1907, the American author
Samuel Moffett was publishing a book under the provocative title *The
Americanization of Canada.*[34] He was suggesting that despite their protest,
"English-speaking Canadians … are already Americans without knowing it"
and announcing the "inevitable" union of Canada with the United States. A
century later, one of the finest connoisseurs of the Canadian psyche, Jeffrey
Simpson, was thus commenting Moffett's argument: "Canadians today are
vastly more 'American' than in Moffett's time, and yet the inevitability of
union with the United States … never materialized".[35]

Morley Callaghan, "the most important Canadian writer of his genera-
tion"[36] explained the bottom-line, in 1928: "walking up Fifth Avenue past
Scribner's bookstore and seeing the window filled with [my book] *Strange
Fugitive,* I thought the world was my oyster".[37] Countless cohorts, from
Ontario, followed and still follow the path breached by Morley Callaghan
and move south. Some severely judge them for that. Others adopt Margaret
Atwood's spot-on formula: "How to say both No, and Yes".[38] In her famous
letter to America, she again furrows:

> We've always been close, you and us. History, that old entan-
> gler, has twisted us together since the early seventeenth century.
> Some of us used to be you; some of us want to be you; some of
> you used to be us. You are not only our neighbours: In many
> cases—mines, for instance—you are also our blood relations,
> our colleagues, and our personal friends. But although we've
> had a ringside seat, we've never understood you completely,
> up here north of the 49th parallel. We're like Romanized

---

33. MARTEL, F. (2010) *Mainstream, Enquête sur cette culture qui plaît à tout le monde.* Paris: Flammarion.

34. MOFFETT, S. (1972) *The Americanization of Canada.* Toronto: University of Toronto Press,
   p. 340.

35. SIMPSON, J. (2000) *Star-Spangled Canadians, Canadians living the American dream.* Toronto:
   Harper Collins, p.340.

36. SNIDER, N. "Why Morley Callaghan still matters". The *Globe and Mail,* October 25th 2008.

37. CALLAGHAN, M. (2001) The *New Yorker stories.* Toronto: Exile Editions limited, p. *ix.*

38. ATWOOD, M. (2004) *Moving Targets.* Toronto: House of Anani Press, p. 69.

Gauls—look like Romans, dress like Romans, but aren't Romans—peering over the wall at the real Romans. What are they doing? Why? What are they doing now?...What can I tell you about yourself that you don't already know?[39]

So, is there a space that clearly belongs to Ontarians and that would, once explored and enlightened, unlock their specific contribution to the common immaterial space? Their contribution, to be sure, but also the acknowledgment that overtime so sorely lacked to its creators? Unless we believe that these creators are condemned to dependence in the face of the powers that successively occupied the first rank in world affairs, Great Britain and the United States, which followed. The relay of the torch between the two Anglo-Saxon nations, a rare historical occurrence, is executed in fluid linguistic continuity. Indeed, the *Pax Britannica* and *Pax Americana* speak the same language. That fact at the same time reinforces and weakens the opportunity for Anglophone creators living elsewhere and that is mainly true for the creators of the Dominion just north of the United States of America. But we know that this opportunity was seized upon by the creators that are caught in these ambiguous circumstances, shared at varying degrees, by many in the world. In the end, Ontarians are not the only ones that have to say yes and no to their big neighbour, and to say so in the same phrase.

Canadians

Lastly, this landscape of the mind is also designed by Canadian events prior or following the Paris Treaty of February 10, 1763. This treaty confirmed British ownership of a vast portion of the North American territory as well as its authority over the dispersed populations that inhabited it. Ontario did not exist then. Upon being constituted, it will discover the singularity of its situation. It finds a Francophone society, with every intention of remaining so, as its Eastern neighbour and with it, a political partner since 1840. West of it, after a wait that lasted a century, four provinces are created, some of which compete with the great central province today on different levels.

Such are the landscapes of nature and of the mind that, for the past two centuries, newcomers from all over the world have witnessed in Ontario. These pictures are transformed by them in the ways Northrop Frye distinguishes as the objective world and that in which we want to

---

39. Idem, p. 325.

live. "It's not the world you see but the world you built out of what you see. ... what you have to do and what you want to do—in other words, necessity and freedom".[40]

What is revealed to immigrants at the first sight of their new environment has considerably changed with time. The first generations of them saw a crude nature that they had to master as well as a homogeneous society to which they had to conform. The most recent generations saw urban spaces that were theirs to appropriate and a heterogeneous and pluralistic society they had to integrate and understand. For close to one and a half century, immigrants to Ontario embarked on heavy ships in British and European ports and had many days over the Atlantic to imagine their new lives. For the past half-century, they leave the world's airports and have but a few hours to internalize a transition that will transform their existence.

> Having, with many of my countrymen, determined to embark for Canada; little dreaming, from the flattering accounts which had been so industriously published respecting that country...I left Glasgow for Greenock, to embark onboard the ship David of London for Quebec along with nearly 400 other passengers...On the 19th of May 1821...and in 28 hours, we lost sight of land...We arrived at Quebec on the 25th of June, [after 34 days on the ocean].

The trip and the challenges it was to bring were far from over. Three hundred sixty six of the travellers got on the road in Montreal towards what is today Ontario.

> Here a very difficult part of our journey commenced, namely, the passing of the rapids of the St. Lawrence...The rapids run with such a force that we were compelled to get two horses to haul every boat...Many of our unhappy countrymen suffered extremely from these hardships, on account of the intense heat of the season, and drinking too freely of the river water...Many of them took badly on the road, and were obliged to remain behind their families many days...When night came, we remained on the riverside. Sometimes, we got access to farmhouses and

---

40. FRYE, N. (1963) The *Educated imagination*. Toronto: House of Anansi Press, p.5.

sometimes not. Others lay in the woods all night... Many died of a few days illness. This journey cost us three weeks.[41]

175 years later, Neil Bissoondath tells of the arrival here of a Japanese girl.

> Toronto: a place where my personality could be free, it was not a city of traditions in a country of traditions. It was America, in the best implication that word held for us Japanese: bright, clean, safe, new. Life experienced without the constraints of an overwhelming past. I shall never forget my joy when, awaking one night, in a sweet from the nightmare, I realized that here I was a young person and not almost an old maid, that by a simple plane flight, I had found rejuvenation.[42]

MILLIONS OF SINGULAR STORIES

Before 1991, close to 2 million immigrants found themselves in these natural landscapes and these landscapes of the mind, and 2.5 million since then. These numbers are impressive. So are the particular stories they conceal.

The act of immigrating is a profoundly personal one. Repeatedly, the Ontarians we met reminded us of that. Except for the fact of acquiring the same citizenship, everything distinguishes the migration experience of each and every one. For instance, the personal history these immigrants lived through up until that moment, that which is imagined in the anticipatory period of reflection, decision-making and wait before the departure for the new country. Finally, there is also the history experienced as a consequence of that choice to migrate and everything that is not included in this too short list of experiences. Thus, in his book *Strangers Within Our Gates: or Coming Canadians*,[43] published in 1909, the father of Canadian socialism James Shaver Woodsworth, an Ontarian, lets a young immigrant speak:

> This may be taken as a typical story of the experiences of a family of immigrants—the dissatisfaction in the old land—the dreams and plans about the new—the father

41. HILLMER, N. & GRANATSTEIN, J.L. (2006) The *Land Newly Found: Eyewitness Accounts of the Canadian Immigrant Experience.* Toronto: Thomas Allen Publishers, p.42.

42. SUWANDA, S. (1994) "The Cage", in *The Whistling Thorn. An Anthology of South Asian Canadian Fiction.* Oakville: Mosaic Press. p.104.

43. WOODSWORTH, J.S. (2006), "Strangers within our gates: or coming Canadians", in Hillmer and Granatstein, *op. cit.*, p.125.

going first to prospect and prepare—the sacrifice made in leaving the old home—the anxieties and hardships of the journey—the hopes that buoyed them—the disappointment in reaching the land of their dreams—the struggles to gain a foothold—the privations of the first few months or years—the gradual making of the home—the move of the young men to the city—their struggles. How much one can read between the lines!

Wherever the bureaucratic lingo implodes with categories and management rules piled on top of one another, wherever a certain official discourse frosts over these lives with euphemisms and platitudes, to say nothing of the rude prejudices that are often allowed, we must conjure up the specific emotions stemming from that exceptional human experience: deciding to change worlds and doing it effectively. That is, definitely leaving a society of origin for another, where one is to reinvent one's life and the lives of those who partake in the adventure. If that experience is made out of relatively common and identifiable material episodes, it also has intimate dimensions, for one to forever hold in one's "hands of the mind", to use Austin Clarke's expression.[44] Hence, the importance of the following testimonials.

For a great number of Ontarians, such change of worlds constitutes an essential element of the conversation they have with themselves, their spouse, children, with their new friends and members of their community. Without being asked to do so, a sizeable half of our Ontarian interviewees referred to that experience, their experience. Thus changing worlds constitutes a prism through which we can evaluate events both close in time and further away. If each new Ontarian physically went from one society to another, it is quite different when you look at other dimensions of his life. He bears, according to Charles Taylor's formula, a multiple identity.

Adriana Rio Nabuco de Gouvêa is a student, Brazilian and Canadian. She relays the philosopher's message in these unequivocal terms:

Getting used to living in Canada was much easier than getting used to living without Brazil. As soon as I settled

---

44. CLARKE, A. "Leaving This Island Place" in *From Ink Lake, Canadian stories selected by Michael Ondaatje*. Toronto: Vintage, 1996. P. 295

down in Ottawa, I began to realize that I was getting attached to symbols of Brazilian identity that had never before been too important to me.[45]

Memory and imagination

Each new Ontarian also contributes to enriching the memory and imagination of his land of adoption, incidental now to his own memory. In the case of Ontario, these latter memories are legion. The Torontonian poet of Polish origin, Marek Goldyn, sheds light on that fusion of memories.[46]

> It's a late hour, my friend,
> But there, in the old country…
> Yet where, in fact, am I?
> In what country?
>
> It's a sleepy hour, my friend,
> But there in the old country–
> What time is it? In which country?
> Here around the Great Canadian
> Lakes
> It's just a little past midnight,
> But there, in the homeland
> The morning is restless

Each new Ontarian also carries with him networks that add to the exponential and entangled cluster of links that already bind Ontario's society to the world. These new networks are often modest, originating in the immigrant's family or the villages from whence he came, stemming from friendship, work or professional relationships. They can also be larger and contribute to Ontario's structural and systemic relationships with major centres of decision-making, of creation, research and innovation. Such is, today, one of the roles of the Diasporas that everywhere become a formidable part of international relations.[47] Ontario is also a conglomerate of Diasporas.

---

45. HILLMER & GRANATSTEIN, *op. cit.*, p.376.

46. *Mosaic in Media 1*, op.cit, p.56.

47. ROY, J.L. (2008) *Quel avenir pour la langue française? Francophonie et concurrence culturelle au XXIe siècle*. Montréal : Hurtubise HMH, p.71.

The worlds from where they came

The first of these migrants arriving in Ontario were Loyalists, slaves or soldiers looking for security and liberty. They were followed by the sons and daughters of Great Britain, who either benefited from the protected routes of the British Empire in the world or suffered from its power. Then came those afflicted by the dramas of the old continent: war and famine in Ireland, poverty in the centre, eastern and southern parts of Europe, the hell of national-socialism and fascism in Germany, Italy, Spain, Portugal and Austria, the terror of communism, the devastation of two world wars, the unfolding of horror in the Balkans.

> On November 23, 1956, when the Communist regime in Hungary was still in a state of disarray because of a month-old and tenacious armed uprising against Soviet dominance by the population, our family crossed the border between Hungary and Austria. We became refugees. This was not an easy decision for our parents. Father was then forty-six years old, and mother thirty-seven. With two young sons, a couple of suitcases in hand, and virtually zero financial resources, they left behind whatever security they had—their apartment, furniture, worldly possessions; all their friends and few remaining family members; father's employment. Without any guarantees about the future, they faced the unknown…
>
> Our parents' first intention was for us to go to Israel. After many hours of deliberations, however, the decision was made to apply for visas to Canada. It was thought that, at our parents' age, it would be easier for them to start all over again in Canada than in Israel…
>
> I left Europe as János Máté and arrived in Halifax as John Mate. I willingly relinquished the name I knew all my life in favour of the promise of easier assimilation. But I was never a "John". That is a very English name, and it always felt foreign to me. The day after our mother died on November 5, 2001, in the midst of my grief, I let go of my immigrant name, John, and returned to the earliest sounds of my childhood, to the name that Mother gave me, János. I was no longer an immigrant[48]

---

48. MÁTÉ, J. dans HILLMER & GRANATSTEIN, *op. cit.*, p.265.

Victims of McCarthyism also came, as did conscientious objectors and other opponents to the Vietnam and Iraq wars. Victims too hailing from the other America, fleeing the regimes of the Brazilian and Argentine generals, the Papa Doc and Chilean colonels, appalled by the enforced disappearances, the summary and extralegal executions, Mexico's misery and the strikes of the Shining Path in Peru. Newcomers also included children of the Caribbean seeking to escape the limitations of their insularity, including those that still plight the Cuban nation.

> The situation in Chile was getting worse and worse. People were disappearing. People were killed ... The children felt terrible, their father was gone, and there was a curfew, and you couldn't go outside. Besides, you didn't trust many people because you didn't know who overhear stories that something has happened with this one, something happened to that one. You just live in fear. You don't know what is going to happen. When I was informed that we were going to leave the country, I was happy and unhappy. I didn't want to leave my family, my father, mother, brother ... But I also wanted to be secure with my children ... I didn't know what to take. I didn't know what was important in the house. I didn't know what was going to happen with the whole house, my car, the furniture, all the photos we had ... For us, it was difficult in Toronto because we had three kids ... we didn't know the city and were always wondering about our family in Chile. We didn't have much communication with them. The newspaper didn't print much about what was going on in Chile ... my husband was always thinking that we were going to leave soon, that the military was not going to last very long and that we were going to return to Chile in two months, three months, no more than six months and then he passed away ... we were left without him in a new country, almost two years after we arrived. We were not allowed to go back to Chile: his name was on a list of those forbidden to return.[49]

49. ENRIQUEZ, G. in HILLMER & GRANATSTEIN, *op. cit.,* p.314.

Others fled the dramas of the African continent: the horrific and criminal Afrikaners' apartheid, the tribal wars in Nigeria, the insanity of Idi Amin Dada in Uganda, the Ethiopian famines, the low skies of the Maghreb and Cairo's Special Forces.

More recently, with laws putting an end to the gross discrimination that affected Asians so harshly for more than a century, increasing numbers have started coming from faraway Asia. Fleeing the cruelly divided Korea, the French lunacy in Indochina followed by America's in Vietnam, the nameless crimes of Pol Pot and the natural and political calamities in Bangladesh, fleeing Pakistan's violence, poverty in the Philippines, secret police in the totalitarian regimes of Jakarta and Tehran, successive devastations in Pakistan, the millennial heaviness of India or the Palestinian drama. They came from Hong Kong, handed over to China by London in 1997, from Taiwan, threatened by Chinese missiles, from the extreme material and spiritual misery of China before Deng Xiaoping substituted state socialism with market socialism, a one-word shift that changed the world. They keep coming from these places but are now carried by a new certainty, the irreversible and eastbound transfer of global power, the emergence of the new Asian hemisphere.[50]

Hailing from the "Canadas"

Ontarians also came, and in great numbers, from Eastern and Western Canada, from the disastrous 1929 economic crisis, from the poverty, endemic unemployment and isolation felt in parts of the country. Among them were some French Canadians, forming a historical and political minority. They too have made the great psychological and physical journey from their lands of origin to the federation's central province.

This internal migration reserves real surprises. The fact, for example, that for half a century, with the very rare exception of a few years, the amount of internal migrants in Canada (from one province or territory to another) has always been higher than that of international immigrants. Thus, in 2005, 300,699 foreigners immigrated to Canada while 315,031 Canadians migrated from somewhere else in the country.[51] These internal population movements fluctuate greatly. If they concern 255,000 people in 2003, their numbers reach 434,000 in 1993 and fall to 370,800 in 2007. In the

---

50. MAHBUBANI, K. (2008) *The New Asian Hemisphere*. New York: Public Affairs.

51. TRAD, K. (2007) *Les caractéristiques du migrant interprovincial au Canada,* Mémoire de maîtrise, Université de Montréal.

period from 1981 to 2007, the balance has tipped in Ontario's favour 16 out of 26 times. Only Alberta and British Columbia have a better record. Twenty five out of 26 for the former, 21 for the latter, but the numbers of people involved there are of a more limited scale. Quebec, for its part, has seen an internal migration deficit 25 out of 26 times and supplies Ontario with half of its Canadian migrants.

Without having exhaustively researched the topic but by simply taking notes along our readings and conversations, our list of names of Ontarian celebrities' born elsewhere in the country kept getting longer. Marshall McLuhan, born in Edmonton; Edwin John Pratt, "the greatest Canadian poet of the 20th century", David French and Michael Cook, all three born in Newfoundland; John Newlove, born in Saskatchewan; Margaret Laurence, born in Manitoba, just like Miriam Waddington; Northrop Frye, born in Sherbrooke, Quebec; Patrick Lane, born in British Columbia without forgetting the author of *Anne of Green Gables,* probably the best known Canadian literary work on the planet, Lucy Maud Montgomery, born in Prince Edward Island. In the words of Margaret Atwood:

> In the early part of my childhood, I had not known any of my relatives, because they lived in Nova Scotia, two thousand miles away. My parents had left Nova Scotia during the Depression because there were no jobs there. By the time I was born, the Second World War had begun, and nobody travelled great distances without official reasons and gas coupons. But although my aunts were not present in the flesh, they were very much present in the spirit. The three sisters wrote one another every week, and my mother read these letters out loud, to my father but by extension to myself and my brother, after dinner. They were called "letters from home." Home, for my mother, was always Nova Scotia, never wherever we might be living at the time, which gave me the vague idea that I was misplaced. Wherever I actually was living myself, home was not there."[52] "My parents were economic refugees from Nova Scotia"[53]

---

52. ATWOOD, *Moving Targets, op.cit.* p.75.

53. *Idem,* p.197.

Finally, that considerable flow of people at Ontario's gates also included adventurers, travel enthusiasts, students that ended up permanently installed, technicians, researchers and scholars hailing from all the world's regions and drawn by the growth and development of that North American territory. Men and women, too, simply wanting to live and know "human happiness", according to the expression of Dr. John Howison, immigrant to Upper Canada in 1820.[54] The good doctor added that the advantages of immigrating to that part of the world "are not altogether chimerical ... but that, in so far as concerns the lower classes of Europeans, they are equally numerous and important as some ... have represented them to be".[55] Our Ontarian interlocutors, coming from every horizon, constantly expressed feelings similar to those shared, close to two centuries ago, by John Howison, all the while signaling the existence still of discriminatory practices.

It is impossible to evoke the Ontarian landscape of the mind without including the crucial contribution of these millions of immigrants and their religious, philosophical, historical, cultural, linguistic and social backgrounds. As we have heard from our witnesses, the migration brings together memories and hopes. As we will see along these pages, it redefines the Ontarian society, stands as the basis of its current constitutive diversity and, doubtlessly, its future crossbred quality.

That society is incomprehensible if we don't take into account these movements which, since Ontario's origins, have led millions of men and women towards the province. Their arrival has reinforced an essential category of this century, one that is also a fundamental to mankind: diversity. In his introduction to the *Canadian stories* he assembled, Michael Ondaatje notes that writers that are the product of immigration, in the second part of the 20th century, have shown a different image of Canada, an image that lies outside the Anglo-Saxon tradition.[56] We will get acquainted with these writers in our chapter devoted to culture.

TORONTO AS A SIGNATURE

Toronto is Ontario's pivotal city. It is the "other Ontario", according to an expression often used by our interviewees. "Don't forget that there are two Ontarios, that of the vast territory outside Toronto, and the metropolis

54. HILLMER & GRANATSTEIN, *op. cit.,* p.38.

55. *Idem,* p.40.

56. ONDAATJE, M., *op.cit.,* p.xv.

itself." The city counts 2.5 million inhabitants. It ranks first in Canadian cities and fourth on the continent in terms of population after New York, Los Angeles and Chicago. It will reach 3 million inhabitants in 2030 and the Greater Toronto Area will go from 5 to 7.4 million in the same interval.

Obviously, the urban fabric in Ontario is not limited to Toronto's, as we have established before. But the metropolis incarnates and is a symbol of the future of a society larger than itself: the Ontarian society. To put it otherwise, this future merges in large part with its personality, reputation and success. Toronto is Ontario's obvious signature.

If Ottawa makes daily headlines, it is for reasons that have little to do with itself. It is rather the result of its status as federal capital and of the will of successive governments to position it as a space of reference for the Canadian experience. Wilfrid Laurier dreamt of making it a model city, just as successful as some European capitals. The ambition was laudable. With time, it appears the result is more modest but certainly not without merit. To achieve that end, considerable resources were allocated to the city; a great number of cultural institutions were set up in Ottawa to the detriment of other big cities in the country, recurring events were created, celebrating the past much more than heralding the future. To the three levels of government that all support the city, the National Capital Commission was added, with significant resources at its disposal.

Second city in the province, the federal capital lacks Toronto's cosmopolitanism, the historical depth of Kingston, the architectural heritage of London, the social heritage of Hamilton, the surprising ethnic singularity of Markham or the industrial clout of Windsor. Ottawa follows another trajectory, that of balance, mistrust and distance between the two principal societies that formed the united Canada of the mid-19th century: the Ontarian and Quebecois societies. These feelings rendered impossible the choice of Montreal or Toronto as the capital of the new federation. Ottawa's choice is the result of a political and institutional logic. It is the capital of a country with multiple societies. The rest is consequential, except of course the legislative, regulatory and judicial capacities that are concentrated there and whose consequences rule the land *A MARI USQUE AD MARE*.

A laboratory of diversity

Toronto is one of the most multicultural cities in the world. The term must be defined. The Ontarian capital is no different than other big cities such as Miami, Los Angeles or New York with regard to the percentage of its residents born abroad. But the plurality of their origins and the volume of the city's visible minorities are what clearly distinguish it. Carol Goar arrestingly described the situation:

> Peer into Toronto's baby carriages if you want a glimpse of the city's future. The face looking back at you isn't likely to be white. Six out of every 10 children born in Toronto belong to a visible minority. And the proportion is rising. Two-thirds of infants have mothers from outside Canada.[57]

Consequently Greater Toronto is a unique laboratory of diversity, of all diversities: religious, ethnic, linguistic, economic and social. In their magnificent book, soberly titled "Toronto", the writer William Kilbourn and photographer Rudi Christ contend that this character imposed itself in the 50s while "over half a million immigrants arrived from Europe and Asia and the British West Indies to enliven the drab countenance of the city. Toronto became a street festival, a parade, a grand bazaar".[58]

According to Statistics Canada, visible minorities will be in a majority situation in Toronto as of 2017 and, in 2031, the population of the metropolitan area will be made up of as much as 78 per cent immigrants or their children, 63 per cent of them belonging to visible minorities; that is 5.6 million people compared to 2.3 million in 2006. According to median population projections, a majority of them, 3.2 million citizens, will be of Asian origin, 1.1 million of them being Chinese and 2.1 coming from Southeast and South Asia.

Half of Toronto's current population is born outside the country and has lived there for less than 15 years. Half of its population is younger than 25 and doesn't have French nor English as their first language. In declining order, after English, the most spoken languages in the city are the Chinese ones, Italian, Punjabi, Tagalog and Portuguese. City Hall's website can be viewed in 53 languages and the famous 311 phone customer service improvement it undertook can answer you in more than 180 languages. The majority of Ontarian cities have developed multilingual services, the intricate Asian and Arabic calligraphies accompanying the better-known European languages characters. Moreover, the communication system of the Ontarian government is also deployed in an open multilingualism.

---

57. GOAR, C. (2006) "Toronto's new lost generation", *Toronto Star*, 3 March 2006.

58. KILBOURN, W. & CHRIST, R. (1977) *Toronto*. Toronto: McClelland & Stewart, p.11.

The city is spread out, difficult to physically come to grasp with. Seen from the CN Tower platform, superb at night in its lighted garbs, its sprawl appears limitless and melts in an infinite space that encompasses it. Coldly set in concrete in parts of its centre, it is installed as well in a natural proximity offered by 1,800 parks and 8,000 hectares of natural areas. Its architectural landscape is puzzling. It has been said that the city lacked vision when it comes to its built heritage, to what needed to be preserved and what is meaningless; said also that its urban planning department was incapable to respect the style and character of its neighbourhoods. Hence the anarchic constructions, isolated towers where horizontality dominates, massive buildings erected on streets that were uniform yesterday still. "Toronto is under attack", Lisa Rochon wrote in 2005.[59] More often than not, the city suddenly appears pretty and offers magnificent perspectives. But more often than not as well, it offers blocked passageways and vistas, mauled beauties and entangled horizons.

Our Torontonian interlocutors expressed a deep attachment to their city. The debate concerning the identity of the inhabitants of the province, whether Canadian or Ontarian, is resolved by a great number of Toronto residents: they profess their priority attachment for the metropolis. They are first and foremost proud Torontonians.

Many of them have insisted on the importance of the "ethnic" villages and neighbourhoods, old, new or on the rise, that give to their city one of its main qualities. Literature, past and present as well, reinforces that assessment. Among others who have shown these villages and neighbourhoods with visible fondness, there stand Hassan Ghedi Santur, Michael Redhill, Rebecca Rosenblum, Dionne Brand, Rabindranath Maharaj, Christian Bode and Hédi Bouraoui.[60] Yorkville, Cabbagetown, Corso Italiana, Chinatown, Greektown, St. Lawrence Market, Kensington Market, Regent Park in full-blown re-creation, Parkdale, the Annex, where great urban planner Jane Jacobs used to live, Queen Street West, the Distillery District, Artscape's Wychwood Barns, Leslieville, all constitute specific, unique and precious places in Toronto's urban web.

---

59. ROCHON, L. (2005) "A towering shame", *The Globe and Mail*, November 3.

60. SANTUR, H.G. (2010) *Something remains.* Toronto: Dundurn; REDHILL, M (2006). *Consolation.* Toronto: Doubleday Canada; ROSENBLUM, R. (2008) *Once.* Toronto: Biblioasis; BRAND, D. (2005) *What we all long for.* Toronto: Knopf; MAHARAJ, R. (2010) *The Amazing Absorbing Boy.* Toronto : Knopf; BODE, C. (1996) *La Nuit du rédacteur.* Ottawa : Éditions du Nordir; BOURAOUI, H. (1999) *Ainsi parle la Tour CN.* Ottawa : Éditions l'Interligne.

A five-pointed star

On both sides of Toronto's University Avenue, which leads to Queen's Park, the province's political centre and historical seat of its government for close to a century and a half, the symbols and places of Ontario's influence and power lunge outwards like the five points of a star: the political, economic, scientific, academic and cultural branches. These branches are sometimes joined to support common undertakings. The conference organized by Artscape in collaboration with the MaRS Discovery District, the Martin Prosperity Institute and the City of Toronto towards the creation of the "Toronto Road for Creative Collaboration ", a kind of project incubator linking art and science, belongs to that category.

On one side of the large and beautiful avenue stands one of the city's—and even the country's—most renowned street: Bay Street. It runs along the tracing of the ancient street opened in 1797 to link Lot Street and the small bay that served as the city's port. It now hosts Canada's banking and financial hub, the equivalent of the Bourse district in Paris, the City in London, Wall Street in New York and Shanghai's financial centre. The majority of big Canadian banks' headquarters can be found there, including the impressive Toronto-Dominion Bank Tower, designed in an association with the famous German architect Ludwig Mies van der Rohe. There, one also finds 75 per cent of foreign banks in Canada, 65 per cent of the country's pension fund societies, the offices of Canadian legal studies as well as those of public relations firms whose texts feed Canadian media daily. This group of institutions and specialized professional services makes up the third financial services centre in North America and the first in Canada. At 303 Bay Street lies, modest in this abundance of steel and glass surging skywards to impressive heights, a low red brick house, the seat of the "Canada First" movement, launched in 1868. Its founders oscillated between strengthening the link with Great Britain and affirming Canada's autonomy. As militants for the maintenance of an exclusively white nation at the north of the American continent, they would be aghast today at the sight of Toronto's racial diversity.

Made up of three divisions,[61] the Toronto Stock Exchange (TMX) is a reminder of the extraverted nature of the country's economy and its links to the world. In terms of market capitalization, the TMX reached $US 2,277.5 billion in 2010, is ranked first in Canada and third in North America and seventh globally. For that same year, 3,670 companies

---

61. The Toronto Stock Exchange, the TSX Venture Exchange and the Montréal Exchange.

belonged to TMX's listed directory and the value of transactions totaled $US 1,383.6 billion. It ranks first in the world in the amount of mining companies listed on the Toronto Stock Exchange. With 1,629 listings in 2011, this sector accounts for two thirds of companies registered on that stock exchange, the remaining third allocated between companies in the fields of energy, life sciences and technologies.

Further to the south, Bay Street crosses Nathan Phillip Square, a large esplanade at the foot of City Hall, a symbol of Toronto's accession to modernity, according to many of our interlocutors. A work from Finnish architect Viljo Revell, selected by a jury among 510 proposals from 42 countries, the building belongs to that category of architectural achievements that embody a city. Its two convex towers evoke feelings of protection and power at the same time. They have been compared to two hands that define the boundaries of a vast and precise space, warm and intense. Fixed in bronze, Winston Churchill stands guard, low-browed, on the plaza, gathering place to demonstrate or celebrate.

As if it were attached to the big avenue and anchored in the neighbourhood, the Discovery District spreads out on two square kilometres in the heart of the city. Its leaders present it as the most important concentration of scientific research centres, houses of higher learning and financial institutions in the country. Between Bay Street and Queen's Park, the MaRS complex includes a wing from the old Toronto General Hospital and two glass towers linked by a transparent passageway. The district feels as if it were magnetically driven by the concept of innovation. Summits on the topic are held there, new companies are incubated there, managers are trained there and advisory services to hundreds of clients from all over the province are dispensed there. The district is a major element in the transformation of the industrial economy that was recently still secure about its pre-eminence and that is shaken today by the strong competition arising out of globalization and, since 2008, by the effects of a financial, economic and social crisis whose outcome remains uncertain. As is the case for the automotive industry, we will see this further. Research in Ontario is not all concentrated in Toronto. It is deployed in the university network of the whole province and in other specialized centres such as Waterloo's Perimeter Institute, a landmark of theoretical physics in the world.

East of the avenue, Yonge Street belongs to the history, imagination and current life of Toronto. It has been immodestly compared to Broadway. It was said to be the longest street in the world in memory of the time it was part of

Highway 11 and stretched from Lake Ontario to North Bay and still further
to the north towards Cochrane, Kapuskasing and Thunder Bay, a distance just
short of 1,900 kilometers. Drawn and built as early as 1785 under the administration of lieutenant-governor Simcoe as a route with the military purpose of
defending Upper Canada, it will be the setting of some major episodes in the
1837 rebellion. It is today at the centre of harsh debates regarding a long-awaited
and often-delayed renovation. Writers have always tried to establish what it is and
what it is not. Didier Leclair drew a singular portrait of it:[62]

> Yonge Street stretched out like a reptile whose length
> would eternally grow. On its flanks, a human fauna moved
> tirelessly, swarming and throbbing, like ants surrounding
> their queen. Oh the egg-laying my eyes witnessed that day!
> The apparitions, the discoveries of races, colours, busy
> storefronts. Yonge Street varied along with its intersec-
> tions: clean, miserable, grotesque. It was decadent in some
> places, shining in others.

On the other side of University Avenue rests another symbol of Ontarian
power. A stakeholder in the Discovery District, the University of Toronto,
created 175 years ago, and its campus offer an architectural blend that
brings gothic, Victorian and contemporary styles together. Vast gardens
and beautiful inner courtyards such as that of the Munk Centre which, in
the middle of the surrounding urban noise, plunge visitors in the peace and
quiet of middle Ages monasteries. Also to be found there, great research
and teaching consortia that have had 10 Nobel Prize winners in their midst
and that are solicited today to partake in the works of Task Force 2030,
created to prepare the university's entrance in its third century of existence. Important Ontarian institutions such as the Royal Ontario Museum
(ROM), the Canadian Opera and the Toronto Symphony Orchestra were
born and developed on the U of T campus. The university also launched and
supported a great number of important intellectual initiatives, such as the
famous *University of Toronto Quarterly*, a true witness of the social, cultural
and political evolution of what they called English and French Canada.

This great urban university belongs to a network of 21 Ontarian
institutions of higher learning, of which six are partially or completely
Francophones. In 2010, they greeted 40 per cent of all Canadian univer-

---

62. LECLAIR, D. (2000) *Toronto, je t'aime*. Ottawa : Édition du Vermillion, p.37.

sity students and an imposing contingent of foreign students. They had 43 per cent of Canadian resources dedicated to research at their disposal and were home to 700 of the so-called Canada Research Chairs.

Alongside the campus and located right next to Chinatown's entrance, the Art Gallery of Ontario (AGO) dominates, imperial in an historical building that dates back to the beginning of the last century and futuristic in the glass addition imagined by the celebrity architect Frank Gehry, one of the most respected signatures of contemporary architectural art. Inaugurated in 2008, that addition doubles the exhibition area of the museum and envelops it in a massive and transparent, changing and magnificent spider web. People will come from very far to admire the vibrant and jubilant work of this Toronto native, who qualifies himself an "organizer of chaos", work which belongs to an ensemble that can also be seen in Bilbao, Prague, Los Angeles, Hanover, Tokyo, Paris and Chicago.

The AGO is part of a series of theatres, galleries, museums and arts schools, many of which have undergone reinvention, or "reformation", as Lisa Rochon would put it.[63] Widely recognized among them are the extension to the ROM, by Daniel Libeskind or that of the Ontario College of Art and Design by Will Alsop. Together, these institutions form an arts district at the heart of the Ontarian metropolis. This proliferation of investments to recreate or create public spaces dedicated to culture are far from being the only signs of Torontonian and Ontarian cultural life. We will return to the topic at length in our chapter on culture.

Some have mentioned the caesura between the old city, where assets are managed, and the ring of new communities that surround it, where an important part of the modernity of the capital is really being built. Toronto's historical centre would show the city through the lens of what has been accomplished while what is being accomplished today is deployed in the periphery, in these suburban cities that grow without pause and where one can find a much more than shopping centres and tightly-built row houses. Rather, it is university and college campuses, professional associations, cultural centres, laboratories and companies that can be seen in increasing numbers there. Networks also, which, due to the diversity of these surrounding cities, link them to the world. So Toronto has little to do with what it was a quarter century ago. It is now bordered by communities where a majority of immigrants, whose vitality is obvious, decide to settle.

---

63. ROCHON, L. (2008), "A monumental moment", *The Globe and Mail,* November 8.

Markham, for example, is host to more than one thousand technological companies specialized in life sciences, a good number of which have parent societies in Asia.

Two moments in history

Two of the architectural achievements evoked here, a new City Hall and the AGO, shed light on two moments of the city's history.

The first of these achievements, the New City Hall has replaced the old 1899 sandstone building, with its low windows, high tower and terrifying gargoyles. Inaugurated during the fiftieth year of Queen Victoria's reign, as we are reminded upon reading the commemorative plaque just outside the main door, Old City Hall represented the spirit of Toronto for close to a century. The New City Hall, slender, warm and transparent cohabits with the Old, solid and enigmatic. Situated next to each other, it's as if both buildings were isolated in their proximity, offering a sight on two parallel visions and two epochs of Torontonian society. Admittedly, the New City Hall occupies all the space. According to Lisa Rochon's strong expression, again, its opening in 1965 immediately transformed Toronto's brand, its signature.[64]

The second of these achievements, the Art Gallery of Ontario, changed face not by juxtaposing two buildings, as was the case for the city halls, but by joining them at the hip. Indeed, the old stone structure now appears enveloped and protected by wide strands of glass. The new city is all contained in the shape and spirit of that envelope. If the New City Hall announced new times, the AGO illustrates it magnificently and undeniably.

Between the two achievements, a time of rupture, marked especially by great citizen struggle such as the one led to stop the Spadina expressway project. Torontonians mobilized and with them, many celebrities such as Jane Jacobs. The author of *The Death and Life of Great American Cities* left her adopted city, which she settled in during the Vietnam War, with vivid memories. With others, and in the spirit of contestations she supported in the United States with regard to the New York transit system and the recognition of civil rights for African Americans, she probably looked on with great satisfaction when Torontonians occupied their City Hall and forced the consortium of elected officials and private interests abandon the Spadina expressway project. That saved the city from the mindless ripping

---

64. ROCHON, L. (2010) "Toronto City Hall: How Finnish Architecture rebranded a City", *Cityspace,* October 13.

of the urban fabric, but it most of all showed the capacity of Torontonians to mobilize for their city, to wage the important fights and to win them. That capacity showed up more than once since.

In 2005, a coalition of citizens is opposed to the construction of a 46-storey tower near the Royal Ontario Museum. The battle is tightly fought, the interests at stake, considerable. City Hall is host to heavy debates which the coalition ends up winning. More recently, with regard to the drastic cuts the current municipal administration suggested, aiming at the Toronto Public Library resources, another coalition of citizens led a relentless fight to force the administration to back down. A friend in Toronto, called from Montreal the night of October 26th 2010 to be comforted after Rob Ford's election, surprises me with a half-worried, half-confident discourse: "Only those who are unaware of the importance of Toronto's social fabric and network of NGOs believe that the new mayor will be able to implement his program. In my opinion, he told me, the fight is just beginning and it is far from certain that Ford will win it". During our many trips to Toronto and throughout Ontario, the importance of that social fabric was constantly verified.

Social cohesion

That five-pointed star also conceals a worrying social reality. Indeed, the Ontarian metropolis suffers from the urban Canadian illness: its status as a creature of provincial capital; the indifference from other "superior" branches of government for these places, these cities, where more than 80 per cent of the country's citizens live; the precariousness of public resources that are conceded to them and that are among the lowest in OECD countries. Cities are regarded as negligible in Canada, along with their governance, their needs and their accomplishments. This is due in part to social cohesion which, slowly but surely, is eroding, as was demonstrated in a 2009 study from the University of Toronto's Centre for Urban and Community Studies. The great city would slowly be splitting into three separate zones: an affluent centre, a poor periphery and a declining zone in between where the middle class resides. It is becoming *"a city of extremes"*.[65] Its biggest challenge, one it shares with all the big cities in the world, is to reinstate places accessible to the middle class. That was confirmed by a recent edition of *Toronto's Vital Signs,* which Royson James summarizes thus:[66]

---

65. WENTE, M. "A tale of two Torontos". *The Globe and Mail,* December 16.

66. JAMES, R. (2009) "A city of disparities", *The Toronto Star,* special section, October 6.

Trends show middle-income families may soon be essentially extinct in the city, even as the economic extremes grow into dangerous spikes of rich and poor ... Between 1970 and 2005, the number of middle-income earners collapsed from 66 per cent to 29 per cent of the city's population. It could fall to 20 per cent by 2025.

Some reports, especially one from the Ontario Human Rights Commission, America's most significant before the government emaciated it, show that xenophobic feelings are not absent from Ontarian cities.[67] Graham Frazer wrote in 1998:

We are too quick to congratulate ourselves. We have less lessons to give to others than we think. Canada remains a country with but a discreet xenophobia, a polite racism, a velvet discrimination, where exclusions are so sly that we often find it difficult to face them.[68]

Canada prides itself in the fact that proportionally to its population, it greets three times as many immigrants as the United States and that it remains the second migration destination in the world, after Australia. But to borrow a title from the *Courrier International,* the people "disappointed in the Canadian dream" are many after realizing that many qualified immigrants' credentials are not recognized, they cannot practice their profession or find the training and integration programs they need. Other cities, such as Barcelona and Vienna, "have a full suite of services to help immigrants launch their own businesses".[69] Complexity of bureaucratic systems or sly discrimination? As a consequence, according to Jeffrey G. Reitz, University of Toronto sociologist, qualified "immigrant earnings in Canada are declining to the lower levels of the United States, where the skill levels of immigrants tend to be lower".[70] That situation is slowly evolving. Michael Ornstein showed in 2010 that the number of lawyers coming from visible minorities is "changing dramatically" in the past years to reach 11.5 per cent in 2006. In 1981, they represented 2 per cent of lawyers aged 25 to 34, compared

---

67. ONTARIO HUMAN RIGHTS COMMISSION (2004), *Paying the Price: The human cost of Racial profiling*, Inquiry Report.

68. FRAZER, *op.cit,* p. 160.

69. ROGEL, N. (2011) "On immigration, Canada could learn from world capitals". *The Globe and Mail,* September 21.

70. KRAUSS, C. (2005) "Some Skilled Foreigners Find Jobs Scarce in Canada", *New York Times,* June 5.

with 20 per cent in 2006. That ongoing progression, however, is sometimes accompanied with dubious practices as these visible minority lawyers are less likely to get a partner status or the same pay scale as their colleagues.[71] Hence the need for constant vigilance and for Torontonians' sustained interventions so that the harmony that is sought between these fragments of the world, that are really the fragments of their city, be reinforced.

The city and the water

Toronto's history is intricately linked to Lake Ontario, which the Iroquois called Skanhdario and whose banks water the city's southern edge, from Etobicoke to Scarborough, with its superb 60-metre high limestone cliffs, the Bluffs. But one can stay in Toronto without really discovering that resource because anarchic urban development has for a long time masked the immense body of water that is a natural boundary. For more than a decade, important works are trying to create a new natural link between the city and the water and thus link up the chain of beauties which, from Brighton to Niagara, make of Lake Ontario's shores one of the provinces true wonders. Among these beauties, one can find the Waterfront trail that runs over 900 kilometres along the Lake and the St. Lawrence River and crosses many parks and natural areas.

Following the recommendations of a task force set up in 1999, the Canadian, Ontario and municipal governments launched a revitalization operation of Toronto's waterfront, one of the great urban redevelopment projects on the continent. The scope of ambitions and investments, valued at $17 billion in 2001 and $43 billion in 2010, is inversely proportional to the past 50 years of built disasters.[72]

Making the waterfront accessible to the public, reducing urban sprawl, creating quality public spaces and viable communities, building affordable and sustainable housing, including in it all places of culture and creativity: such are the great stated objectives. As the rocky debates that followed the present municipal administration's intentions to put an end to the public facet of that broad plan have shown, Torontonians approve of this plan and appreciate what has already been accomplished. As a result, Mayor Ford yet again had to abandon his intentions in that regard. The central section of the waterfront has been revitalized, 16 public parks were created or

---

71. MIDDLEMISS, J. (2010) "Faces of Ontario law firms altering 'dramatically'", *The National Post*, July 21st.

72. WATERFRONTORONTO, *Annual Report 2002-2003*; Waterfrontoronto; *Management Report 2010-2011;* Waterfrontoronto, *Economic Impact 2010-2011*.

modernized, undulated platforms installed, as well as playing fields, trails and beaches and a boardwalk of close to 2 kilometres now flank the port. Lastly, the East Bayfront is in complete renovation. Six thousand residential units are being built there; so are vast commercial spaces and, in 2012, the neighbourhood will welcome more than 3,000 students that will attend George Brown Colleges's new waterside campus. The plan's implementation is spread until 2025 and, without undue modesty, aims at giving Toronto a waterfront that can rival any of the most accomplished waterside cities in the world. That's a rendezvous, in about 15 years, to appreciate this broad restoration.

JOHN WILDGUST

At the heart of Toronto's financial district, John Wildgust invites us to breakfast in a Belgian bistro that offers clean lines and fusion food. All around us, a forest of glass and steel springs up. There, lodged in the sky, are the headquarters of Canadian financial institutions and big banks. Raising his glass, our host issues a resounding "Welcome to the centre of the universe". That surprising icebreaker requires further explanation. The conversation lasts 2 hours. The waitress speaks to us in French, a language that Wildgust also commands perfectly after a long stay in Quebec City. He has a rare knowledge of the country, having pitched his PR agent and journalist's tent in the main Canadian cities for more than 30 years.

Born in Stratford, John adopted Toronto as his city. He loves his city and defends it tooth and nail for its quality of life, its proximity to large bodies of water, which protect it from severe winter conditions, its ethnic diversity, which links it to the world, and its constantly improving cultural offer. The oral argument is elaborate. Of course, the descendants of Europeans, of which he is, have become a minority and the visible minorities are now rather a majority. But that fact does not trouble him at all. "Toronto managed to attract and keep a constant flow of immigrants from all over the world, and more recently, from faraway Asia". He likes this kaleidoscope of races, languages, attitudes and customs and underlines its harmony. Despite some pitfalls and specific problems in such or such community, that coexistence was and remains, in his judgment, marked with the signs of concord.

In a few words, John just summarized a century and a half of history. The journey between the white man's world, defended with laws, regulations and defensive measures and that other world made up of persons and communities from every ancestry.

John's identity lies first in Toronto, that city of all "establishments" that regularly "votes red and green", left or centre left. We know, since the municipal election of 2010 and the federal election of 2011, that Greater Toronto can also vote blue. John's identity is also Ontarian, especially "when one visits the other regions of the country, the Texans of Alberta and the Californians of British Columbia". Here, we don't have to live with "confrontation and shameful discrimination" as they do in the United States, but with something else, difficult to define and emanating from that long practice at negotiation. For John, Ontario is at the epicentre of that attitude that defines Canada's specificity.

That position, according to our interlocutor, is not without problem. Toronto is not the most popular elsewhere in the province. Never was. Fault is found with its power, its arrogance and its appropriation of everything. Clearly, it is envied for "its durable success". Maybe John knows that, but in 1867, Upper Canada was named Province of Toronto and Lower Canada, Province of Quebec. The reaction was at once negative. Under pressure from regions that were unflinching in their opinion that the city of Toronto took up enough space already, that appellation was abandoned. That day, the province of Toronto became the province of Ontario.

The big city is not the most popular in the rest of the country either. It is blamed for absorbing everything from wealth and talent to population. It is faulted for that insidious control of the country's soul through its control over the main written and TV media whose self-conceit, especially in the case of the public broadcasting network, is inversely proportional to its number of listeners and viewers. *The Globe and Mail*, is left unscathed by these critiques. It is in a separate category and, since its creation in 1844, remains politically independent, even though it recently supported numerous initiatives from the Harper government. Some of its signatures are among the most reliable in Canada. It is not clear if it is venerated due to its age, which is normally accompanied with wisdom, or for its modernity, which recently was gladly demonstrated with this new layout and graphic design, both magnificent. The *Toronto Star*, although it has the higher readership in Canada, is less renowned at both the edges of this impossible country. That paper is said to be liberal and indeed it is. Sometimes, it is so close to Toronto's life that one has the feeling, reading it, to insert oneself in that "polyphonic murmuring" which, according to Dionne Brand, can be heard in the Queen City. *The National Post* irritates liberal minds but they still read it for some of its unique analyses. The Sun is an embodiment of the tabloids which, in the motherland, rummage through trash, both at the historical and street levels. They exaggerate, say the purists... they ask the questions that are on most minds, reply its makers.

More than two thirds of all Canadian magazines published in English are published in Toronto. Since the middle of the 19th century, a significant number of general magazines were launched in Toronto, from *the Canadian Journal* in 1850 to *Toronto Life* more than a century later. Some were short-lived, others resisted better to the competition from American magazines which, in the long run, have dominated the choices of Canadian readers. Some titles clearly belong to the intellectual, cultural and political history of Canada and Ontario: *the Queen's Quarterly*, launched in 1893, the *Toronto Saturday Night,* in 1887, which became, two years later, *the Saturday Night, the Canadian Forum,* in 1920 and the *Maclean's,* known as such since 1911 but born six years earlier under the title *Business Magazine,* whose political and cultural influence today is predominant.

But the Ontario press is larger than that produced only in Toronto. Each medium-sized city has its own daily newspaper, each community its own daily, weekly or monthly publications. In Toronto, the foreign language press accounts for more than 50 titles and an impressive circulation: more than 225,000 for the Indian press, 175,000 in the case of the Chinese press, 75,000 in Spanish and 50,000 for the Pakistani and Caribbean press, all of which are good relays for information about cultural activities in the communities. Cultural centres programs are announced, as well as exhibits, workshops, conferences and concerts offered by Torontonians or by creators coming straight from the homeland. Always present too, well-placed advertisement for the programming of OMNI Television, the TV of all languages and all stories.

John also confesses some worries.

> How are we to keep the heart of the city alive and beating? What can we do to prevent its centre from wilting away while big and powerful suburbs, the infamous 905 area, thrive and extend their reach as far as "cottage country", that refuge for Torontonians looking for peace and nature? How are we to avoid the strengthening of a crown of poverty between the centre and the periphery? How can we reshape the Ontarian economy and replace the great industrial sector that made Ontario's fortune, especially

since the Automobile Pact ... unless the Chinese come here to build the cars of the future!

HOWARD ASTER

Howard Aster is a publisher. And a great one at that. The catalogue of the publishing house he founded, Mosaic Press, proves it without a doubt. It has more than 500 titles. Some were penned by recipients of prestigious prizes: one Nobel, twelve Governor General's Awards and many more. The enterprise is local and global. It has networks and partners in more than 30 countries. It partakes in every European and American book fairs. The man that brings most of this to life greets us in his house, filled to the brink with books, engravings and memories, in the centre of Old Oakville.

Founded in 1827, the city first made a living with its port and with the export of pine and oak for the construction of the Empire's ships in the 19th century before becoming a vast kitchen garden that supplied Toronto and a sought-after holiday resort. In the little streets that lead to the lake and to our host's sanctuary, one house out of two displays its history, the date it was built, its function in the community, sometimes the names of its past inhabitants. Some are modest, others lavish with gardens of great beauty even in the February cold, but they all are witnesses of a unique history and, with these little signs reminding passersby of a sure attachment to an almost bicentennial heritage. And at the end of Oakville's Waterfront Trail, segment of the 900-kilometre pathway stretching along the lake from Niagara to the border with Quebec, Toronto shows itself, distant and majestic.

Here we are in a different Ontario, patrimonial, scenic, bucolic almost. Oakville is worth the trip for the harmony of its historical neighbourhood, its old beauty as well new, its relationship with water, which linked it to faraway shores. But that vision can be mistaking; Oakville is also a great industrial city. On the other side of the highway which splits the city in two, in the northern lands, the Ford empire installed its Canadian headquarters and Canadian branch, and in doing so, contributing to the development, growth and prosperity of a modern city.

Howard greeted us, him too in French, as would an old friend. Warm and welcoming was the family dining room, hot were the wine and the homemade soup and superb the conversation. He opens his address book to us, insists that we visit Hamilton, London, Oshawa and many more communities. You will meet there the great Ontarian families who developed these regions. You will learn the history of the labour and social movements and of the political baronies that guided the history of the province and of the country. He suggests we meet some authors, offers us a few "essential" reads and promises long and heterogeneous lists of personalities that we "absolutely must meet". He will be true to his word and deliver these lists, opens these doors, many of these people, his friends having greeted us and greatly enriched our Ontarian encounters.

With him, we dive back in the October Crisis, the Meech Lake and Charlottetown sagas, the imperial reigns of Trudeau and Mulroney, that of Chretien as well, this "geographic and social centrist"... and what has happened to the country since. We appreciate the quality of "coast to coast" information, or lack thereof, exchange thoughts on the intellectual laziness that befalls the country, the lack of boldness of Canadian publishers whose risks are all covered by a grants system that is both generous and corrosive for innovation and the hard work implied by the conquest of local and foreign markets.

If ever for a moment we hint at an insidious form of nostalgia for a country that no longer exists, and maybe never existed, Howard stokes the ashes and passionately evokes the new authors, "his" new authors. With their recent experience of the country, they fertilize the scorched earth of our debates and remind us of the dramas of oppression that often brought them to our shores. Many titles in his catalogue illustrate this intermingling of races and horizons, this enrichment of imaginations, those that are planted here and those that hail from other bountiful lands. Their authors come from everywhere, the Caribbean, South Asia, Africa and the Americas. Devotedly, Howard lists them without forgetting the poets, filmmakers, producers, pollsters, directors and other sociocultural architects. They may be the ones that show us the country as it is becoming. As John Wildgust did before him, Howard talks of the shift from a time of uniformity to one of diversity. He sees in that shift the unprecedented conditions of a new human, social and cultural experience.

The conversation has little to do with all the others we've had until then. Here are old-stock Canadians, no doubt cosmopolitan but rooted in the ancient lands of Lower and Upper Canada, their memories filled with episodes that made Canadian history and headlines for the past half century but that probably do not resonate with a good amount of new citizens. They are also interested and fascinated, however, by the new sedimentations that enrich the country's immaterial landscapes. Honey Dresher, the great lady of Montreal's cultural diversity, brought about this encounter. She was right to insist. "Passage obligé", she said. A mandatory, crucial and fortunate visit.

Howard talks of the new conditions of his passion, which is also his profession: the international dimension of literary market, the emergence of new electronic supports and platforms, global competition for the illustration and the printing of books. We promise to see each other again and have kept that promise since, more than once. Speaking of books, not cars like our friend John Wildgust, it is Howard's turn to mention Chinese competition. More than 2 million immigrants to Ontario are of Asian origin. From everywhere in Asia but predominantly from China and India.

Like many of our interlocutors, Howard is insistent when it comes to the Ontarian diversity. We left Oakville convinced that it was time to explore it in making connections with the communities that embody it.

THE COMMUNITIES

> In the vast western landscape, Rahul Bhardwaj told us, Ontario's situation is almost unique insomuch that the diversity here is a component of the province's fabric and that it quickly imposed itself as THE dominant value. Diversity! Either it is a dominant value or it isn't. That choice is foundational; every other debate sits at the margin of that one.

This appreciation from our witness, Rahul Bhardwaj, kept drawing our attention as we went along our exploration of Ontarian society and could not help but observe its accuracy over almost all of the province's territory. Windsor's mayor, greeting us in his City Hall, is of Lebanese origin. The publisher of the *London Free Press*, giving us a tour of his newsroom, is of Italian origin. The economist and former high-ranking official at the United Nations that we met a McMaster University in Hamilton is of Syrian origin. The national vice president of OMNI Television if of Belarusian descent. The director of the University of Toronto's Desautels Centre for Integrative Thinking is from Romania. The president of the Toronto Community Foundation is of Indian origin. Toronto's Poet Laureate is of Trinidadian origin. The president of the Maytree Foundation also comes from India, as does the Principal of U of T's Mississauga campus. However incomplete, this sample shows that diversity is a primary, immediate and constitutive data for whomever observes Ontarian society today. It is obvious in Toronto and in a great number of medium-sized Ontarian cities.

Such diversity first belongs to people. Ontarians are diverse in their indomitable individuality, marked by their origin, by the moment of their arrival, their reasons for migrating, their age, education, religion, socioeconomic position, their understanding of the fundamental principles of the country, especially the language. A large and magnificent literature shows the singularity of the experiences of those who chose to settle in Ontario. No other life looks like that of little Samuel in Rabindranath Maharaj's *The Amazing Absorbing Boy*,[73] whose memory is filled with his island's landscapes, festivities, people, alive or not. But Samuel's steps, looks, contacts and conversations span the distances between Regent Park, Union Station, Nathan Phillips Square, Toronto's subway stations and its public library. There he meets people of modest means, often living in difficult conditions. They wear heavy coats and "they all looked faded, like dematerializing comic book ghosts".

Ontarians are also diverse within each community. This fact is demonstrated by the religious pluralism—Muslim, Christian and atheist—within the Arabic community; the religious and linguistic pluralism of members of the Black community; the ethnic, religious, linguistic and cultural pluralism of the Indian community and of those others from South-East Asian countries; the linguistic, ethnic and cultural pluralism of the Chinese community.

That diversity is also that of the communities themselves. Indeed, Ontarians are diverse because of the plurality of communities that together form the Ontarian society.

It explains the large number of associations, organizations and federations which, in Ontario, avail themselves of such or such ethnic group or subgroup. In almost all the different Ontarian communities, the plurality of associations and pluralism of representation dominate as the expression of the variety of experiences, situations and geographic, cultural and spiritual affiliations. Dionne Brand showed the links that can exist between members of different communities, the feelings that bring them together beyond any difference, the natural set of human interrelations, their mutual assistance as well as the joys and sorrows they share.[74]

This positioning does not make the personal interests and needs of these new Ontarians disappear. They all have different philosophical, ethical,

73. MAHARAJ, R., *op.cit.*

74. BRAND, D., *op. cit.*

political, social and environmental backgrounds and values, and professional interests that, beyond cultural or ethnic affiliations, explain their participation in groups to which they don't necessarily belong culturally or ethnically. The discovery of Toronto by Maharaj's little Samuel is first that slow appropriation of a city whose citizens hold all the stakes and challenges of the world in their hearts and spirits.

We have observed such diversity as it truly appears, including with its community component, all through our Ontarian adventure. It in no way looks like the gross caricatures of communitarianism that are made in France, notably, where its rejection has the weight of dogma. Blinded by a kind of irrational fear of identities, the supporters of that conception are dangerously distancing themselves from real society. Truth be told, no community is homogeneous. All are plural and fragmented, often divided. Furthermore, they exist through the engagement of some in a sea of indifference towards others. In an interview with a French magazine, *Le Point*, Charles Taylor states the essential:[75]

> If I define myself as communitarian, it is not because I want to contribute to the blossoming of different communities within one state. I am a communitarian in the sense that I think solidarity between individuals is important and that society is not an indifferent ensemble of individuals: it is an ensemble of communities, visible or not. The communitarian movement is born in Anglo-Saxon countries in reaction to the neoliberal theses that wanted to reduce state intervention and challenge the collective mechanisms of solidarity. It is a reply to those who, like Mrs. Thatcher, think that society doesn't exist, that there are only individuals. That said, this does not correspond to the reality or problems to which individuals in a minority are confronted, such as North Africans that are discriminated in the hiring process... Of course there are oppressive communities. It is the role of the state after all to defend individuals against those. But it is absurd to think that all are so. To think that is simply not seeing that community solidarity often serves as a support to individual freedom.

---

75. TAYLOR, C. " le pape du communautarisme ", *Le Point*, 28 juin 2007, p.82.

What does "community solidarity" mean? What are its aims and utility, especially in a society as diverse as Ontario's? Who can better answer these questions than those who live that diversity? We went and met them to get their testimonies. We had to choose and ended up discussing with people from the Chines, Italian, Indian, Black, Arabic and Francophone communities. We could have chosen otherwise but it appeared to us that these communities, with their weight in terms of current and future demographic, sociological and historical importance, constituted a suitable selection.

VICTOR WONG

In the modest offices of the Chinese Canadian Council, installed in the heart of Tong Yen Gai, Toronto's historic Chinatown, Victor Wong greets us with a contagious friendliness. The man is knowledgeable about the history of the country and of immigration to it and mindful of the equity and justice reserved to Chinese immigrants, including Tibetans, with whom his organization maintains an ongoing dialogue. He reminds us that Ontarians of Chinese origin constitute one of the province's most important visible community. The same goes for Toronto, and their presence is also felt in a great number of Ontarian cities, among them Ottawa, where they also form the first minority, in Kitchener-Waterloo, Guelph, Kingston and in the towns around Toronto, especially its northeastern crown. And their numbers could double as of 2031. The expression visible " minority" is defined by the Employment Equity Act as "persons, other than aboriginal peoples, who are non-Caucasian in race or non-white in colour".

Three main ideas are retained from our long conversation. Ideas that sketch a unique profile of the Chinese community: the weight of history, a typology of that community and the specific character of Chinese immigration.

The weight of history

The historical file is loaded. Using the force of law, Canadian lawmakers, provincial and federal, enact and impose the worst systemic discriminations and denials of justice to the Chinese; those wishing to immigrate to Canada and those that were already Canadian citizens.

One thinks of the fate reserved to the 17,000 Chinese workers from the province of Kwangtung who, between 1880 and 1885, came to Canada to build the western section of the Canadian Pacific railway in Alberta and British Columbia. More than 4,000 of them did not survive the task. The others are left to fend for themselves in utter destitution once the great work is completed. They are rejected here and without the possibility of a return to China.

One also thinks of the infamous head tax, set at $50 in 1885, raised to $100 in 1900 and further up to $500 in 1903, the equivalent of two years of salary at the time. The 1923 *Exclusion Act* also comes to mind, effectively ending all Chinese immigration for a quarter century until it was finally abolished after the war, in 1947.

Finally, one thinks of the formal negation of political rights, the right to stand for election and the right to vote among them, which, in the case of Canadians of Chinese and Asian origins, will also be abolished in 1947. That odious discriminatory policy was first a result of provinces having the prerogative to set the rules that applied at the federal level. In 1920, the Dominion Elections Act determines that the federal right to vote is under federal jurisdiction, not provincial. Twent eight years will pass before the right to vote is granted to Canadians of Asian descent.

During that long period, it was said that the Chinese spoke an incomprehensible dialect and that their customs were strange. They were feared and, as a consequence, they were kept down. Aside from these outrageous laws, they were treated with contempt and often violence. The Chinese presence, effective or apprehended, or more broadly any Asian presence, was the source of reprobation and refusal all over the country. The case is disturbing and conclusive: urban riots in the West that "threaten to leave Chinatown and the Japanese quarters a wreck;,[76] editorials in the East declaring that they are not our brethren and in that sense, they cannot "help us to develop along those lines that Providence has chosen us, or that we have chosen for ourselves. His presence is a hindrance and not a help".[77] Racist interventions in the House such as that pronounced by a member of Parliament (MP) in 1922:

> It is desirable that we should have a white Canada and that we should not become a yellow or mongrel nation. This is a great national question and our future progress and prosperity are at stake.[78]

---

76. HILLMER & GRANATSTEIN, *op. cit.,* p. 119.

77. *Idem,*p.116.

78. *Idem,* p.178.

The same year, *Maclean's*, in its May 15 edition, asks the following question: "Shall we bar the yellow race?"

And two decades later, right in the middle of the Second World War, a little girl follows the movements on the busy quays of Hong Kong.

> A Canadian official looked at us and then turned to one of
> his colleagues and said: What are those people doing here?
> They are not white! Well, they're on the list. Why don't
> we just leave them there? ... The man who had spotted us
> had other things to do, so he turned away. And by turning
> away, we were destined for Canada, even though we were
> Chinese, even though we were Oriental, even though we
> were not wanted.

That little girl was born Poy. She will become Clarkson, Adrienne Clarkson, Governor General of Canada from 1999 to 2005.[79]

Decades will go by before finally, in 2006, the federal government responded to the campaigns led by the Chinese Canadian National Council, asking for a formal apology from Canada for the suffered discriminations. These demands also included symbolic reparations to the persons that were submitted to the head tax, and to their spouse if these persons had passed.

Describing that chapter of Canadian history as "unfortunate", and evoking the "deep sorrow over the racist actions of our past", Prime Minister Harper declared the following to the House on June 26, 2006:

> I rise today to formally turn the page on an unfortunate
> period in Canada's past, a period during which a group of
> people, people who only sought to build a better life, were
> repeatedly and deliberately singled out for unjust treatment.
> I speak of course of the head tax, ... as well as the other
> restrictive measures that followed. ... This tax remained
> in place until 1923 when the government amended the
> Chinese Immigration Act and effectively banned most
> Chinese immigrants until 1947. ... The Government of
> Canada recognizes the stigma and exclusion experienced
> by the Chinese as a result. ... We also recognize that our
> failure to truly acknowledge these historical injustices has

---

79. CLARKSON, A. (2008) *Heart Matters*. Toronto: Penguin Books, p.11.

prevented many in the community from seeing themselves
as fully Canadian.

Stephen Harper was right to mention that these policies "prevented many
in the community from seeing themselves as fully Canadian". This is most
probably where the Chinese community's interest in that tragic fragment of
the country's history stems from. Our interlocutors in that group all evoked
it. The multiplication of research and intervention projects is proof of that
and cinema has made the topic a recurrent one.

Victor no longer restrains himself and destroys the idea of a homogeneous community. His words concern the Chinese community specifically
but describe a plurality that prevails in almost every community.

> You have the very old ones, like my grandfather, who paid
> the infamous head tax and who, after the Second World
> War, had their family, or what was left of it, join them. You
> have the Hong Kong workers who, afraid of the Cultural
> Revolution, chose to leave. You also have the first wave of
> so-called immigrant investors, from the same territory,
> who feared the repercussions of the events of Tiananmen,
> and decided to leave; then the second wave, made up of
> those who took the same decision when it appeared increas-
> ingly clear that the British government was about to hand
> the colony over to Beijing. Then you have the more com-
> fortable Taiwanese, worried with the permanent incidents
> in the Taiwan Strait. Finally, you take into account the
> 300,000 Chinese immigrants that came in the last decade,
> without counting those that came from third countries,
> Asian or elsewhere in the world. Major differences exist
> between all these categories. The firs example is the lan-
> guage they speak. The first immigrants from China came
> in high numbers from the Guangdong province and spoke
> a dialect close to Cantonese. The ones that came from Hong
> Kong spoke a different dialect also issued from Cantonese.
> The recent 300,000 speak Mandarin, which was little
> established here but is now starting to impose itself in the
> public space, the people that speak it being more present,
> seeking more information, more involved, etc. In short,
> our community has its own linguistic problems!

Two Chinatowns

The old Chinatown in Toronto's centre was for long the sole common space of the community. All the stereotypes were then condensed in that territory: laundries, restaurants, suspended Peking ducks, the exotic fruit stalls, pharmacies specialized in traditional medicine. It took shape as an answer to the need for an enclave to face the discrimination the Chinese suffered. The old neighbourhood has been partly destructed. In the 60s, the *Save Chinatown* campaign partially protected the historical district from the demolition the city's administrators had planned to build Toronto's new city hall there. Despite the protests, the expropriation took place and two thirds of the neighbourhood were torn down. The community remembers this painful episode and it is explained with the three following reasons: implemented in the middle of the 50s, the decision to demolish was made much before, in 1947, when Chinese citizens did not have the right to vote; the decision was part of the assimilation ideology popular at the time and which was contradicted by the very existence of a Chinatown; lastly, the idea of a "modernistic" plan justified the demolition in order to make room for a city hall that would fit these criteria.

Worlds meet in what remains of the historic district today, the Western world which surrounds and visits it; an Asian world of abundance, diversity, commerce and hard work. The old neighbourhood has been revitalized. It now boasts legal firms, banks, financial institutions, specialized boutiques, currency traders, travel agencies and stores offering all the world's technological products. These additions have not altered the energy, colour or life of the historical neighbourhood. But Tong Yen Gai no longer has the monopoly of Chinese life in Toronto, even if it remains the symbolic centre of the community. No longer is it the mandatory destination of newcomers.

Northeast of the city, Chinatown Two sprawls on the territories of Richmond Hill, Markham and, in part, Scarborough. The duality is not only geographic. It also translates a stark difference between levels of schooling, financial capacities and social status.

The contrast between Toronto's two Chinese cities is striking. The first is true to the image we have of a large Chinatown in a North-American city. The second is apparently less spectacular. In the train that takes us there, the users are young, urban and hip. The station opens on wide arterial roads where the automobile dominates. Walking is not common there, contrary to the old Chinatown, where each step reserves a surprise. At first sight, the second city looks like an American suburb, with multilane avenues, residential developments, shopping malls and big industrial parks. But it is much more than an ordinary suburb. It hosts hundreds of corporate head-quarters as well as high technologies and life sciences companies. It lacks no ambition either. Markham does not hesitate to present itself as the high tech capital of Canada and, with Richmond Hill, as the Bay Street of the north. Some neighbourhoods in these cities have over 50 per cent of citizens that are of Chinese origin; public display signs reflect that reality.

Very symbolic, Markham's Varley Art Gallery owns Avron Yanovsky's famous Bethune Mural. That work was painted for the Communist Party of Canada as a tribute to Norman Bethune, a Canadian doctor, a hero in China and, in his country, a passionate advocate for universal health care. The work was finished in 1965 and then installed at Toronto's Norman Bethune-Tim Buck Educational Centre.

The Chinese Cultural Centre of Greater Toronto, one of the most impor-tant such centres in North America, can also be found there. Entirely funded by the community, this beautiful establishment, inaugurated in 1988, brings together the traditional Chinese architectural style and the clean lines of the minimalist style. After a 2006 extension, that time with Ontarian govern-ment financial support, this centre fulfills its predictable missions, especially that of teaching and improving the knowledge and understanding of the Chinese culture and languages. It also developed relations with different Ontarian communities that use the facilities for their own activities. That proximity a reality that was evoked by many of the people we spoke to, that is, the fact that the Chinese community is more readily welcoming in its own institutions than present in those of others.

If the centre is first known for its quality cultural programming, it also initiates significant humanitarian interventions such as the creation of a coalition at the time of the 2003 SARS crisis, a fundraiser to the benefit of the victims of the 2004 tsunami and the creation of an assistance service for Ontarians wanting to adopt Chinese children. Some of these programs exclusively aim at the younger generation, which was officially recognized through the creation of an autonomous council. First among such programs is the offer of a study trip to China. The Chinese Cultural Centre also shel-ters the Asian Business and Cultural Development Centre, dedicated to the links between Asia and Ontario in these fields.

The Centre is an ideal gathering place for Ontario's Chinese community. It is in that house that victories of Patrick Chan, the Canadian figure skat-ing champion, were celebrated. It is there also that the Chinese authorities, represented by the Vice President of the People's Republic, have chosen to introduce Canadians to the Shanghai's world exposition and invite them to participate. Finally, the Centre often welcomed the principal dancer with the National Ballet of Canada, Chan Hon Goh. Daughter of two famous Chinese dancers, born in Beijing and coming to Canada in 1976, the artist imposed herself on the world stage as one of the finest classic ballerina of the time. She shared her life in a book that was superbly received by national and international critics.[80]

In downtown's Chinatown, one has the feeling of running into folks whose gaits and faces betray the extraordinary reality of immigration, of that desired, complex and harsh crossing from one world to the other. In Markham and Scarborough on the other hand, one has the impression of meeting inhabitants of Shanghai, rather young and welcoming, with a love for cars and fashion, having found and activated the levers of their economic ambitions.

Some belong to privileged categories, such as the specialized technicians who settle down with ease in the areas were high tech firms are present, Kanata, just west of Ottawa, for instance, or again, Markham and Scarborough. There is also the category of immigrant investors and professionals, many of them returning from whence they came after a shorter stay. A significant number of Chinese immigrants are rather modest, however, without a firm control of the country's fundamentals and, consequently, form a quasi-autarkic community. There are many reasons for that, but a lack of proficiency in English ranks high among them. That explains the multiplication of services in the languages immigrants understand and the quest for jobs in companies and firms that operate in these languages. That is not a virtuous circle. For Victor Wong, it has disastrous consequences. "It shuts off the community, leaves workers with modest and vulnerable jobs within the community and explains their low levels of participation and engagement in volunteer work as well as their relative absence from public employment, including elective positions."

Along the conversation, we realize that Victor knows Karen Sun, our first guide in this discovery of the Ontarian Chinese community.

KAREN SUN

We met Karen in the nicely renovated and illuminated building of the Centre for Social Innovation, at 215, Spadina Avenue. This was the setting

---

80. HON GOH, C. (2002) *Beyond the Dance, a Ballerina's Life*. Toronto: Tundra Books.

for a long discussion about her community. The young woman works for the Toronto Chapter of the Chinese Canadian National Council. She fights for "the promotion of equity, social justice, civic participation and respect of diversity". From categories that are more or less abstract and that include hundreds of thousands of people, she takes us to particular and individual experiences, starting with her own.

Educated as an environmentalist, Karen admits her own surprise to find herself "in social and ethnic issues", serving the Chinese community of Toronto. She sees in that a proof of the systemic discrimination that afflicts visible minorities. In her case, it is not a question of the famous foreign diploma and credentials recognition: "I was born in Canada and graduated from the University of Guelph".

She evokes her recent and current work: the organization of an information and training session for recently-arrived Chinese women. She informs them of their new rights and compares the differences between the Canadian and Chinese legal systems. In return, these women share with her their often difficult situation: non-proficiency in English and the quasi-permanent isolation that results from it, intergenerational distance, domestic violence and other such hardships. Karen also mentions the publication of a book that brings together the testimonials of old Chinese immigrants' experiences, their difficulties and successes in going from one world to the other, their adaptation, or not, to the reality of Ontarian society. She doesn't fail to mention the translation of these eyewitness accounts by young Torontonians of Chinese origin as a way to maintain the links between the "ancients and the moderns".

The youth! Karen, among them, declares that they integrate faster and must live in two permanently conflicting universes, that of their family and that of their new environment. But all of them are confronted to inescapable imperatives: learning the language, finding a job, appropriating the social and legal norms of their new society and coupling the ancestral values of their country of origin with those prevailing in their new country.

Karen speaks of her pride at being Canadian, in the 80s. She now feels Torontonian, living "in the bubble" that covers the city. Between these two identities, Ontario occupies a place that is hard to define. In her mind, the question needs to be asked otherwise. She refuses to consider herself a minority, that status given to her by "others, all the others". Paradoxically, all her work aims at strengthening minorities, at fostering solidarity and coherence between the fragmented parts of the Chinese community and at building bridges between the very different worlds of the Hispanic, African and Southeast Asian minorities. The point is to push back against social and professional exclusion, which comes in great part from the loss of the value that was attached to their diplomas, specializations and experiences which, incidentally, got them to be accepted by Citizenship and Immigration Canada.

What Karen is telling us, we will hear again from many sources and in every community: poverty, disrupted families, indigence and isolation of many elderly people, discrimination, depression stemming from a confused identity. All of this drama is part of a broader feeling of having lost, for some, the hope of a better life, which was the motivation behind their move to Canada. For others, fortunately, we talk of exiting that transition period and the control of their lives consistent with their aspirations. At the end of our meeting, Karen hands us a copy of the book she mentioned, the one with the testimonials from old immigrants from China. It makes for a wonderful read.[81]

They are the stories of Yuncai Sun, who "fabricated" a map of the Toronto subway in Mandarin, allowing hundreds of his friends not proficient in English to circulate comfortably and break their isolation. Of Guohua Leung, who challenges himself to learn a language he doesn't know, English, at a high level, in order to fulfil his dream: be an interpreter for Chinese immigrants in Toronto's hospitals. Of Lyuan Yang who, in order to escape sadness, writes *Hong Kong's Essay,* a nomad's memoir. Of Ziwei Bao, who creates an elderly choir, now a staple in the community, a frequent guest in its festivities and even for great cultural gatherings in Nathan Phillips Square; the group's first album was an instant success. Of Doug Hum, who mobilized the community to request for apologies from the Canadian authorities for the infamous head tax, to put an end to what he felt were "racist" programs on CTV, qualifying Chinese Canadian students as "foreign" and to obtain, in the school system, the first teachings of the Chinese language and history.

These stories illustrate the multiple paths taken by a community in order to shape and assert itself. They render other stories, better known and sometimes spectacular ones, possible. That of Adrienne Clarkson, who became Governor General, of Raymond Chang, businessman, philanthro-

---

81. CHINESE CANADIAN SENIORS (2007). *My Story,* Toronto: The Chinese Canadian National Council, Toronto Chapter.

pist and Chancellor of Ryerson University, of Susur Lee, world-renowned chef, of Olivia Chow, member of the Canadian Parliament, of Jean Lumb, businesswoman and recipient of the Order of Canada. The list of Chinese Canadians whose exceptional contribution to society is worthy of mention runs quite long.

ALBERTO DI GIOVANNI

The discourse is as ample as the big and lovely house we are in, the Centro Scuola e Cultura Italiana, created to "showcase the place that Canadians of Italian origin have taken in the country's mosaic and to assert their identity". The Italian community holds a unique place in the history of Ontario. Its members constitute the biggest European minority in the province after the British and their contribution to its development has been significant.

Barely constituted as a country at the end of the 19th century, Italy sees more than 7 million of its children leave it for the shores of the Americas between 1889 and 1920. Canada profits little from this first great wave of Italian immigration. Eighty thousand Italians chose it then, compared to 4 million who prefer the United States and 3 millions in Latin America, with roughly two thirds going to Argentina and a third in Brazil. One reason for that is the Canadian policy of the time, which favoured Britain and other northern European countries as the origin of new Canadians. As of 1920, the Italian source is simply blocked because again of restrictive Canadian policies that reflected "racialist and xenophobic notions in Canadian public opinion and politics", according to the leaden words of sociologist Nicholas DeMaria Harney.[82] The policies of fascist Italy are also at play, as they strictly limited the amount of emigrants.

Things were entirely different following the Second World War. Indeed, in a few short years, the Italian Canadian population jumped from 150,000 to more than 600,000. Many of them settle in Toronto. In littler groups, others choose the mining and forest lands of the north, the agricultural valley of Niagara, the industrial cities of Windsor, Hamilton and Guelph as well as the federal capital.

"Petit peuple", as some of our French friends would say: construction labourers, carpenters, bricklayers, masons, plasterers, assistant plumbers, electricians and farm labourers for men and the women were linen maids, laundresses, factory workers and housekeepers. The nature of Italian immi-

---

82. DEMARIA HARNEY, N. (1999) *Eh, paesan! Being Italian in Toronto.* Toronto: University of Toronto Press, p.19.

gration in Canada evolved substantially between 1950 and 1980. If, after the war, 12.6 per cent of newcomers held non-manual jobs and 62 per cent had manual ones, these proportions were reversed after 1980. Nonetheless, the stereotypes concerning Italian immigrants endured despite the fact that this immigration changed and its members fill the urban landscape with high towers, apartment buildings, schools, hospitals, highways and boulevards.

Historian Franca Iacovetta remembers the 1950s and 1960s in her important book *Such a hardworking people, Italian immigrants in post-war Toronto:*

> I grew up in a crowded southern Italian immigrant household in an ethnic neighbourhood in downtown Toronto. Some of my earliest and most vivid recollections are of the evenings when my parents would come home from work. My mother used to arrive first, following a day's shift in the industrial laundry where she repaired tablecloths, hotel sheets, and towels. Having spent the day under Nonna's watchful eyes—my grandmother spent much of her adult life in Canada helping to raise her children's children ... my father, a bricklayer (and, later, a subcontractor), would not be home until dark. Soon after my mother's arrival, the other women of the household came home: my aunt, who lived upstairs with my uncle, cousin, and grandparents; and then "the lady downstairs," whose family rented the basement flat...I shared my bedroom—the main-floor living room—with two younger brothers and the family TV set. My parents slept in the dining room, and two older brothers occupied a third-floor attic room. At night, I would listen in on my parents' conversations. I can still hear the adults gathered around the kitchen table, endlessly discussing how to get jobs, the daily grind at work, and the struggle to get ahead. Amid the talk was the constant refrain: "siamo lavoratori forte" [we are such hardworking people]. It is a refrain that in the years between 1946 and 1965 was also heard on the lips of sympathetic outsiders who marvelled at the remarkable capacity the Italians had for hard work.
>
> ...

The late 1940s, the 1950s, and early 1960s were a time when our parents, as newcomers to this land, performed the dangerous or low-paying jobs that others shunned, spoke little English, and sometimes found themselves the victims of abuse. At the same time, they proved immensely resourceful, exhibiting a tremendous capacity for hard work and a talent for enjoying life, and each other's company, even in adversity.[83]

Such were the lives of a great number of Italian immigrants: solidary, painstaking, congested, committed, modest, abused but not without its joys. A life with laundresses as mothers, bricklayers as fathers, aunts, uncles and cousins living one floor up, women renting the basement with their families, parents sleeping in the dining room, little brothers sharing the living room with their sisters and their big brothers' beds in the attic. At the heart of this little world, critical engines roll on: hard work, some exploitation too and some simple happiness. The Second World War will come and break these promising arrangements with the internment of members of the Italian Canadian community, collectively suspected of sympathizing, and even more, with the regime of the Duce, ally of Nazi Germany.

To see the native land again

For these folks, life also resided in the link they maintained with their country of origin to feed simple joys, to keep in touch with the family, to enjoy phone conversations and announce births, weddings or deaths of close relatives or distant cousins.

A true anthology, the poignant description from Frank G. Paci of one of these phone calls announcing the death of Assunta to his aunt Pia, who had stayed in her remote village of Novilara. The line is bad, so is the spoken Italian, the old lady's voice is weak and filled with emotions. She explains that she no longer lives in the village but on a distant farm. That is why she received the telegram so late. Little used to the small machine, she says she's scared of making a call so far in the world. "An accident, they tell her; a train accident, replies the old lady, it's the hand of God". Then the forceful reminder of Assunta's intense and unaccomplished desire to see the country again, and to see her sister Pia. And these last sentences of a chaotic and painful conversation that reached every dimension, those of time and

---

83. HILLMER & GRANATSTEIN, *op. cit.*, p. 275.

distance, those of steady affection and vivid memories: "She hadn't seen her in over 30 years. From that day in the train station in Pesaro when she left with a suitcase and her trousseau trunk to go across the ocean to America".[84]

Assunta's dream to see Italy again materializes for a lot of people; the dream of visiting the childhood village to renew relationships with dear ones, to satisfy curiosities on the faith of the uncle who settled in Buenos Aires or Sao Paolo, of the cousin that became a Californian, of the dandy neighbour who tried his luck in Sidney and the family's youngest, living somewhere in Eastern Europe. About his village of San Giorgio, Fortunato Rao observes that:

> We have people in every country of Europe including Russia. From San Giorgio we have a large number of people in every country in South America, all over the U.S., Canada and Australia, you name it. Everywhere you find San Giorgesi and they went there for only one thing, to work. The people have emigrated all the time from San Giorgio since the world was created.[85]

That kind of international family tree, with roots planted in this village as in so many others explains the nature and importance of the transnational networks of the Italian diaspora, of men and women from all diasporas. It also allows one to understand the nature and diversity of their amalgamation in a given country. Nicholas DeMaria Harney, in *Eh Paesan!*, inventories the associations bringing Italians together in Toronto: more than 38 in 1954, 240 in 1984, 400 at the end of last century.

The Italian Ontarian community is getting bigger and organized. Toronto's Italian Cultural Institute opened its doors in 1976, its Italian Chamber of Commerce a few years later. The community is developing around three complementary value systems: family, work and solidarity, the latter well illustrated with the creation of a mutual aid society and with the pooling of family and clan resources to reach otherwise unreachable objectives. And a fourth value: the ambition of these families with regard to the education of their children, more than just an ambition, it is actually the ultimate goal of their misadventures, their efforts and their savings.

---

84. DI GIOVANNI, C.M. (2006) *Italian Canadian Voices: A Literary Anthology, 1946-2004.* Oakville: Mosaic Press.

85. HILLMER & GRANATSTEIN, *op. cit.*, p. 244.

In a simple sentence, Caroline Morgan Di Giovanni says it all: "Children attended university for the same reasons that brought their parents to cross the ocean: make life better". And the movement is considerable. Nicholas DeMaria Harney reminds us that in 1971, 56 per cent of Canadians of Italian origin had attended school for less than 9 years and only 5 per cent had completed their secondary education. "Make life better": the objective had been passed on from the parents to their children. In 1981, 56 per cent of Italian Canadians of the 15 to 25 age group attended schools and their high school registration level was just below the national average. In other words, the schooling level's growth rate for the children of the Italian minority was superior to that of other Canadians.[86]

Inferno... Paradiso

Alberto Di Giovanni has been director of his cultural centre for 20 years with a seemingly everlasting passion. Born in Italy and educated in Toronto, the man is prolific, precise and general all at once. We tour "the house" with a guide that is evidently happy. Here's the Carrier Art Gallery, superb room dedicated to Dante. There's a facsimile of the *Divine Comedy*'s manuscript, 17th, 18th, and 19th century editions of the masterly work, famous illustrations signed by Gustave Doré, by Amos Nattini, of the Alinari studio and by Salvator Dali, a superb collection of contemporary Italian artists' works, oil-paintings, etchings, collages and sketches representing the three eternal places: *Inferno, Purgatorio and Paradiso*. The library is remarkable, for its collections as much as for its muffled and studious ambiance. The centre also holds numerous rooms where the Italian language and civilisation are taught; that's its first vocation.

I bring to the attention of our host the fact that he makes references to Canada to the point of never evoking Ontario. I ask him about the notion of identity. After a moment, he says: "An Ontarian identity, I don't know. An Ontarian society, most certainly".

Our questions interest Alberto Di Giovanni, but he incorporates them to his, as if he were mixing grape varieties to make a more complete wine. He readily states that "1967 marks the entry of Canada in the modern era, and he believes Montreal's world exposition is the pivotal moment of that shift". In his opinion, that event is an advent. Beyond the ups and downs of the time, our interlocutor evokes a major phase of "liberation from colonial mentality and a true moment of reflection for all. For Italians as for others.

---

86. DEMARIA HARNEY, N., p.21.

Finally, this country started to think itself as something else that an addition to a declining empire".

Without being asked for it, Alberto shares with us his understanding of Canadian multiculturalism. It has little do to with scientific studies, conflicting statistics, funding of great and not so great events and political recuperation. He remembers a speech by then Secretary of State Gérard Pelletier, "a great intellectual who understood much better than Pierre Trudeau, that bureaucrat". In that speech, the politician stated that multiculturalism is consanguine to the country in part because of the historical presence of Aboriginals. Our host followed by stating the omnipresence of multiculturalism in modern Canadian society.

"The government defined the policy, nothing more, nothing less. The favourable way it was greeted was not political at first, according to Alberto. For him, that greeting is explained by a shared feeling by many, a kind of personal acknowledgement. Multiculturalism first concerns human beings as human beings".

Mr. Di Giovanni thinks that this policy marks, for the Italian community, the shift from a time when it was ostracized to one where it is finally recognized, from inferno to paradiso.

> We Italians were no longer a minority whose members were condemned to do the hard work, especially in the construction sector. We were still partly that, but also many things other than the stereotypes, the prejudices and the platitudes filling the paternalistic speeches that locked us up. We were also artists, writers, lawyers, doctors and we already knew that, but others pretended to ignore that… Of course, we were now citizens of our country of adoption, but we came from elsewhere, from Italy, and our rich cultural heritage crossed the seas with us. In our bags, there was also that thing, both impossible to negate and to define, that thing which stayed within us, creating permanent conflicts between school values and family values and which fed an increasing feeling of emptiness, confusion and tension emerging from the clashes between these two worlds: our natal Italy and the country in which our children were born. We had to educate our educators and put an end to an extreme form of Anglicisation which, in

many cases, pushed people to change their names. That's what was deep within us and that we had to find ways to exteriorize. That's the true origin of this house in which you stand. That's what multiculturalism has changed.

Listening to Alberto Di Giovanni's argument, my mind drifts to the beautiful poem from Ontarian writer Celestino de Juliis :

I own a house now. My father sowed his seeds in his back-yard, and reaped the lettuce and tomatoes. He had known who he was when his hands formed the cheese drawn from the milk of his flock.

Having come here, he was less sure and worked in factories or construction sites. He made his own wine and slaughtered still the Easter Lamb for us. He loved what were his own with little show and fewer words. The language never yielded to him, strong as he was.

I wrote the numbers out on a sheet so he could write his cheques, pay his bills... My youth was spent in shame of him. My tiny face would blush, my eyes avert on parents' night when he would timid come to ask in broken syntax after me.

In my backyard I have my grass and flowers and buy my produce at Dominion. My eyes avert in shame now that I ever was that boy.[87]

AJIT JAIN

Canadian publisher of *India Abroad,* the important monthly magazine of the continent's Indian community, Ajit Jain belongs to the school of thought which bets on successful insertion, a kind of contagious victory for immigrants against the obstacles implicated by their status.

The term for them is visible minorities, but they are, in the truest sense, invisible. And invisible they remain, until—unless—they manage to acquire a face, a voice, a reputation that resonates with the mainstream. Easily said, not as easily done—consider that members of these minorities come from their native lands, programmed through generations

87. DIGIOVANNI, C.M., *op.cit.* p. 141.

of genetic typecasting to a particular ethos. And then they find, in their adopted land, that nothing they have lived through and learnt is applicable anymore, and are forced to navigate through an alien cultural, social and economic ethos. In the midst of such struggle, how acquire a face, a profile, a reputation that transcends invisible barriers?[88]

If, on the world stage, many ask themselves about the compared future power of China and India, it appears that in Ontario, according to median projections, the Indian minority will overtake the Chinese one in terms of numbers in the coming years. With 950,000 members in Canada in 2008, 600,000 in Ontario, the Indian minority could reach 1.3 million members by 2020.

The relatively recent arrival of Indians in Canada seemed to have spared them the tragic fate reserved to Canadians of Chinese, Japanese, German or Italian origins, marked by the racism that dated back to the end of the 19th century and found its roots in 20th century wartime suspicions. But such is not the case. Discriminated against in the United States, at the beginning of the 20th century, Indians seek refuge in Canada, mentioning their status as British subjects and the obligations of the Crown towards them. But upon their arrival, they are amalgamated with other Asians and are rejected, sometimes violently.[89] Following difficult negotiations between the Indian and Canadian governments, the famous "continuous passage" clause is adopted, virtually making Indian immigration to Canada impossible for half a century. This will lead to the Komagata Maru drama.

> The main struggle in which East Indians were involved stemmed from the attitude of the dominant society towards them. The dominant society wanted to keep Canadian soil free from another Asian "defilement," East Indians in this case. To achieve this objective, the dominant society, at first, tried to exclude East Indians from Canada. By 1914, it had effectively managed to close the door to East Indian immigration. Meanwhile the dominant society sought also

88. JAIN, A. (2008) "The power list", *India Abroad*, September 2008.

89. BHATTI, F. M. (1980) , "A Comparative Study of British and Canadian Experience with South Asian Immigration", and RAJ, S., "Some Aspects of East Indian Struggle in Canada, 1905-1947" in K. Victor/Gordon Hirabayashi, *Visible Minorities and Multiculturalism: Asians in Canada.* Toronto: Butterworths, p.43.

to extinguish the East Indian presence in Canada by eliminating the possibility of its self-perpetuation. It tried to
make it impossible for resident East Indian men to bring
their wives to Canada. It was hoped that such an approach
would make Canada free from the undesirable East Indian
element within a generation.

...

The dominant society had several reasons for exclud-
ing East Indians. It was feared that the admission of East
Indians, even in small numbers, would be injurious to
the advancement and preservation of Anglo-Saxon civilization and pre-eminence. Among the English-speaking
people at the time, it was generally believed that they
represented the pinnacle of human evolution and achieve-
ment...It was feared that the admission of the "lesser
breeds" into Canada would frustrate the realization of
"this noble destiny."[90]

The Komagata Maru drama deserves mention or reminder, however brief. On May 23, 1914, the steamboat Komagata Maru arrives at
the Vancouver Port with 376 British subjects of Indian origin onboard
(12 Hindus, 24 Muslims and 340 Sikhs), wishing to settle in Canada.
According to federal authorities, their arrival infringed on the *Continuous
Passage Act* enacted by the Canadian government in 1908. This Act
required immigrants to arrive to Canada on an uninterrupted journey
from their country of origin, a practically impossible itinerary to respect
for immigrants from the Indian subcontinent. Consequently, their disem-
barkation is forbidden for two months and both parties accept to submit
their dispute to the tribunals, which allow 22 Canadian citizens to dis-
embark and order the Komagata Maru to leave the port of Vancouver and
return to India with all the other passengers. A riot breaks out on the boat
and the authorities open fire. Twenty nine passengers are hit, 20 fatally
so. That tragedy reminds us of another, unfathomable and unbearable:
Canada's refusal to greet the 900 Jewish passengers of the S.S. St. Louis
that are trying to flee Nazi Germany.[91]

90. RAJ, S., *idem*, p. 65.

91. ABELLA, I. & TROPER, H. (2000) None *is Too Many, Canada and the Jews of Europe, 1933-1948.*
Toronto: Key Porter.

The first minority

Fifteen years after the Second World War and following the lifting of the restrictive laws that heretofore blocked their coming to the country, Indians started to take the road towards Canada. Since then, the flow has been constant and increasing. Between 1996 and 2001, the Canadian population has been growing at a rate of four per cent; make that 30 per cent for the Indian community. In 2001, two thirds of the members of that minority were born abroad, compared to eighteen per cent for Canadians as a whole. Sixty five per cent of those Indo-Canadians were born in India and the other 35 per cent coming from Pakistan, Bangladesh, Sri Lanka, south and east Africa, the great Indian Ocean region and, in smaller numbers, from the Caribbean.

Close to 60 per cent of the members of that large minority live in Ontario compared to 26 per cent, 10 per cent and 6 per cent respectively for British Columbia, Alberta and Quebec. According to the most recent data, that choice towards Ontario is strengthening. It is, in fact, a choice for the greater Toronto metropolitan area where, at the turn of the century, 350,000 Indians had taken up residence.

The profile of the Indian community is truly unique. Its diversity is well-known. It is ethnic, linguistic and religious. In 2001, 34 per cent of Indo-Canadian are Sikhs, 27 per cent are Hindus, 17 per cent Muslims, 16 per cent Christians and 4 per cent are without religious affiliation. Given its numerical importance and religious diversity, this minority contributes greatly to Ontario's new religious pluralism.

At the sociological level, the community sets itself apart with its relative youth. In 2001, 39 per cent of its members were less than 24 years old, compared to 32 for all Canadians, and another 33 per cent of its members fell in the 25 to 44 age group. In sum, 72 per cent of Indo-Canadians are less than 45, compared to 63 per cent for the country's population as a whole.

A distinctive feature of that community is its high education rate and a widespread command of English. The language is spoken by 85 per cent of its members when they arrive on Canadian soil; that should normally constitute a significant comparative advantage. Almost two thirds of male and female 15 to 24 year-old are enrolled full time in school. That number is 55 per cent for Canadians as a whole. Twenty six per cent of the community's adults have a university degree, compared to 15 per cent for other Canadians and when it comes to graduate diplomas, the ratio is 2 to 1 in their favour, especially in mathematics, physics, computer science and applied sciences. Indo-Canadian women between 25 and 37 years of age belong to the country's most educated group; 58 per cent of them have a university diploma while in the non-immigrant population of the same age group, only 25 per cent do. Furthermore, that community stands out with a much higher marriage rate than Canadians in general, 61 per cent versus 50 per cent, and a level of non-marital unions and 5 times inferior to the Canadian average. The same low compared numbers apply to single parenthood in the community. It is also worth noting that its members are little likely to live alone, including the elderly; 4 per cent compared to 13 per cent for other Canadians.

Abstract past – Abstract future

At the political level, members of that minority say they feel a deep sense of belonging to Canada as well as a strong attachment towards their ethnic or cultural group. Ontarian authors with links in these two worlds have made these the objects of their tales, like Aenita Desai's *Winterscape* and the splendid Uma Parameswaran short story *The Door I Shut Behind Me*. Who are they, she asks herself when she observes Indian immigrants living in Toronto.

> What are they? Indians or Canadians? They had not changed their food habits; the women had not changed their costume; apparently they were a close-knit ethnic group; still far from being assimilated into the general current of life around them. Yet they were as far from the Indian current. They shied away from talk of their return. They hoped to go back, they said, but Chander felt their hope was for a time as far in the abstract future as their memory was for an abstract past. Like the mythological king, Trishanku, they stood suspended between two worlds, unable to enter either, and making a heaven of their own.[92]

Maybe that is the real situation if immigrants, all immigrants, settling thus between the country of origin and the host country. It is, according to Shyam Selvadurai a "marvelous open space represented by the hyphen, in which the two parts of my identity jostle and rub against each other like tectonic plates, pushing upward the eruption that is my work."[93]

92. PARAMESWARAN, U. (1990) "The Door I Shut Behind Me", in *Selected Fiction, Poetry and Drama*. Madras: Affiliated East-West Press, p.67.

93. SELVADURAI, S. (2005) *Story-Wallah: Short Fiction from South Asian Writers*. New York: Houghton Mifflin Company, p.1.

In little time, the visibility of the Indian community in Ontario imposes itself. Hindu temples and mosques start appearing. The former are home to gurus and swamies, the latter greet imams from here and abroad. Religious festivities and cultural activities are displayed in the public space. Abdullah Hakim Quick, imam of the Jami Mosque in Toronto and a PhD student in history at University of Toronto thus traces back the origins of the Muslim community of South Asian origin:

> Being a South Asian Muslim in the sixties and seventies in Ontario forced the individual to develop a dual personality. Outside of the home he or she was very much a part of Canadian society, adopting most of the recognized customs. Inside the home, the South Asian Muslim family constructed an environment similar to that of India and Pakistan. A type of "cocoon" was developed where the visitor, on entering the Muslim home, would be enveloped by the smells, sounds, and sights of home life in South Asia. Relationships were also the same, in that the South Asian man expected to be the absolute ruler of his home and his children were expected to be quiet and submissive.
>
> This obvious contradiction has led to tension, division, and often violence in the home. The South Asian Muslim woman, for example, could not bear all the responsibilities of the household for economic pressures forced her out of her home and into the workforce. Contact with feminists also affected her outlook on the role of the husband and father. Fatigue, depression, and misunderstanding have combined with cultural isolation and resulted in a very high percentage of family feuds and broken homes. Consequently, children growing up with this tension have inherited a disillusioned outlook on their family, culture, and religion.[94]

The community could not remain indifferent to such acute social problems. It decided, after consulting with the elders, to accelerate the development of its institutions and places of worship multiply, the Jami Mosque

---

94. QUICK, A.H., " Muslim Rituals, Practices and Social Problems in Ontario ", in *Polyphony*, vol.12, Toronto: Multicultural History Society of Ontario, p.120.

and U of T's Hart House Multi-Faith space among them. Services were organized to accompany deaths in the community, but also weddings, births, the
Festival of Fast-Breaking, Eid al-Fitr and thus, the communities close ranks.
To their functions as spiritual guides, imams added those of social advisors
with regard to issues such as domestic violence, juvenile delinquency and
mental illnesses...Mosques thus became a second cocoon for South Asian
Muslims, protecting them from the ills of Canadian society.

> The eighties have witnessed a new phase for the South
> Asian Muslim community. Thousands of Muslims have
> entered Canada, and the sense of security for the estab-
> lished immigrants, coupled with a better understanding
> of the laws and rights of citizens, has enabled the Muslim
> community to enter the mainstream of Canadian life and
> begin demanding recognition and benefits....In 1989,
> attendance at the two largest "Eid-ul-fitr" gatherings
> reached twenty thousand. This was one of the largest
> public Islamic gatherings in North America! Planning
> is now in progress for the establishment of Islamic social
> organizations designed to bring together the expertise
> of professionals and religious scholars. South Asian doc-
> tors, lawyers, accountants, and social workers are at the
> forefront of this move to address the growth of family
> problems by using the best of both worlds.[95]

As important as they may be, it is hard to rally the younger generations
behind these evolutions. Even under the protection of the cocoons that are
the family and the mosque, one group expresses its opposition to arranged
marriages, to household traditions and to Asian ways in general. A second
group renews with its faith and experiences a kind of fusion between its
culture of origin and that which prevails in North America. A third group,
finally, declares itself as completely agnostic.

Linguistic ease and advanced schooling: these advantages should normally facilitate job access for the members of that community. Indeed, the
men and women that belong to it are more likely to find work and do so
in the manufacturing sector and in the scientific and technical fields. If
these data appear rather favourable, they come with others that are less so:

---

95. *Ibid.*

revenues inferior to the national average and, for 20 per cent of workers of Indian origin, inferior to the low income cut-off. A high proportion of the elderly, too, with low disposable incomes. And finally,

> about half of those in the East Indian community have experienced some form of discrimination. Indeed, 49% of Canadians of East Indian origin had experienced discrimination or unfair treatment based on their ethnicity, race, religion, language or accent in the past five years, or since they arrived in Canada. A large majority (87%) of those who had experienced discrimination said that they felt it was based on their race or skin colour.[96]

Ajit Jain knows all of that and much more. He has a precise understanding of that balance sheet, of its assets and liabilities, and he believes it does not justly reflect the situation of his community. Many of its members, in his opinion, have acquired an image, a profile and a reputation that transcend every visible and invisible barrier. He evokes Canada's new relations with India, the visits of the Premier of Ontario in the great Asian democracy, the economic cooperation that is being put into place and the quality of insertion of so many in the Ontarian society. He gives me two copies of his publication, *India Abroad*, both dedicated to the impressive *Power Lists*.[97] Reading those, one better appreciates the exceptional contribution of so many Ontarians of Indian origin in almost all sectors of society.

LINCOLN M. ALEXANDER

The year was 1968. The first Black Canadian was entering the House of Commons which had, at the time, only one female MP out of 264. Lincoln M. Alexander was elected in the Ontarian riding of Hamilton West. He will be re-elected three times.

The son of immigrants from the West Indies, his mother was a cleaning lady and his father a railway luggage handler, "one of the rare jobs then accessible to a coloured man". Born in Toronto, the new MP lived in Harlem and served in the Second World War as a radiotelegraph operator in the Canadian Army. As an adult student, he obtained his Bachelor of Arts at McMaster University and a Bachelor of Law at Osgood Hall. At

96. Statistics Canada, *The East Indian community in Canada*, 2007—Number 4, http://www.statcan.gc.ca/pub/89-621-x/89-621-x2007004-eng.htm.

97. "The Power List", *India abroad*, september 2008 and august 2009.

the beginning of the 1950s, he belonged to a restricted club of 4 or 5 Black Ontarian lawyers. After being refused by the big law firms, he joined the country's first interracial one. "Nobody said it, but Black meant you were seen as incompetent."[98]

His election, his accession to the Cabinet in 1979 and his nomination to the function of Lieutenant-Governor of Ontario in 1985, three ground-breaking achievements, drew the attention of the national and international press. First president of the Canadian Race Relations Foundations (1996), created by the federal government in connection with the Japanese Canadian Redress Agreement, Lincoln Alexander championed the equality rights guaranteed by the Canadian Charter of Rights and Freedoms. He led a vast pan Canadian campaign against racism and made headlines again in 1999 by declaring "racist attitudes and institutional racism are still very much alive. In my view, we still have a long way to go ... We want Canadians to fight racism wherever it rears its ugly head—in schools, in hockey rinks, in workplaces, on the street, and yes, even in Parliament."[99] Such declarations are surprising at first, for anyone who hasn't read the memoirs of Lincoln Alexander.[100]

The man is moderated but he is not without conviction and courage. At the end of that formidable career, Alexander chooses to share his life story. At each step of that life, the spectre of racism in all its shapes and form, from the most subtle to the most brutal, casts its cold shadow over that Black man and his community. "After all, this was the WASP Toronto of the 1920s and 30s where people with my parents' and my colour of skin were barely sufficient in number to constitute a minority group. Blacks at the time made up a sliver-thin portion of the city's population, and racial prejudice abounded.[101] Lincoln Alexander felt that racism in elementary school, as did Cameron Bailey, one of our witness; he felt it in high school, in the Army "none of the 3 services at the time—army, navy and air force—were interested in having blacks"[102], in the public services,[103] in his quest

98. BROWN, W. (2002) "L'honorable Lincoln M. Alexander, Premier Canadien de race noire élu à la Chambre des communes ", *Perspectives électorales*. Ottawa : élections Canada.

99. *Idem.*

100. ALEXANDER, L. M. (2006) *Go to school, you're a little black boy*. Toronto: Dundurn Press.

101. *Idem*, p. 18.

102. *Idem*, p.39.

103. *Idem*, p.43.

for employment after he left the Army,[104] at U of T's Law Faculty,[105] in his contacts with law firms,[106] upon purchasing a house[107] as well as during the first phase of his political career.[108]

Austin Clarke built his remarkable body of work on that overflow.[109] He described a society, the Ontarian society, whose consciousness is, according to Sonnet L'Abbé's words, "unable to rest, troubled by the visible, deep social divisions along racial lines that Canadians wish were the stuff of history, but which we still confront".[110]

In his functions as lieutenant-governor, Alexander forcefully denounced racism and wished for significant actions to be taken in order to change what had to be changed. One of his interventions before the Ontario Chamber of Commerce remains famous because of its content and the controversy it then stirred. Was it appropriate for the Crown representative to take sides that clearly? The man at the centre of the debate had no doubt about it since his own story was so entrenched in the continuing centenary struggle for the recognition and implementation of equality rights for all men and women, irrespective of their skin colour.

Diversified, as all other visible Ontarian communities are, the one that brought together the Black population is also one of the oldest. Its arrival in Ontario stems from two of modern history's major events: the Independence of the United States and the long battle for the abolition of slavery.

The very first Black community in Ontario is composed of Loyalists fleeing the United States, convinced that the Imperial British system will be more favourable to them than the new American republic. In the decades that followed, until the American Civil War and even further in time until the adoption, in 1865, of the 13th Amendment abolishing slavery, that initial Black community saw its ranks swell with the arrival of thousands of slaves seeking liberty and a life freed from the extreme racial and legal

---

104. *Idem*, p.54.

105. *Idem*, p.61.

106. *Idem*, p.65. The same ostracism affected Law graduates of Jewish origin.

107. *Idem*, p.70. In that case, discrimination affected citizens of Jewish, Italian, Polish and Chinese origins or simply those born abroad.

108. *Idem*, p.96 and 217.

109. CLARKE, A. (2008) *More*. Toronto: Thomas Allen.

110. L'ABBÉ, S. "Toronto the black", *The Globe and Mail*, September 27 2008.

discriminations they had suffered for generations. That movement grew further because of the War of 1812 and the American *Fugitive Slave Law* of 1850 authorizing slave-owners to recuperate "their goods, that is to say, their slaves" that fled to the North, and use force in order to do so.[111] In a letter dated October 12, 1850, preserved at the Ontario Archives, S. Wickam thus summarizes the situation: " ... for the law is so now all through the United States that the slave holders can take their slaves were ever they can find them ... My advice to all colored people to stay in Canada wither they are free or fugitives".[112]

Even if it goes beyond the reach of our work, we relate this episode of Ontarian history because of the solidarity movements that have made possible for these fugitives to cross from the United States to the colony of Upper Canada. Beyond the political debates and ideological choices of the time, these movements have involved a great number of citizens and institutions without whom theses crossings would simply have been impossible. Ontarian historian Fred Landon was the first to recreate the epic story of that perilous voyage of slaves coming from many American borders states but also the faraway southern states of Virginia and North Carolina, for instance. He also documented the system that made these passages possible, the famous clandestine railway that outsmarted the American services with coded terminology, messages and symbols. He also brought to light the conditions of their installation in the communities of Southwestern Ontario. That fragment of history is modestly but powerfully reconstituted at the North American Black Historical Museum, inaugurated in 1981 in Amherstburg,[113] one of the destinations of fugitive slaves.[114] It is also related in the documents of the time preserved at the Archives of Ontario and displayed during the exhibit titled *The Black Canadian Experience in Ontario 1834-1914: Flight, Freedom, Foundation*, a joint project between the said Archives and the Ontario Black Society.

---

111. BENJAMIN, D. (1856) *A North-Side view of Slavery. The Refugee:or the Narratives of Fugitive Slave in Canada, related by Themselves, with an Account of the History and Conditions of the Colored Population of Upper Canada.* Boston: John P. Jewett and Company.

112. Archives de l'Ontario, Code de reference : F499MU2885.

113. LANDON, F. "Amherstburg, Terminus of the Underground Railroad ", in *The Journal of Negro History,* Association for the study of African American Life and History, 1925, vol. X.

114. One can see, in the Archives of Ontario, a modest map called *Southwestern Counties of Canada West.* It depicts the main settling centres of the coloured population in 1855. Reference Code: Brochure 1855, no 41.

Abolition of slavery

The abolition of slavery stirred a lively debate in Upper Canada. It engendered the creation of interest groups such as, in 1851, the Anti-Slavery Society of Canada and, in 1859, the Association for the Education of the Coloured People of Canada. It motivated the launch of journals dedicated to the defense of former slaves' interests, such publications as 1851's *Voice of the fugitives* and 1853's *The provincial Freeman*, created and run by a Black woman, Mary Ann Shadd. The same battle is at the heart of these initiatives: the abolition of slavery. Opinions were by no means unanimous on the topic; the colony itself having in its midst an important number of slaves and defenders of the *status quo*.[115] But it had the support of many Ontarian personalities, Blacks and Whites, religious and civil, among others that of George Brown, the publisher of the *Toronto Globe* who opened his pages to the movement, and Oliver Mowat, who will be Ontario's Premier between 1872 and 1896. These local initiatives join the international abolitionist movement; they are inspired by it and contribute to strengthening it. For the 150th anniversary of the Anti-Slavery Society of Canada's creation, Library and Archives Canada organized, in 2001, an important exhibit about that major episode in Ontarian history.

These abolitionist movements have also found important support in the local imperial administration. Some, such as Lieutenant-Governor John Graves Simcoe promote significant initiatives, for instance the 1793 Act against Slavery which, although it does not abolish slavery, forbids the importation of slaves in the colony and plans the gradual emancipation of the children of slaves that live in it. In 1829, Lieutenant-Governor John Colborne summarizes the position of the colonial leaders to visiting Americans in these words:

> Tell the republicans on your side of the line that we royalists do not know men by their colour. Should you come to us you will be entitled to all the privileges of the rest of His Majesty's subjects.[116]

Four years later, in 1833, the imperial Parliament abolishes slavery and, in 1842, Great Britain and the United States sign the Webster-Ashburton

115. LANDON, F. "Evidence is found of Race Prejudice in Biddulph, 1848", in *Ontario's African-Canadian heritage: collected writings*. London: London Free Press, p.95.

116. ULLMAN, V. (1969) *Look to the north star: A Life of William King*. Boston: Beacon Press, p.84.

Treaty that aims at eliminating slave trading between Africa and America. In 1865, following the victory of the Union forces, the USA adopt the 13th Amendment which abolishes slavery in that country. A page of world history was thus turning, as was a page of Ontarian history. Indeed, the slavery question had been debated for decades in the colony. In large proportion, the elite of the time, administrators, religious leaders and many citizens militated for its abolition, contributed to the settlement of thousands of slaves fleeing the United States, to their installation and the development of their communities.

The legal abolition, however, does not put an end to all the practices so deeply rooted in history. The question of slavery is followed by that of the rights of Black citizens. As was demonstrated by Lincoln Alexander's testimonial and by the works of great Ontarian writers, the question flows through the contemporary history of the province as it does that of America.

More than a century and a half separate two major documents illustrating the perennial nature of the issue of Black citizens' rights in Ontario: the 1843 petition of Hamilton's "People of Colour" to the Governor General[117] and Stephen Lewis' 1992 report on racism.[118] Both call for the protection of the law to guarantee the fair treatment of young Blacks, with regard to the public schools they can attend at the middle of the 19th century and with regard to their safety, access to jobs and educational

---

117. "Dear Sir,

The people of colour in the Town of Hamilton have a right to inform your Excellency of the treatment that we have to undergo. We have paid the taxes and we are denied of the public schools, and we have applied to the Board of the Police and there is no steps taken to change this manner of treatment, and this kind of treatment is not in the United States, for the children of colour go to the Public Schools together with the white children, more especially in Philadelphia, and I thought that there was not a man to be known by his colour under the British flag, and we left the United States because we were in hopes that prejudice was not in this land, and I came to live under your Government if my God would be my helper and to be true to the Government. I am sorry to annoy you by allowing this thing, but we are grieved much, we are imposed on much, and if it please your Excellency to attend to this grievance, if you please Sir. I have left property in the United States and I have bought property in Canada, and all I want is justice and I will be satisfied. We are called nigger when we go out in the street, and sometimes brick bats is sent after us as we pass in the street. We are not all absconders now we brought money into this Province and we hope never to leave it, for we hope to enjoy our rights in this Province, and may my God smile upon your public life and guide you into all truth, which is my prayer and God bless the Queen and Royal Family.

The Coloured People of Hamilton"

118. LEWIS, S. (1992) "Racism in Ontario" in *Report to the Premier*. Toronto: Office of the Premier.

services at the end of the 20th. "We are called nigger when we go out in the street, and sometimes brick bats is sent after us as we pass in the street" write the Hamilton petitioners to whom the chief of police agrees with. In his report, the man wrote:[119]

> I regret to say that there is a strong prejudice existing amongst the lower orders of the Whites against the coloured people. The several Teachers as well as others acquainted with the extent of this prejudice fear that if coloured children are admitted into the schools the parents of the greater part of the White children will take them away.

150 years later, after riots that shook Toronto in the 1990s, Stephen Lewis declares that:

> What we are dealing with, at root, and fundamentally, is anti-Black racism. ... It is Blacks who are being shot, it is Black youth that is unemployed in excessive numbers ... it is Black kids who are disproportionately dropping-out.

A plurality of origins

The expression "Black community" is quite ambiguous. It includes a plurality of very diverse origins and situations.[120] The descendants of the Hamilton petitioners are its oldest fragment. That community would be much more numerous if Canadian policy had not severely blocked Black people's entry in the country. That policy, clearly stated in 1911, prohibits the landing of "of any immigrants belonging to the Negro race, which race is deemed unsuitable to the climate and requirements of Canada". That policy was to be lifted in 1953 and 1962, when these climatic and racial restrictions were withdrawn from the law.

---

119. ARCHIVES PUBLIQUES DE L'ONTARIO (2003) *Documenting a Province. The Archives of Ontario at 100. Chronique d'une province. Le centenaire des Archives publiques de l'Ontario.* Toronto : Queen's Printer for Ontario.

120. All statistical information in this publication referring to African, the African community, Canadians of African origin or people of African origin denotes people who reported African origins either alone or in combination with other ethnic origins in response to the question on ethnic origin in the 2001 Census or 2002 Ethnic Diversity Survey. See also Anne Milan and Kelly Tran, *Blacks in Canada: a long history*, Statistics Canada, 2004.

In 2006, there were 473,765 Ontarian citizens of African origin. That generic term included a plurality of national origins with specific languages and cultures. That number was severely criticized and those critics are very old. It has been said that they were very much below the reality.[121]

These citizens belonging to Black communities share some characteristics; they are, for instance, younger than the average of citizens in a province that a majority of them chose to settle in, except Haitian immigrants. Their population growth is higher than that of other Ontarians and they have a much lower rate of retired people, 24 per cent of which live with their families compared to 5 per cent for Canadians as a whole. Furthermore, they are fewer to acknowledge mixed ethnic roots. Finally, upon landing in the country, a very strong majority has a good command of one of the official languages of Canada and knows one or many other languages.

These same citizens from Black communities, however, differ on many other levels. If a distinctive majority of Ontarians from Africa are not born here, it is a whole different story for Jamaican Canadians, whose second generation members make up the main part of the community. Another difference concerns the educational levels, very high for Ontarians of African origin to the point where it surpasses the country's averages by 5 per cent. The difference is remarkable. Indeed, 71 per cent of Africans aged 15 to 24 are enrolled in school programs compared with 57 per cent for the same age group nationally.

These better-schooled men and women are paradoxically less employed than other Canadians, 11 per cent less in 2001, and even more so for the 25-44 age group. That tendency is slightly reversed for the 45 to 64 year-old. The women of the Black community are more affected by that difficulty to find work. These disparities can be seen when it comes to compensation levels, where they can reach 20 per cent less for members of the Black communities. These gaps have repercussions on the levels of disposable income upon retirement; they are 10.5 per cent lower than the average disposable income of other retired people and, in the case of retired Black women, that number is 30 per cent. Put together, these situations create very high poverty levels in the community. It is estimated that 39 per cent of its members have revenues below the poverty level, compared to 16 per cent for all Canadians and that 47 per cent of its children below 15 years old live in poverty compared to 19 per cent for all Canadian kids of the same age group.

---

121. MORRIS, D. & KRAUTER, J.F. "The Negroes" in *The Other Canadians, profile of six minorities*. Toronto: Methuen, 1971, p.40; CLARCK, G.E. *Le visage complexe des noirs au Canada*. Montréal : McGill News, Winter 1997.

What do these troubling numbers hide?

They doubtless reveal the continued ambiguity with regard to the treatment of racial issues in this country. One will remember the content of the debates surrounding the arrival of slaves in the colony throughout the first half of the 19th century: a genuine sympathy and an active and decisive support from many, as we have heretofore mentioned, but at the same time, an opposition just as determined that could only be silenced, publicly at least, by the law from the London Parliament that abolished slavery in the entire British empire in 1833.

After that, the old demons changed faces and the power of the law was deployed to limit, and even stop, Black immigration in this country for a century. Climate, alleged maladaptation of immigrants from the tropics[122], strategies aimed at discouraging Blacks from immigrating,[123] reservations towards them when it comes to opportunities offered to other immigrants,[124] recognition by tribunals of segregated schools,[125] or discrimination in terms of access to public places.[126] Two reports, one from 1909 and the other 1949, both by senior administrators of Canadian immigration, draw the same conclusion.

At the beginning of last century, William J. White, immigration inspector, writes to the designated Canadian Minister: [127]

> With the colored people as with others, there are exceptions. We have already a number of them in portions of Western Canada and I believe them to be superior to most of these I saw in the south, and if there is any best, I think we have secured the best, and secured only those who will make good citizens, but the risk of the emigration of a

---

122. *"One of the conditions for admission to Canada is that immigrants should be able to readily become adapted and integrated into the life of the community within a reasonable time after their entry. In the light of experience it would be unrealistic to say that immigrants who have spent the greater part of their life in tropical or semi-tropical countries become readily adapted to the Canadian mode of life which, to no small extent, is determined by climatic conditions. It is a matter of record that natives of such countries are more apt to break down in health than immigrants from countries where the climate is more akin to that of Canada."* House of Commons Debates, Session 1952-53, Vol. IV, p.1351.

123. HILLMER and GRANATSTEIN, *op. cit.* p.127.

124. MORRIS, D. and KRAUTER, J.F., *op.cit*, p.43.

125. *Idem*, p.45.

126. *Ibidem*, p.48

127. HILLMER and GRANATSTEIN, *op. cit.,* p.126.

large number who would prove undesirable is so great that
I feel it would be wise to take such action as would prevent
any more of them making homes in Canada.

At the middle of last century, A. L. Jolliffe, director of immigration, writes to the designated Canadian minister:[128]

Generally speaking, coloured people, in the present state
of the white man's thinking, are not a tangible community
asset, and as a result, are more or less ostracized. They do
not assimilate readily and pretty much vegetate at a low
standard of living. Many cannot adapt themselves to our
climatic conditions. To broaden the regulations would
immediately bring about a large influx of coloured immigrants. Quite realistically, this would be, in my opinion, an
act of misguided generosity.

Such was, for close to a century, the state of mind of Canadians towards
their Black fellow citizens. And, to quote immigration director Jolliffe again,
"as a result, they are more or less ostracized". That "more or less" reflects a
whole range of recurrent discrimination in terms of lodging, that being in
contravention of Ontarian law, of employment, of access to public services
and to recreational activities; all these forms of discrimination often validated
by the tribunals.[129] If the civil and political rights of the citizens belonging to
that minority are the same as those of all other citizens, the general immigration policies and judicial decisions are instrumental in their negation. Thus,
in 1924, such a decision by an Ontarian court ruled in favour of a restaurant
owner who was refusing Blacks in his establishment. In 1939, the Supreme
Court of Canada confirms the decision from a Quebec court which accepted
the argument of a tavern owner who refused to serve beer to a Black man.
Commenting on that decision from the highest tribunal in the country, the
editorial of the *Dominion Law Report* says the following:[130]

This would appear to be the first authoritative decision on
a highly contentious question and is the law's confirmation
of the socially enforced inferiority of the colored race.

---

128. *Ibidem.*

129. MORRIS, D. and KRAUTER, J.F., *op.cit*, p.46.

130. HILLMER and GRANATSTEIN, *op. cit.*, p.239.

To face that systemic and historic discrimination of Black citizens, the reaction was being organized to guarantee their full legal rights to members of the community. That reaction is led by victims themselves, regrouping in many associations, such as the important Canadian League for the Advancement of Colored People and by civil society stakeholders like the Canadian Congress of Labour and the Labour Committee to combat Racial Intolerance, created in Winnipeg in 1946 and quickly spreading all over the country.

A first law against racial discrimination

The Ontarian political authorities also reacted in decisive fashion. In 1944, the provincial government introduced the first legislation in the country against racial discrimination. In 1950, it amended the Labour Relations Act to have it include provisions for fair employment practices and have it meet the requirements of the United Nations Universal Declaration of Human Rights and also passed legislation that aimed at ending discrimination in housing. Finally, in 1958, it created the Ontario Anti-Discrimination Commission, which will become, in 1961, the Ontario Human Rights Commission, which it endows with a Human Rights Code, another first in the history of the federation. The same year, Ottawa unanimously adopts the Canadian Bill of Rights, so dear to Prime Minister John Diefenbaker. In the society, behaviours evolve slowly, very slowly. In 1960, the City of Toronto hires its first Black cop, Larry McLarty. That former Jamaican policeman will be the only coloured cop in Toronto for many years. For Black History Month in 2009, he remembers with humour those days not so far back in time: "When people saw me in the street, they didn't believe what they saw and were surprised; some even asking me if I was a real cop".[131]

According to an important Statistics Canada survey dedicated to ethnic diversity and published in September 2003, prepared during the 5 previous years, a third of respondents that are members of the black community declare that they have been discriminated against or victims of unfair treatments because of their ethnicity, race, religion or accent. A majority of them state that these situations stemmed from their race or skin colour and that this discrimination occurred in their work environment, especially when they were applying for a vacant position or promotion.

---

131. MAMHU, D. "Oui, tu peux… Au service de la police de Toronto", *Le Métropolitain*, semaine du 4 au 10 février 2009.

MOHAMMED BRIHMI

A splendid royal rug from Rabat adorns the entrance of this gorgeous Moroccan enclave in the heart of Toronto, on Front Street close to Union Station, the busiest train station in the country. Mohammed waits for us at the bar, surrounded by taffeta curtains, Aladdin lamps and beautiful low furniture imported from the Cherifian kingdom. The music and the smells come from faraway Andalucía and the mounds of spices that can't be missed in the Kasbah of Marrakech.

This Ontarian, without complex, is visibly happy in a country that spelled success for him. He enumerates his identities with pride, "Canadian of Moroccan origin, Arabic-speaker, Francophone and Muslim". He loves Toronto, "its windows on world cultures that are constantly renewed". But he worries about the presence of numerous disadvantaged neighbourhoods and the poverty of many Torontonians.

Dissident in his country, student in Quebec, trilingual, UN official, Ontarian elected municipal official, spokesperson for Franco-Ontarians, political activist with contacts in Ottawa, Quebec City and Queen's Park, his integration is accomplished, to say the least, as is his citizenship. Of Canadian history, old and current, he has a deep knowledge, probably deeper than that of many "old-stock" Canadians. He has the answer to any question on Canada's storyline since World War II and especially on recent events in Quebec and Ontario. He knows the theses, their authors and stake-holders. He was himself one such stakeholder and witnessed many of these events first hand. He furthermore has the distinct feeling of belonging to a significant minority, along with 300,000 Ontarians of Arab background.

Their origins illustrate the diversity of these minorities: Christian and Muslim Arabs from the Maghreb and the Mashriq, from the Gulf countries, from Iraq, Egypt, Palestine and Jordan; Muslims from India, Malaysia, Indonesia, Iran, Bangladesh, China, the Caribbean and sub-Saharan Africa. One world or many worlds. They first arrived from Syria and Lebanon, in 1880, fleeing the regressive politics of the Ottoman Empire.[132] They have not stop coming since, and especially in the immediate postwar period: 36,500 in the 60s, 133,000 in the 90s. Mohammed insists: diversity is the very essence of this community. Unfortunately however, we have taken the habit of mixing things up, especially Arabs and Muslims, although more

132. ABU LABAN, B. (1981) "The Canadian Muslim Community: The need for a new survival" in *The Muslim community in North America*. Edmonton: University of Alberta Press.

than 50 per cent of Arabs living in Canada are Christians. Another mistake is to identify Muslim Canadians too quickly as being from the Middle East while a great many number come from Southeast and South Asia.

Mohammed talks of these communities' emblematic figures, the immigrant investors that made it and set up important businesses here, discreet and powerful executives such as Nadir Mohamed, President and CEO of Rogers Communications, some great intellectuals and scientists whose names we don't hear enough.

September 2001

When asked about 9/11, he qualifies the effects of the tragedy on his community as a "descent into hell". Irrational and omnipresent, the hostility towards Arabs and Muslims, all put in the same basket, has resulted in such aberrations as the arson of a Sikh temple in Hamilton. It was taken for a mosque! Some of his friends wanted to change names, especially the young ones. The season was difficult, "but since then, the storm somewhat quieted down". Besides, in his opinion, it didn't only have negative effects. It strengthened solidarity and led to the creation of associations such as those within universities, for instance. But these steps forwards were often slowed down by safety policies that were justified in terms of their nature but often unjust in their implementation.

Mohammed pays great attention to the debates that pit, in Ontario as elsewhere in the world, the defenders of a conservative view of Islam and of the social and moral rules that stem from that view against those who seek to bring together Muslim tenets and requirements entailed by the human rights doctrine and policies, such as equality and fairness. For him, the latter are clearly a majority in Ontario, but the media attention is rather focused on the radicals or those thought to be so, comforting the prejudices of many.

Mohammed knows well that the issue of Arabic and Muslim presence in the West has been hotly debated for decades, as demonstrated in 1986 by Ali M. Kettani's important *Muslim Minorities in the World Today*.[133] He also knows that that question, first a European one, has crossed the seas in September of 2001 and has spread in the Atlantic zone, including in Canada. Witnesses to that are the cases of Maher Arar,[134] Abousfian Abdelrazik,

---

133. KETTANI, A.M. (1986) *Muslim Minorities in the World Today*. London: Mansell.

134. PITHER, K. (2008) *The story of four Canadians tortured in the name of fighting terror*. Toronto: Viking Canada, 460 p.

Abdihakim Mohamed, Suaad Hagi Mohamud, Hassan Almrei, Mohamed Mahjoub, Adil Cherkaoui and Mohamed Harkat, concluded most of the time with losses for the Canadian government decided by tribunals and displayed in Judge Dennis O'Connor's report. The unique and tragic case, also, of Omar Khadr, that 15 year-old captured and accused of killing an American soldier. At the moment these words are written, Omar Khadr, the only Western national still held in Guantanamo Bay, is being tried by an American military tribunal. Three decisions by federal courts and one by the Supreme Court of Canada have not shaken the federal Government's will not to repatriate him. *"Bring Back Omar Khadr"*, titled a *National Post* article in August 2010. "Canada is the only Western nation that has not yet negotiated the return of its citizens from the Cuban base used to house U.S.-captured terror suspects, and this [trial] is a good opportunity to remedy that situation."[135]

Finally, there's the case of these 18 Toronto terrorists who were thinking of "taking over this country", "murdering the Prime Minister" and shed blood in Parliament,[136] and the troubling tales of training camps, explosives fabrication and secret hideouts that regularly made headlines and contributed to give substance to the worst apprehensions.

All these cases have made two categories of victims. First, Canadians of Arab origin or of the Muslim faith because of a climate that favoured the terrible notion of collective guilt. Second, Canadian institutions in charge of intelligence, of counter-espionage and, in part, of the country's diplomacy because of a lack of transparency. For its part, the judicial system has demonstrated integrity and independence, partly restoring the country's honor.

In the global and continental climate of the past years, these events have strengthened reactions such as rejection, scorn and discrimination towards Canadian Arabs, as census-linked surveys and analyses continue to show.

Mohammed is of the opinion that the request concerning the application of sharia law in Ontario was issued by a small number of people who did not succeed in imposing their will and, without denying its existence, holds the presence of more radical Muslim elements as a tiny faction with no roots or impact in the community. He thinks that "most Canadian Arabs, whether Christian or Muslim, have left their country of origin for reasons linked

---

135. WALCOM, T. "Bring back Omar Khadr", *The National Post*, August 10 2010.
136. O'TOOLE, M. "Toronto 18' man pleads guilty, set free", *The National Post*, 21 January 2010.

with the respect of liberties or because of the difficult economic conditions that prevailed over there. Nothing is more contrary to their project than to come here stir disarray". Mohamed rejects the theses that that keep finding historical or cultural excuses to justify radical Islam. A victim himself of a regime that was hostile to liberties, he has lost none of his convictions and refuses to believe that violence is the right answer to combat violence.

We treated ourselves to a visit of the Canadian Arab Federation (CAF) offices in Scarborough. They were mostly empty and the people on duty were none other than the executive director at the time, Mohamed Boudjenane, and two or three volunteers, where not long ago, numerous teams were holding information sessions for newcomers as well as English classes, job training sessions and other basic services. A war of words has created this void by leading the federal government to put an end to the substantial financial support it granted the CAF, which was considered, for the 10 years leading to that point, as a useful partner of the federal Department of Immigration.

This was the result of some positions expressed publicly by the CAF with regard to the Israeli-Palestinian conflict, positions that federal authorities assimilated to anti-Semitism. Even after CAF members qualified the terms used by their president Khaled Mouammar as regrettable, Minister Jason Kenney subjected the financial support of his Department to a change in CAF leadership and the recognition of "Canadian values", broadly speaking. But the rift between both parties was so deep that it had become impossible to bridge. A case of extreme dissidence from the Federation or mere stubbornness of the federal authorities? Suffocation of the freedom of expression of a group which does not benefit from public favour or a discourse made in public that can be likened to barely disguised support of terrorist groups? It is difficult to be an Arab in the West, difficult to be an Arab in Canada and difficult to be an Arab in Ontario.

Mohammed is a proud Ontarian. He steers clear of these political quarrels all the while exerting all the prerogatives of citizenship. He has lost nothing of the pride of his origins, but he enriched it with the additional pride that arose from what he has accomplished in his country of adoption. For him, it is possible to be an Arab in the West, in Canada and in Ontario.

FRANÇOIS BOILEAU

Since 2007, François Boileau is the French Language Services Commissioner of Ontario, a sort of watchdog for "the Francophone population to live, grow and prosper in their language" in Ontario. The man is direct and competent, some describe him as audacious, others use the term courageous. He belongs to that category of Canadians that have a view of the country that is rooted in its history, past and future. He greets us in his downtown Toronto office and introduces us to a team that's made up of Francophone Ontarians, both native ones and some that come from all over the world and that belong to that linguistic minority which, in Ontario, is also a historical minority.

A French past

Ancient and current, the relations between Ontario and the French civilization and language express a geographical, historical and political situation that is unique on the continent.

Before being British or Canadian, the territory of Ontario belonged to the king of France for more than two and a half centuries. « Toronto was under French suzerainty longer than it has been a city », observe Willian Kilbourn and Rudi Christ.[137] With the objective of placing the Ontarian experience in the very long run, provincial historiographers remind us of its distant French past, identified as the "history of the French presence in Ontario". They bring up the list of French discoverers who first explored and named the Ontarian territory.[138] It is an impressive list: Samuel de Champlain, Étienne Brulé, Jean Nicollet, Adrien Jolliet, the Jesuits Isaac Jogues and Charles Rymbaut, the Sulpicians Francois Dollier de Casson and René de Bréhant de Galinée. They remind us that Jean Talon, the famous intendant who wanted to build settlements on these new lands "for the future greatness of New France and the honor of France". But in Paris, Colbert insists: "We must gather up in the St. Lawrence valley, come together in order to better defend ourselves against an eventual enemy".[139] They also remind us that Ontario's toponymy is witness to that old French presence,[140] so much so that the government had to establish a policy with regard to the Linguistic Treatment of French Geographic Names in Ontario. Then, the first European establishments on Ontarian territory are French, such as Fort Frontenac, erected in 1673 where Kingston now stands, numerous fur trad-

---

137. KILBOURN and CHRIST, op. cit., p.8.

138. ARCHIVES PUBLIQUES DE L'ONTARIO (2003) *Documenting a Province. The Archives of Ontario at 100. Chronique d'une province. Le centenaire des Archives publiques de l'Ontario.* Toronto : Queen's Printer for Ontario.

139. VACHON, A. ; CHABOT, V. et DESROSIERS, A. *Rêves d'Empire, le Canada avant1700.* Ottawa : Archives publiques du Canada, p. 65.

140. LAPIERRE, A. (1981) *Toponomie française en Ontario.* Montréal : Etudes vivantes.

ing posts, including the famous Michillimakinac post, built in 1680 at the junction of Lakes Huron and Michigan.

Neighbouring Quebec

Ontario's relationship with the French civilization and language is not exhausted by this interest for its distant past. Far from it. That relationship also accompanied the province throughout its history, ever since the British conquest of 1759-60, due to its geographic proximity and to its political links with Quebec, the sole Francophone majority society in North America.

Since 1791, Ontario shares a long border with Quebec. From 1791 to 1840, at the time called Upper and Lower Canada, both lived side by side as distinct entities linked by a strong movement of persons, ideas and goods that will do nothing but grow until today. From 1840 to 1867, the Anglophone and Francophone provinces are part of a so-called Union polit-ical regime. Then in a third period, from 1867 to this day, they belong to the same federal system. In short, both provinces have been political partners for almost 175 years and were brought to deal with such singular proximity. This link also stems from the constant migration of Quebecers to Ontario which, for the past two centuries, and today still, has profoundly marked both societies. They allowed, for instance, the emergence in Ontario of a Francophone minority whose story has been the object of numerous studies and analyses.[141] That link is enriched by the installation in Toronto, these past 2 decades, of branches from a significant number of Quebec's finest corporations and by the decision of the Quebec and Ontario governments to create a "common economic space", the 4th most important on the continent. This aim was recorded in the Trade and Cooperation Agreement concluded by both governments in 2009. The neighbouring societies are thus perma-nently reminded of that cultural and linguistic duality in North America.

In the long run, political and strategic partnerships are forged between groups and individuals from both provinces. These partnerships can be found in federal political parties and in Canada-wide organizations. They are also forged between the two provincial governments themselves. One

141. GERVAIS, G. "L'histoire de l'Ontario français (1610-1997)", in THÉRIAULT, Joseph-Yvon (dir.) (1999) *Francophonies minoritaires au Canada — L'état des lieux*. Moncton : Éditions d'Acadie, p.161; CORBEIL, J.P. ; GRENIER, C. & LAFRENIÈRE, S. (2006) *Les minorités prennent la parole : résultats de l'Enquête sur la vitalité des minorités de langue officielle*. Ottawa : Statistique Canada, 2007; LABRIE, N. et FORLOT, G. (1999) *L'enjeu de la langue en Ontario français*. Sudbury : Prises de paroles ; BOUDREAU, F. ; COTMAN, J. ; FRENETTE, Y. and WHITFIELD, A. (1995) *La francophonie ontarienne : bilan et perspective de recherche*. Hearst : Le Nordir.

needs only think of the alliances between Lafontaine and Baldwin, Mowat and Mercier, Robarts and Johnson, Peterson and Bourassa, among others, and of the recent rapprochements between the governments of Jean Charest and Dalton McGuinty. One also thinks of the Ontarian intellectuals who, especially in the decades that coincided with the Quiet Revolution or immediately followed it, have studied Quebec and made it the subject of their research and interventions: Kenneth McRoberts, Stephen Clarkson, Graham Fraser and Margaret Atwood, among others.

Certain events in one of those societies have had important consequences on the other. According to many English Canadian authors, Quebec's new self-assertion in the 1960s has not only radically transformed Quebec. It also changed the country. In his famous text *Across the River and Out of the Trees*,[142] Northrop Frye states that "the discovery of a new French-Canadian identity through the Quiet Revolution was the crucial factor in consolidating a similar sense in English Canada". Indeed, the Quiet Revolution, the political surge of the Quebec sovereignist option, the creation by René Lévesque of the sovereignty association Movement are at the source of major political initiatives taken by Queen's Park. The Confederation of Tomorrow Conference, for instance, which was organized in Toronto in November 1967 by Premier John Robarts, against the will of the federal government.[143] The conference was dedicated to the accommodation of Quebec's demands. There's also the strong commitments made by the government of Queen's Park with regard to the status of the French language and the Francophone minority in Ontario at the 1971 Victoria Constitutional Conference.[144]

That positioning of both provinces as significant vis-à-vis has always had important consequences. In the long run, it engendered all the expected forms of favourable and inimical relations between two capitals belonging to the same federal political regime: alliances between political leaders and families; converging positions of the provinces when confronting the central power, development of bilateral cooperation and more recently, the signature of a wide-ranging agreement that symbolizes a multisectoral rapprochement. It also engendered its share of oppositions just as significant,

142. FRYE, N. (1980) "Across the River and Out of the Trees" in *The Arts in Canada: The last Fifty Years*. Toronto: University of Toronto Press, p. 6.

143. ROY, J.L. (1978) Le débat constitutionnel Québec-Canada, 1960-76. Montréal : Leméac, p.139.

144. *Idem*, p. 225.

each capital with its best interests at heart, understandably. In the recent period, these oppositions have bubbled to the surface in the cases of North American free trade,[145] of the patriation of the Canadian Constitution and the creation of a unique Financial Markets Authority for Canada. These relations go beyond politics. With varying degrees of intensity, the academic and intellectual fields of both societies have also had significant rapports, and especially with regard to Quebec's status in the Canadian picture.[146]

Ontario's Francophonie

Ontario's relations with the French civilization and language are also fed by the presence on its territory of citizens whose identity is an integral part of that civilization and that language.[147] Homogeneous for most of its history, the Franco-Ontarian community was first composed of immigrants from Quebec and Acadia. Today, the community is in full mutation due to the growing numbers of Francophone immigrants that choose to settle in the province. These past years, numerous groups reflecting the presence of francophone African communities were created in Ontario[148]. The transformation of the Association canadienne française de l'Ontario into the Assemblée de la Francophonie de l'Ontario (AFO) in 2006 illustrates that mutation. Haitians were among the first to join the new AFO. They were followed by Europeans and Maghrebis, who in turn paved the way for the thousands of young Africans who followed them since. Six hundred fifty thousand people strong, L'Assemblée represents the first Francophone minority in Canada.

Let us only remind the reader of the exceptional resilience of that Franco-Ontarian minority in the face of important rights denials such as the tragic Regulation 17 of 1912, which declared English the only language of instruction in Ontarian public schools, thus denying Francophones the right to have

---

145. CLARKSON, S. (2002) Canada's *Secret Constitution: NAFTA, WTO and the end of Sovereignty?* Ottawa: Canadian Centre of policy alternatives.

146. KEITH, W.J. & SHEK, B.Z. (1980) *The Arts in Canada: the Last Fifty Years.* Toronto: University of Toronto Press.

147. For a chronology of the Ontarian Francophonie, it is wise to consult the work of SYLVESTRE, P.F. *L'Ontario français au jour le jour : 1 384 éphémérides de 1610 à nos jours.* Toronto: Éditions du Gref, 2005.

148. Union provinciale des minorités raciales et ethnoculturelle francophones; Association de la diaspora africaine du Canada; Diversité et futur; Association africaine de la ville Reine; Association tchadienne de l'Ontario; Association africaine francophone de formation continue; Association marocaine de Toronto; Association cinéma masques d'Afrique. Others are shaping up, in the Ivorian and Congolese communities.

public schools that taught in their language. That decision was challenged by the Association canadienne-française d'éducation de l'Ontario in front of London's Privy Council, a challenge that was followed by 200 legal recourses against the infamous Regulation, which will finally be abandoned in 1927. Today, that minority accounts for 12 school boards which, in 2009-2010, were funded for $1.2 billion. One also thinks about its extreme combativeness to gain a long-denied recognition,[149] its capacity to build numerous local or provincial coalitions that allowed it to fight some crucial fights and win them.[150]

As a minority within Canada, Franco-Ontarians benefit from the limited but real rights guaranteed by the Constitution Act of 1982 and the Official Languages Act of 1988.

That community today enjoys acknowledgement, status and legal protection defined and guaranteed by a law unanimously supported by the Ontarian Legislative Assembly. It also benefits from a swell in membership due to a new inclusive definition of the term Francophone. These gains are neither fortuitous nor circumstantial. They come in the wake of the secular mobilization of a network of organizations, associations and groups that are all federated by the Assemblée de la francophonie de l'Ontario. They come as a result also of the unstopping tension made of proposals, failures and successes, of which the Sommet de la francophonie ontarienne, held at U of T in 1991 is a strong example.

---

149. Historically, the first great battle was on the issue of the use of French in public schools, a battle marked by significant crises, notably those of Sturgeon Falls (1971) and Penetanguishene (1976). The most recent struggle concerned the safeguarding of the Hôpital Montfort, Ontario's sole francophone research hospital.

150. Here is an incomplete list of these coalitions and the remarkable diversity of their reach: the *Association canadienne-française d'éducation d'Ontario (1910)* to become *l'Association canadienne-française de l'Ontario* in 1969 and will transform itself in the *Assemblée de la francophonie de l'Ontario en 2005* (75 francophone organizations); the *Association multiculturelle de l'Ontario, Association française des municipalités de l'Ontario, Association des professionnels de la chanson et de la musique, Regroupement des organismes du patrimoine franco-ontarien,* the Fédération des Caisses populaires de l'Ontario (1946), Conseil de la coopération de l'Ontario (1964), Bureau franco-ontarien du Conseil des Arts de l'Ontario, Assemblée des centres culturels de l'Ontario, Fédération des élèves du secondaire franco-ontarien, Fédération des aînés francophones de l'Ontario, Association des juristes d'expression française de l'Ontario, Association des enseignants en enseignantes franco-ontariens, Regroupement des gens d'affaires de la Capitale nationale (1984), Club canadien de Toronto (1986), Regroupement des intervenantes et intervenants francophones en santé et en services sociaux de l'Ontario (1990), Chambre économique de l'Ontario (1991), mouvement des intervenants et intervenantes en communication radio de l'Ontario (1993), Association interculturelle franco-ontarienne (1992), the *Table féminine francophone de concertation de l'Ontario (1992)* and the *Coalition francophone pour l'alphabétisation.*

Following a tradition that dates back to 1982, the leaders of Ontario's Francophonie regularly adopt a road map that takes the form of a strategic plan which serves as a guide and gauge in their actions. These plans have had significant effects in education, health and justice, as we will see. They also played a decisive role in the creation, in 1985, of TFO, the only franco-phone television network in Canada based outside Quebec and significant cultural festive rendezvous like the Festival franco-ontarien and Toronto's Franco-Fête. Lastly, they provide the community with its own symbols, such as the Franco-Ontarian flag. Finally, the Ontarian government has a Department dedicated to the Francophonie.

The French Language Services Act

Adopted unanimously by the Ontario members of the Provincial Legislature. the French Language Services Act gives French a legal status in the Legislative Assembly, where both official languages can be used in the debates and other proceedings. This Act stipulates that the Assembly's bills must be presented and enacted in both English and French and that all public statutes that were enacted after the coming into force of the Revised Statutes of Ontario, in 1980, are to be translated into French and enacted again by the Assembly. The law also states that the regulations the Attorney General considers appropriate to translate will be so, before being submitted to the Executive Council or the other regulation-making authority for adoption. Lastly, the law sets up a comprehensive plan with regard to the "right" to services in French. According to Linda Cardinal, director of the University of Ottawa's Chaire de recherche sur la francophonie et les politiques publiques, this law introduces a linguistic framework in Ontario, "a way to govern languages".

> A person has the right in accordance with this Act to com-
> municate in French with, and to receive available services
> in French from, any head or central office of a government
> agency or institution of the Legislature, and has the same
> right in respect of any other office of such agency or insti-
> tution that is located in or serves [a designated] area.[151]

There are 25 such designated areas today.[152]

---

151. *Idem*, article 5.

152. They cover the cities of Toronto, Hamilton, Ottawa, Sudbury, Mississauga and Brampton, plus the regional municipalities of Niagara such as Port Colborne, Welland and Pell, eighteen counties such as the cities of Windsor, Belle River, Tilbury, Rochester, Pembroke, Penetanguishene, London and Kingston.

The intentions of the legislator are vast, as the Act's important preamble show:

> Whereas the French language is an historic and honoured
> language in Ontario and recognized by the Constitution
> as an official language in Canada; and whereas in Ontario
> the French language is recognized as an official language
> in the courts and in education; and whereas the Legislative
> Assembly recognizes the contribution of the cultural her-
> itage of the French speaking population and wishes to
> preserve it for future generations; and whereas it is desirable
> to guarantee the use of the French language in institutions
> of the Legislature and the Government of Ontario, as pro-
> vided in this Act.

This reminder of the status of French as an "official language in the courts and in education" is a reference to three laws. The Courts of Justice Act of 1984, which gives French and English official language status in the judicial system. The Education Act of 1968, which recognizes Francophones' rights to receive an education in their language at the elementary and secondary levels and the 1986 legislation on school governance which guaranteed Francophones proportional representation within the English school boards and a control on the budgets and programs of French schools. On the same year, the Metropolitan Toronto French-Language School Council was created.

Even the supporters of the French Language Services Act thought that it would remain incomplete as long as there was no authority to verify the implementation of its obligations. That absence was filled in 2007 following the nomination of a French Language Services Commissioner (FLSC) with the power to conduct investigations into complaints received[153] or of his own initiative, with the capacity also to make recommendations with regard to the law's enforcement.

As Ontario's first French Language Services Commissioner, François Boileau has signed three annual reports.[154] The man is seasoned, an astute

---

153. 351 such complaints in 2009-2010.

154. Office of the French Language Services Commissioner, First annual report of the French Language Services Commissioner, *Paving the Way, 2007-2008*; FLSC 2008-09 Annual Report: *One Voice, Many Changes*; FLSC 2008-2009 Annual Report: *Open for Solutions* Toronto, Office of the French Language Services Commissioner.

strategist, demanding and he does not lose sight of his targets.[155] He congratulates and reprimands, visits communities as well as deputy ministers, develops a comprehensive vision that plans for the quick settlement of the more pressing issues and at the same time, for the planning of a complete regime centred on an "active offer of quality services" and "the implication of Francophone officials in the development of policies as set out in the law", says the Commissioner himself. He works for the optimal development of public services offered in French in all Ontario, including by organizations to which the Ontario government delegates responsibilities. In his 2009-2010 report, the Commissioner grew impatient in the face of governmental inactivity when it came to French services delivered by such third parties and he requested a regulatory framework. The Commissioner reminds us of the Supreme Court decisions, and especially the Beaulac decision in which:

> the Supreme Court of Canada reiterated the true purpose of language rights, namely the search for substantive equality. In recalling this purpose, Honourable Justice Michel Bastarache, writing on behalf of the Court, confirmed the collective nature of language rights in this case. The same is true of the language rights recognized in the French Language Services Act. Despite the fact that it is based on the individual and the recognition of individual rights, its Preamble implies that there is a need to recognize the rights of the community that speaks this language and the government's obligations with respect to this community. In other words, without a community and without society, a language no longer fulfills its primary function, which is to transmit and act as a vehicle for that community's culture.[156]

These principles have important consequences. They imply, among other things, that the "policies and programs will need to be adapted to the special needs of this community".[157] The creation by the Ontario government of 12 French-language school boards in 1995, 27 years after the first

155. Office of the French Language Services Commissioner, *Letter to the Honourable David Caplan, Minister of Health and Long-Term Care regarding the proposed regulation*, November 12 2008; *Special Report on French Language Health Services Planning in Ontario*, Toronto, Office of the French Language Services Commissioner, 2009.

156. *Paving the Way, 2007-2008, op. cit.* p.17

157. *Ibid.*

French-language public high school opened in Welland in 1968, allows us to measure the road traveled.[158]

In the field of health care, some provisions of the Local Health System Integration Act of 2006 planned for the creation of a French language health services advisory council as well as the participation of Francophones in the implementation of these services. That council has been set up and its members are high calibre ones. The above principles have been reaffirmed and strengthened by the Supreme Court decision in the case of Desrochers v. Canada of 2009 in which the Court confirmed the principle of substantive equality in the provision of government services in both official languages. That substantive equality is not limited to the linguistic provision of services; it must also lead to distinct services, where necessary, due to the particular needs of the official language minority community.

Linda Cardinal is one of the true specialists of these complex questions. She does not hide the importance of Ontario's French Language Services Act. But in a noticeable intervention, she suggested important expansions to it. They include, among others, the entrenchment of the Act in the Canadian Constitution, the Commissioner's accountability to the provincial Parliament, the adoption of a mechanism to analyze the situations differently as they apply to the community as well as the requirement that in the case of French-language services being transferred to third parties, these transfers should be accomplished with "a favourable view" to their Franco-Ontarian beneficiaries.[159]

An inclusive definition

In 2006, 578,040 Franco-Ontarians lived in the province. There were 630,000 in 2010, or nearly 5 per cent of the Ontario population. That growth comes as the consequence of a political decision by the government to accept an inclusive definition of the term "Francophone".

Initiated by Franco-Ontarians in 2006 with the transformation of the Association canadienne française de l'Ontario into the Assemblée de la Francophonie de l'Ontario, that inclusive definition was further devel-

---

158. Pressed hard with demands from Franco-Ontarian wishing to have an adequately-funded school system, the provincial government created, in 1967, the Committee on French Language Schools in Ontario, or Beriault Committee. Bills 140 and 141, both constitute implementations of some of that committee's recommendations, the former setting up French-language public secondary schools and the latter creating French-language advisory committees.

159. See the interesting and important works of the *Chaire de recherche sur la francophonie et les politiques publiques* on the University of Ottawa website http://www.sciencessociales.uottawa.ca/crfpp/eng/index.asp.

oped by a working group at Statistics Canada,[160] adopted by the influential Trillium Foundation, recommended by the French Language Services Commissioner in his 2008 report, and was finally accepted by the Ontarian government in 2009. It was felt this new definition better reflected "the evolution and diversity of Ontario's Francophone communities", in the government's words.

For statistics gathering purposes, Francophones were previously defined as only those whose mother tongue is French. They were essentially descendants of Quebecers, or French Canadians, that came to Ontario to build the railroad or were drawn by the possibilities offered by agriculture or by the mining and forest sectors between 1880 and 1920. They were also Quebecers who, year after year, continued to cross the border and settle in Ontario.

But the new inclusive definition captures those whose mother tongue is neither French nor English, but who have a particular knowledge of French as an Official Language and use French at home. Consequently, Franco-Ontarians made an immediate gain and a long term gain that will probably prove even more significant.

That decision takes into account the ongoing and important growth in Francophone immigration in Ontario since 1996 due to a provincial policy centred on that growth.[161] This policy includes welcoming them in French and various social proposals to help live a better life in Toronto, and in French. At that time, Francophone immigrants accounted for 4.8 per cent of all Franco-Ontarians. Ten years later, that proportion exceeds 16 per cent at the provincial level and 50 per cent of Franco-Torontonian as well as 20 per cent and 15 per cent of Francophones in Ottawa and Hamilton.[162] That pool of French speakers is also filled with a million Ontarian students who, in 2006, were opting for French as a second language; that's 49 per cent of the potential clientele, with 120,000 of them choosing French immersion programs.[163]

---

160. CORBEIL, J.P. and BLASER, C. (2007) *The Evolving Linguistic Portrait, 2006 Census: Findings*, Ottawa, Statistics Canada.

161. GUIDE D'ÉTABLISSEMENT DE L'ONTARIO (2009) *Nouvel arrivant au Canada*, numéro 22. Toronto: Centre francophone de Toronto.

162. DE VERDIER, K. and NANGUY, F. (2004) *Vivre en français à Toronto/The French Side of Toronto*. Toronto: Les éditions Franco.

163. CANADIAN PARENTS FOR FRENCH (2008) *French Second Language Education in Ontario, Report and Recommendations to the Ontario Minister of Education*. Toronto: Canadian Parents for French.

So who are these new Franco-Ontarians? The French Language Services Commissioner answers that question for us.[164]

> The new definition applies to newcomers who know French and who speak French in the home, even though it is not their mother tongue. Take, for example, a family from Algeria. This family may be more likely to speak Arabic in the home and may also know English; however, the second language spoken in this family's home is French. For this reason, this family is considered a Francophone family.
>
> This new definition also applies to exogamous families, with one Anglophone parent and one Francophone parent. In Ontario, exogamous couples now represent close to 65% of Francophone families. Unlike the method of calculation that is based on the language spoken most often in the home, which is often English, the method of calculation used by the Ontario government means that families that also speak French in the home are considered Francophone. Many children from exogamous families attend a French language school.
>
> These children needed to be taken into consideration as well, and recognized as Francophones.
>
> Interestingly, more and more young people are identifying themselves as "bilingual" or as "Canadians", that is to say, people who are bilingual. This is the important issue of identity. Most of the time, these young people are from exogamous families; they live in French and participate in activities in the community.
>
> These young people also needed to be included in the definition of Francophone and that is exactly what the new definition does.

A rescue operation for the Francophone minority, according to some; a minority whose future is threatened by demographic stagnation and the aging of its members[165] as well as by the reverse trend in the general

---

164. BOILEAU, F. "La portée de la nouvelle définition de la population francophone", *Le Droit*, June 6 2009.

165. GOVERNMENT OF ONTARIO AND ONTARIO TRILLIUM FOUNDATION (2009) *Profile of Ontario's Francophone Community*. Toronto: Government of Ontario and Ontario Trillium Foundation.

provincial demography, which is growing and thus diminishing the relative importance of that minority. Reality check, according to others, who remind us of the ongoing rise in the immigration of French speakers, of their needs and expectations in terms of public service in their language, especially in education, health and justice. These expectations are shared by other non-Francophone immigrants, the Chinese community being cited often, who also wish to have access to French services. These evolutions are complementary, as are the two worlds they link: the Franco-Ontarian community, whose numbers are dwindling, and the French-Speakers that are the result of immigration, insertion and diverse sociological evolutions, whose numbers keep on growing.

The effort of the Ontarian state in support of the Francophone community and of French speakers all over its territory is real, significant and observable. Almost all printed and electronic public documents that were consulted in the purpose of writing this book were available in French, as were a good amount of official texts from Ontarian public and private institutions. That effort was recognized in June 2009 by the United Nations. Indeed, on the tour the UN dedicates to the public service, Secretary-General Mr. Ban Ki-Moon presented a Certificate of Recognition to the Ontarian government for the importance it attaches to "providing quality services to Ontario's Francophone community".

CONCLUSION

Such are the Ontarians and the advanced society they organized for themselves in little more than 2 centuries. Its history clearly shows the passage from one vision of diversity to another. From one that was hostile to it, Ontario evolved towards another which acknowledges, integrates and promotes it as a fundamental value and not just as an objective reality. According to their own experiences and their vantage viewpoint, our interlocutors were unanimous in their assessment of that unfinished and irreversible passage. For them, that quasi-utopic gamble is a successful one.

Prevailing in the central province until after World War II, the first of these visions favoured a homogeneous world ethnically, culturally and linguistically. That was the modern Western scheme of things at the time, a period in which immigrants and those who greeted them belonged to the same world in terms of values. The traditional relationship between majority and minorities was the country of adoption's main framework. Even if the political rhetoric tells of a welcoming and tolerant history, the truth lies else-where. For a long time, a very long time from the middle of the 19th century to the middle of the 20th, a tight preference was given to White Christian immigrants, preferably Anglophones. Some have qualified these hundred years as our "racist past" and tried to demonstrate that the history of immi-gration to Canada was in no way a "success story".[166]

The country will have to wait for the reform and immigration law of 1967 in order to see systemic discrimination eradicated and common standards implemented in the selection of men and women wishing to acquire Canadian citizenship. In the interval, a long-lasting century-old interval, racial selectivity dominated spirits, discourses and laws. That theme was absent from our initial project, but it imposed itself forcefully after each meeting with Ontarians. Indeed, the people we spoke to, espe-cially in the Asian and Black communities, spontaneously addressed it as a persistent element of the relation with their country of adoption. The issue, which especially interests younger Ontarians, is not only an Ontarian issue. But it is them Ontarians that made us realize the weight of memory in human societies.

The second of these visions imposed itself in the last decades of the 20th century. It transformed the Ontarian society's DNA, having it become heterogeneous, multiethnic, multicultural and multilingual. That mutation did not come by easily, but it is inescapable today, the diverse Ontarian communities virtually poised to become a majority in the very near future. As we have stated the effort of the Ontario Government in support of the Francophone community and of French speakers all over its territory is real, significant and observable. This also is express a radical change and an effec-tive recognition of the historical and political uniqueness of this community.

That passage radically changed civil society by feeding it with a consider-able amount of associations created by the communities and by contributing to the renewal of the social, economic and political leadership of Ontario. It also contributed to the fact that the Ontarian society is opening up even more to culture, to the plurality of its numerous sources in the world and to the diversity of its expressions, which can all be seen and heard in Ontario.

Incomplete, the state of things poses unique challenges to the Ontarian society, all the while protecting it from the inherent traps of the majori-ty-minority relationship. It places the society in an unprecedented situation

---

166. HILLMER & GRANATSTEIN, *op. cit.*, p.3

that brings together social practices, interethnic relations, intercultural experiences, permanent sharing of public spaces, common resources and different leaderships. That situation is the conflation of shared encounters, objectives and values, the breeding ground for the development of reciprocal benevolence, the sphere where unity is created and where identity is shaped. Both unity and identity do not swallow up the plurality of affiliations; they rather submit it to experiences that leave it in a new sphere which defines the affiliations of Ontarians. That vision is not theoretical. We have observed it time after time during our Ontarian journey, in university classrooms and kindergartens, with boards of directors, staff, administrative executives, NGO bosses and cultural teams that all greeted us.

Ethnic, cultural and linguistic diversity constitutes the background reference and the daily fact of life for Ontarians. Dionne Brand, famed Ontarian author and currently Toronto's Poet Laureate, beautifully expresses the new sound that replaced the Victorian discourses.[167]

> Name a region on the planet and there's someone from there... In this city there are Bulgarian mechanics, there are Eritrean accountants, Colombian café owners, Latvian book publishers, Welsh roofers, Afghani dancers, Iranian mathematicians, Tamil cooks in Thai restaurants, Calabrese boys with Jamaican accents, Fushen deejays, Filipina-Saudi beauticians; Russian doctors changing tires, there are Romanian bill collectors, Cape Croker fishmongers, Japanese grocery clerks, French gas meter readers, German bakers, Haitian and Bengali taxi drivers with Irish dispatchers. That was the beauty of this city; it's polyphonic murmuring.

That murmuring is not only heard in the metropolis; as was demonstrated earlier, it echoes all over Ontario because indeed, if the immigrant population mainly settled in the GTA, it is also present in other Ontarian cities and regions.

From our encounters with the leaders of different communities, we have learned that the diversity that so defines Ontario is also ingrained within each of the communities. Religious, cultural, linguistic, social and political plurality in the country of adoption mimics that of the countries of origin

---

167. BRAND, D. (2005) *What we all long for.* Toronto: Alfred A. Knopf, p.4.

to such a degree that no immigrant community can be said to be homogeneous. That is a significant realization. It contradicts some apocalyptic views of diversity as a negation of common citizenship, as an acid in which acquired values dissolve and with them, so would social cohesion and some components of the rule of law. We have also learned that solidarity within the community manages quite a large number of issues that non-immigrants do not even imagine exist.

Finally, that passage from the ancient vision of diversity to the current one has had effects on the political and judiciary powers, which had to take into account in their analyses and decisions the needs and expectations of all these communities. The passage has not set anything in stone, and it never will. Diversity as a value is at the heart of that gestation. Due to its demographic and political weight, it is likely that the set of references emerging in Ontario spill over the province's borders and make themselves felt on the entire federation.

In 2031, the number of Ontarians will vary between 16.3 and 18 million, depending on the estimate we use, the average or the high estimate. John Wildgust will be disappointed: Ontario shall not be the centre of the universe. The province however will keep and strengthen its central place in the federation. Indeed, that same year and according to the same estimates, the four eastern provinces, plus Quebec, will have populations of 10.7 million while the western provinces plus Yukon, the Northwest Territories and Nunavut will account for 12 million people. With Quebec and its 8.38 million people, British Columbia with 5.46 and Alberta with 4.11, Ontario will be far ahead and account for 42 per cent of the Canadian population.

Its preponderance at the national level and its continental rank—it places 5th behind California, Texas, New York and Florida among the 64 states, provinces and states of the United States and Canada—will both be secured. It will owe that position to the favourable net migration that will guarantee an estimated population growth of 27 per cent for the coming two decades, representing 3.3 million people. The province will by then welcome 55 per cent of the immigrants that chose Canada as their new adopted country and its population growth rate will be higher than the national average due in part to the higher fertility rate of women from visible minorities compared to their fellow female citizens. The country's natural population growth will probably turn negative towards 2020. Then, immigration will become the only source of population increase.

That growth will ensure for Ontario a certain demographic superiority and, consequently, its predominance in the Canadian federal system. In 2030, Ontario will have greeted more than 7 million immigrants, strengthened its status as a society composed of diverse communities with the resulting challenges and advantages. Society without a majority, it will live off multiple convergences and countless identity blends that will be the materials of an unprecedented model of togetherness.

That Ontarian power of attraction would not have been as consistent and dense had it not been for an economy that was able to absorb these millions of immigrants and guarantee them one of the most enviable standards of living in the world. Some have doubts about the province's capacity to do so in the decades to come and, as a consequence, downsize all the forecasts, including demographic ones. Others believe, on the contrary, that Ontario will manage to pull through with the transformation of its economy, so deeply affected like all western economies, by the "shifting wealth" at the world level. All central, these questions are treated in the chapter that follows. Dedicated to the Ontarian economy, it explores its ongoing mutation from being a fragment of the continental economy to a fragment of the global one.

CHAPTER 2
A CHANGING ECONOMY

AT THE TURN OF THE MILLENNIUM, Ontario accounts for close to 40 per cent of the Canadian GDP, for more than 50 per cent of the country's industrial activity and for 51 per cent of its exports. Toronto's financial centre ranks 3rd in North America and 7th internationally. Such is the considerable capital erected by successive generations of Ontarians. According to John Ibbitson, that success is "the root metaphor of Ontario".[1]

The Ontarian economy today is facing two considerable challenges: a new competition in the production of goods and services at the global level and the emergence of new creditworthy markets that comes with the weakening of the American market. Ontario shares these challenges with all the economies of the Atlantic zone, for which the global transformations and effects of the 2008 crisis were more severe than in any other part of the world.

The moment is particular. Our Ontarian interlocutors seek the good formulas to bring together the strong historical performance of their economy with the effects of the global market mutations and those, calamitous, of the cataclysm that have eroded its great manufacturing sector since 2008. A fragment of the continental economy, Ontario was brutally affected by the collapse of the big American market. In a brief period of time, the source of the province's prosperity became the cause for its difficulties and worries.

This American crisis and its aftermath are not like the other cyclical slumps that have marked the history of contemporary American capitalism. Roger L. Martin, dean of the University of Toronto's Rotman School

---

1. IBBITSON, J. *Loyal no more. Ontario's Struggle for a Separate Destiny*. Toronto: Harper Collins, p.4.

of Management and one of the continent's most respected thinkers of economic systems, feels the reasons for said collapse lie with the systemic mutation of American capitalism. In his judgment, for the past 35 years, we have given priority to the expectations market rather than to the real market; priority to the returns for board members and shareholders rather than to the goods and services for consumers. As long as these priorities are not reversed, all the reforms will be vain and the system as it is has "the ability to destroy our economy and rot out the core of American capitalism".[2]

That posture and its repercussions are felt at the very moment an unprecedented geopolitical and geo-economic transformation is tipping the West's financial, scientific and technological resources towards the East. That is the equivalent of European powers taking progressive control of the world in the 16th century. The international community is already rattled by it particularly since the American and European economies find themselves in a delicate phase of their history. The obvious abuses from American financial institutions, including banks, and their irresponsible risk-taking weakened not only themselves but the states that are in their debt as well. In that calamitous context, Canada has shown true resilience since 2008. But one must certainly not draw the conclusion that the country is immune to all the consequences of what happens elsewhere in the world; unless one believes that all the country's workers will find jobs in Alberta. Consequently, the need to think and build the future differently imposes itself without a doubt.

Ontario is confronted to that considerable need in a time when none of what has been gained can be considered guaranteed; neither traditional components of the private sector nor public policies, and especially those concerning the fiscal transfers and programs that are at the heart of the relationship between the federal, provincial and territorial levels of government. These uncertain times, coupled with the federal laissez-faire of the first Harper years, strengthened the conviction of those who think that this "country of regions" must recognize these regions' legitimacy and capacity to lead their own development, especially given the fact that their interests have become more specific and difficult to have converge. Hence the rise in regionalism or provincialism in Canada, including in Ontario.

What are Ontario's interests in those global, continental and Canadian conditions? This chapter tries to outline the Ontarian ongoing debates, hypotheses and propositions about that unprecedented situation, whose

2. MARTIN, R.L. (2011) *Fixing the Game*. Boston: Harvard Business Review Press, p. 31.

outcome will have important consequences on their living standards and those of every Canadian.

THE WORLD'S MOST IMPORTANT MARKETS

The undeniable success of the Ontarian economy has many explanations. There's the geopolitical positioning that offered it uninterrupted access to the most important world markets for more than two centuries: the British Empire and the United States of America. Add to these prodigious external markets, the Canadian domestic market, which was built on the foundations of the national policy of John A. Macdonald, great figure in Ontario and Canada's history.[3]

That privileged access to core world and Canadian markets was Ontario's luck, one which 8 to 10 successive generations have successfully exploited, making their economy one of the most advanced on the planet. That favourable course of events certainly defines Ontario's past, but it also sketches the current challenges: securing or staying tied to the world's core markets, producing goods and services that answers their demands.

Ontario's economic success is manifest and it has had multiple effects. For instance, it allowed for a high level of foreign investment, especially from Great Britain and the United States, for the development of a vast industrial sector and, more recently, of a services sector, as well as making the erection of a world-class financial centre possible. That success has enabled the constant flow of millions of immigrants that came and added themselves to the Ontarian society. It sustained a high level of employment and services offered to those, from all over the world and Canada, who found in Ontario the living conditions they were looking for. Finally, it sheds light on the important Ontarian contribution to the Canadian socioeconomic experience, from fiscal equalization to all the public and social policies that distinguish the Canadian federation from the American republic.

LEN CRISPINO

Len Crispino immigrated to Ontario in 1957 when he was 9 years old. Decades later, he returns to his native Italy as an official representative of the province and then he came back to Toronto in leadership position. His is an impressive journey, instructive about the inclusive policy towards immigrants.

---

3. WAITE, P.B. (1975) *Macdonald: His Life and World*. Toronto: McGraw-Hill Ryerson Limited.

The man, engaged in the transformation of Ontario's economy, welcomes us in the large conference room of the Ontario Chamber of Commerce that he presides. We're in early April of 2011. We evoke his personal and professional itinerary, which "would probably have been impossible elsewhere in the world, especially in Europe". We talk about the cultural diversity of the Ontarian society he witnessed growing "like a beautiful and gigantic tree". From this vantage point, our eyes gaze on the vertical city, majestic in the light of that day. Our host also sees the other horizon, somewhat hazier, that brings us to his office: the state of the economy three years after the beginning of the crisis "that changed everything, as it had to".

> We have to say goodbye to the idea of a going back to our prior situation in many sectors, especially the car industry, just as we must absolutely penetrate new markets. That conviction is strong in times of economic crisis when the American market is crumbling. We know we can't depend solely on that market. However, when the situation improves, we go back to our routine. We have considerable capacities to enter new markets but we make do with a minimal part. We must take much more vigorous and sustainable initiatives, invest in this future, fix ambitious objectives for ourselves: the doubling of our exports, for instance. We also have to realize that our currency is at par with the American dollar and that the days of a weak Canadian dollar are gone and not likely to come back anytime soon.
>
> If the federal government doesn't take these initiatives, Ontario's government has to. And it must succeed all the while knowing that such necessity constitutes a shared responsibility; the state can't accomplish everything by itself. Hence our idea of organizing the Ontario Economic Summit. For the 7th straight year, public authorities, companies, unions, universities and NGO's are all invited to think together about the stakes at play and the challenges of economic growth and development. These summits strengthen that culture of shared responsibility and maybe that's their biggest achievement.

Four clear messages stand out after our meeting with Len Crispino: say goodbye to a return to our prior situation, put an end to the dependence on the American market, penetrate new markets and fix ambitious objectives for ourselves.

A major stress

This assessment is shared by many. Ontario's Task Force on Competitiveness, Productivity and Economic Progress has established it without complacency in its 2009 report, which also bears the signature of the well-known Martin Prosperity Institute.[4]

> In each of our previous reports, we have observed the basic good health of our economy and that of our most important trading partner, the United States. But the prevailing scene is starkly different. Our North American economies and all economies around the world are under significant stress. A mood of pessimism and panic has set in among ordinary Canadians and our business and public leaders... Everywhere there are signs of weakness. Manufacturing is very weak; unemployment is starting to move up after a long period of nearly full employment; new house sales are weak; government deficits are back with a vengeance.

Disastrous semesters have followed prosperous growth years. A clear need for transformation has followed a long stretch of periodic adjustments to the Ontarian economy. Four years after the start of the crisis, the situation has been partly rectified, as demonstrated by the investments of companies in plants and machinery since 2010, even if "Canada's biggest trading partner is going to be an ocean of uncertainty for years to come".[5] But the province's public debt is still hefty; in 2011, exports are falling and after 7 consecutive negative trimesters, GDP has fallen in the middle of the year, industrial production has weakened and employment is stagnant. Thus, even the most optimistic commentators consider that exiting this crisis will take a long and difficult time "reflecting the deep and lasting damage caused by the financial crisis".[6]

---

4. MARTIN PROSPERITY INSTITUTE (2009) *Opportunity in the turmoil*. Toronto: Institute for Competitiveness & Prosperity / Martin Prosperity Institute.

5. SIMPSON, J. "Recession Recovery: We've only just begun", *The Globe and Mail*, June 29 2011.

6. THE CANADIAN CHAMBER OF COMMERCE (2009), *Economic Outlook 2010: On The Road To Recovery*. Toronto: The Canadian Chamber of Commerce, p. 2.

To the significant stress that has weakened all the economies of the Atlantic zone, including Ontario's, one can add, in that particular case, some converging factors that are also likely to weaken, with time, its economic results. These fragilities are threefold: a slow downturn in the fundamentals of the Ontarian economy that preceded the 2008 crisis, a weakness in terms of stakeholders' competitiveness, productivity and innovation in the industrial and commercial sectors and, lastly, a clear delay in the penetration of the emerging markets. So, it is not the 2008 crisis that has produced the idea of transforming the province's economy. That idea preceded the crisis since it imposed itself at the beginning of the present century. The crisis has but strengthened it.

> Ontario is in the midst of a global economic transformation. While this transformation to a knowledge or idea-driven creative economy has been underway for more than three decades, the current financial and economic maelstrom has accentuated its importance.[7]

The following diagnosis is about the Ontarian economy. However, parts of it also affect the economies of Canada's other provinces and regions.

Fundamentals of the Ontarian economy

At the turn of the millennium, the performance of the Ontarian economy appeared solid. However, in the years immediately before the 2008 crisis, its fundamentals showed signs of tripping. Thus, if the crisis' repercussions on the exports volume were major, their continuing fall had begun as early as 2004-2005. Furthermore, manufacturing output has been wobbly since 2000, going from stagnation to modest rises. In the same period, the balance of payments slipped into deficit and the secondary sector's manufacturing jobs are falling to the profit of so-called administrative jobs. Lastly, if the crisis slowed the mining sector and if the forest sector crumbled following the sharp fall in the US construction industry, both these important sectors were already affected by the new competition of some emerging countries on the American market.

These signs of weakening find some of their origins in faraway lands where production capacity and the ability to do business have started to change the world. Serious observers were wondering, well before the crisis, if Ontario was giving up on its usual role as the engine of Canada's economic growth.

---

7. MARTIN, R.L. and FLORIDA, R. (2009) *Ontario in the creative age.* Toronto: Rotman School of Management, p. 1.

The province's employment growth rate between October 2006 and 2007 was at 1.5 per cent compared to 2.3 per cent for Canada and the growth in disposable income was 5.5 per cent in Ontario compared to 6.2 per cent in nationally.[8] Finally, the GDP growth rate has been consistently falling, from 4.8 per cent in 1996-2000 to 2.1 per cent in 2000-2005. It will stand at a mere 0.8 per cent in 2006-2010.[9] According to Ontarian economist Serge Coulombe, "Ontario is no longer the locomotive of the country's economic development since 2002".[10] An older diagnostic by the Task Force on Competitiveness, Productivity and Economic Progress in 2003 established that the weak innovation and productivity indexes of the Ontarian economy triggered its falling behind at the national and continental levels.[11]

Competitiveness, productivity and innovation

Questions on competitiveness, productivity and innovation were asked well before 2008. Study after study, the relative performances of Canadian and Ontarian firms were documented and debated. Compared with the United States and OECD countries, these performances appeared weak and well below the threshold necessary to conquer new markets and impose themselves in new strategic sectors. In its 2011 report, the Science, Technology and Innovation Council pointed to international evaluations relative to the productivity of labour in the country:

> In terms of growth in labour productivity, the Institut européen d'administration des affaires ranked Canada 95th of 132 countries. The International Institute for Management Development (IMD) in Lausanne, Switzerland ranked Canada 45th of 58 countries. Part of Canada's low international standings in productivity growth is attributable to the fact that developing countries have a much greater potential for rapid productivity growth through technological convergence or catch-up from low productivity levels. Among 33 advanced economies in the IMD standings, Canada's productivity growth ranks 24th. As Canada's pro-

8. VALLIÈRES, M. " L'Ontario piétine ", Montréal, *La Presse*, October 6th 2007.

9. THE CONFERENCE BOARD OF CANADA (2011) *Provincial Outlook Long-Term Economic Forecast: 2011*. Toronto: The Conference Board of Canada.

10. BELLAVANCE, J.D. " Péréquation : le portrait ", *La Presse*, January 12th 2010.

11. CAMPBELL, M. "Study finds Ontario is falling behind", *The Globe and Mail*, December 4th 2003.

ductivity continues to lag despite macro-economic reforms intended to improve economic performance, economists are increasingly focusing on a lack of innovation in Canada as a contributor to poor productivity performance.[12]

A vast 2009 survey of 6,233 Canadian companies with over 20 employees and more than $250,000 in business earnings gave tangible form to these troubling rankings.[13] It dealt with 4 innovation categories: organization systems, products, processes and marketing. Only 19 per cent of companies surveyed consider the introduction of new goods and services as a strategic objective and but a third says it wants to introduce, in the long-run, improved practices in terms of business processes, marketing and management. Innovation and marketing for new products rank third in the list of long-term objectives for all companies. These data explain the low level of investment in research and development, with the exception of certain specific sectors. According to the survey's results, that level has fallen in the last years.

Benefiting from the advantages of the American market's proximity and from the abundance of its own natural resources, factors that "insulated us from the rest of the world",[14] the Ontarian and Canadian corporate cultures have integrated few innovation requirements, if any, that a more competitive situation would normally have warranted.[15] They gave in to the ease stemming from that proximity and access to the world's biggest creditworthy market. Consequently, Canadian businessmen that have worked within a free trade treaty with the United States for the past 25 years have been less sensitive to the formidable evolutions and opportunities offered by the world market. That culture was also infused with the effects of a weak Canadian dollar and the commercial dividends such a situation created in the short run.

---

12. Science, Technology and Innovation Council, *Imagination to Innovation: Building Canadian Paths to Prosperity*. Ottawa: Government of Canada, 2011, p. 3; COOPER, S. *Canada's Disturbing Productivity Performance*. Toronto: BMO Nesbitt Burns Economics, March 2011.

13. The 2009 Survey of Innovation and Business Strategy (SIBS) was issued by Industry Canada, Foreign Affairs and International Trade Canada as well as Statistics Canada.

14. GRIFFITHS, R. (2008) *Canada in 2020: Twenty Leading Voices Imagine Canada's Future*. Toronto: Key Porter Books Limited, p.10.

15. THE CONFERENCE BOARD OF CANADA (2009) *How Canada Performs*. Toronto: The Conference Board of Canada.

Bar those from British Columbia, the exports of every Canadian province to the United States reached at least 70 per cent of their total exports. Only those of Alberta and New Brunswick surpass Ontario's on the American market.[16] Following many who had said it before them, group of CIBC economists evoked, in June 2011, the general effects of that proximity and situated these effects in the Ontarian context.[17]

> Ontario's predominant focus on its major and lucrative trading partner in the US has seen it largely ignore other markets and opportunities. While much discussion has taken place over the years about the need for Ontario to broaden its trading partners, until recent times the strength of the economic relationship with the US has precluded any real need to build ties with other markets. However, the rapidly changing global economy is dictating the need for Ontario to broaden its trade perspectives.

Speeches and interventions on innovation, or the lack of it, abound in recent administrative, political and prospective Canadian literature. In a straightforward paper published in July 2010, Ontario's Premier reminded us that his government proposed the five year Open Ontario Plan aiming to increase the productivity of the province's industrial sector. That plan included proposals such as the elimination of the capital tax that year and the introduction of a harmonized sales tax. Such improved fiscal measures mixed with the value of the Canadian currency create an environment that is more than favourable to capital investment in machinery, equipment and other industrial supports.

> In spite of our considerable efforts to make Ontario more competitive, as an economy, we're coming up short on productivity. From 2001 to 2008, the average productivity in the U.S. grew by nearly 2 per cent a year. In Canada, productivity grew by only 0.7 per cent. Canada used to rank as high as third place out of 20 OECD countries in productivity in 1960, but lately we've slipped to 16th of 31 OECD countries. …Productivity isn't about working longer hours at

---

16. CIBC, *Provincial Forecast*, February 1, 2011.

17. TAL, B; RANGASAMY, K. and ENENAJOR, E. (2011) *Spicing up the Ontario-India Economic Relationship*, Toronto: CIBC World Markets Inc.

the office, the factory or the job site. Productivity is about businesses making the right kinds of investments so that our people can maximize their time on the job more effectively. It's about giving them the tools they need to get the job done.

And that's where Ontario businesses are slipping. We know that, relative to the competition, our businesses under-invest in machinery and equipment, training, research and development, and information and communication technology. These are all important drivers of productivity, and we have to do better.[18]

A year before, John Manley insisted, while interviewed by Paul Wells from *Maclean's*:[19]

I don't think you could say that innovation is deeply in the DNA of our Canadian business enterprises. We have built prosperity, up to and including this decade, on a fairly basic paradigm: we are rich in natural resources. We're good at harvesting them. And we have built a manufacturing and processing sector, and to some degree a services sector, which has been quite successful in exploiting access to the U.S. market. ...

But, he says the "world is changing so quickly that the inability to find ways to adapt to the changing environment is detrimental, not only to the business sector, but to the country's prosperity as a whole".

"Innovate or perish." John Manley could not have been any clearer.

THE CRISIS

Apart from the United States, Ontario may be the hardest hit by the 2008 financial and economic crisis since the province's economy was so seamlessly integrated with the continent's. We have already evoked some specific effects of that crisis on Ontario and Ontarians. These effects have produced general situations that changed, for an unpredictable period, the province's public finances and its economic capacity when compared to its Canadian partners.

---

18. MCGUINTY, D. "Ontario's productivity challenge: Step up, business leaders", *The Globe and Mail*, July 2nd 2010.

19. WELLS, P. "Innovation isn't in Canada's DNA", *Maclean's*, July 24th 2009.

After managing an increase in financial resources between 2003 and 2007, and then having balanced successive budgets during that period, and in compliance with the Fiscal Transparency and Accountability Act of 2004, the Ontarian government suddenly saw its financial situation deteriorate in considerable proportions.

Planned to reach $14.1 billion in the 2009-2010 fiscal year, the deficit rather jumped to $24.7 billion, according to the Ontarian government's Economic Statement of October 2009. This situation had disastrous consequences for the government, especially fiscal consequences: 48.1 per cent decrease in corporate income taxes collected as well as personal income taxes because of the explosion in unemployment, less than 25.5 per cent in the sole automotive industry between October 2008 and October 2009.

The hope of a return to balanced budgets as of 2017-2018, as is anticipated, appears little likely in the absence of a strong economic recovery in the United States, which no one predicts. That return to equilibrium could also stem from tighter financial management and a more rigorous control on spending. But will we be able to avoid drastic budget cuts in education and social programs, which represent two thirds of provincial spending in Ontario? The notion of a major rise in corporate income tax is so contrary to economic recovery that it is only evoked in marginal circles. And in such context, how are we to maintain a good level of public investment that would be likely to contribute to the transformation of the economy and to its modernization, competitiveness and, ultimately, its output?

The Drummond commission forecasts are troubling. It assessed the 2011 budget scenario with its goal of balancing the budget by 2017-2018 and concluded that it would not likely lead to balance. Then it builds a status quo scenario taking into account the deterioration of the economic outlook and concluded "that the deficit would more than double to $30.2 billion in 2017–18 and net public debt would reach $411.4 billion, equivalent to just under 51 per cent of the province's GDP." To avoid that outcome, it devised a preferred scenario that would balance the budget in 2017–18 in consequences of deep cuts in public spending, 17 per cent lower than in the Status Quo scenario. All public services budget should be reduce by 2.4 per cent on a yearly basis for six years at the exception of Health, Education and Social services budget than will expand by 2.45, 1 per cent and 0.5 per cent respectively.

The economic returns of the provincial economy have fallen below the 3-year weighted average of its fiscal capacity relative to all of Canada. That position is explained in part by the 2008 crisis as well as by the income growth of Alberta, Saskatchewan and Newfoundland. For the first time in the country's history, Ontario is collecting equalization payments.[20] Thence came its demand for a "New Deal" for itself and a fairer return of parts of the $20 billion that, according to many convergent assessments, represents the gap of what it contributes to federal public finances and what it receives in return from the federal government.

There are two main causes for that degradation. If the first of these causes is conjunctural, although the circumstances that define it could well mutate and become structural, the second will only be strengthened in the coming decades. The question is surely not for Ontario to substitute one type of integration for another, but rather to acknowledge their complementarity, which expresses the new totality that applies to all.

Both causes are inseparable. The financial and economic crisis illustrated the ongoing transition towards a multipolar financial world. It certainly did not reduce the United States to insignificance. However, it hurt America's preponderance and brilliantly illustrated the new capacities of these other countries.

Whether they are mere factors unrelated to the crisis or a direct effect of it, recent data show a slow but real movement of Canadian and Ontarian exports towards emerging countries. EDC titled a 2011 report *The Diversification Dividend*,[21] and in an analysis from April 2011, Statistics Canada demonstrated that the share of Canadian exports to Europe and Asia is showing slow but sure signs of growth.

SHERRY COOPER

Her conferences, books and media interventions have made a communication star of the former Executive Vice President and Chief Economist at BMO Financial Group when it comes to local and global economy. Indeed, Sherry Cooper's assessments on the national and international state of things are always anticipated because of their reliability and originality.[22]

---

20. It is recognized that a few times and for short periods in the past, the province could have benefited from that redistributive policy.

21. EDC, *The Diversification Dividend: Global Export Forecast – Spring 2011,* Ottawa, EDC, June 2011.

22. In 2010, Sherry Cooper received the Lawrence Klein Award for U.S. forecasting accuracy because of her predictions for the 2006-2009 period. She arrived first among fifty renowned economists that were considered for the award.

In 2001 before many others, she mentioned the arrival of economic turbulence as a consequence of the new global economic and social order. But her prediction does not stop there. In the presentation of her book, *Ride the Wave,* one can read that "wild economic times are coming. Exciting times. They are harbinger of a radically new global economic and social system, one that will deliver unprecedented wealth. But, before we get there, we'll have to survive years of gut-wrenching economic volatility".[23]

She greets us in the Group's comfortable offices at the corner of King and Bay, in the financial heart of Toronto.

> What happened in 2008 looks nothing like those cyclical crises that affect an economy's evolution at regular intervals. Considerable changes were then affecting the Unites States, whose market represents a third of Canada's economy, doubtlessly more for Ontario. The industrial basis of the province was wrapped in a swirl of complex situations, old and new. To insufficient productivity were added a sudden and major decrease in exports, especially but not exclusively in the automotive industry and concurrently, the significant rise of the loonie made exports even more difficult. For its part, the financial services sector witnessed a compression of activities that led to a high level of postponed investments and of layoffs. So, the period is particular and times are hard. We now know that we must absolutely increase our productivity and place innovation at the rank of national priority, where for a long time we prioritized science and the discoveries if fostered. We also know that we have to diversify our production and our markets. The rise of technological firms in the Kitchener-Waterloo area and in Toronto is encouraging. Of course, we don't have the equivalent of Silicon Valley, but that sector must absolutely become an engine of our economy, she muses, before concluding.
>
> And we have to support that sector more firmly. How can we compensate for our objective inferiority towards the United States? Over there, sponsors, champions and

---

23. COOPER, S. (2001) *Ride the Wave, Taking Control in a Turbulent Financial Age.* Toronto: Financial Times, Prentice Hall, Introduction.

patrons abound, their financial capacity as well as their willingness to help tech firms are significant. This comes from the entrepreneurial and risk cultures that are very strongly engrained in our neighbours but which we lack here. Plus, in the United States, there are a great number of financial firms and they often have deep roots in the communities, as local banks do, for instance. That proximity is instrumental in the acknowledgement and funding of start-ups that benefit from local networks that are already in place. Contrary to Quebec, with the savings and credit unions of the Mouvement Desjardins, Ontarian entrepreneurs don't have access to such local financial services. Our banks don't fill that need.

Place innovation at the rank of national priority, where for a long time we prioritized science and the discoveries if fostered. Sherry Cooper's world is fascinating, her dialectic subtle, her intuitions and predictions considered oracles by fellow economists!

The car industry

One cannot study the crisis and its effects without referring to the automotive industry, which, at the beginning of the 21st century, accounts for $100 billion in Ontarian exports, close to half a million jobs, and contributes to the general prosperity of the province and that of it great southwestern region. The very idea of its decline spells economic and social tsunami. The steps taken by Premier McGuinty at the beginning of the crisis are thus quite understandable. "It's no secret now we're talking to Fiat. We're talking to India, we're talking to China, to folks in Germany", he said.[24] India offers real opportunities to the Ontario car industry, opportunities that are assessed by the work of the Automotive Innovation Council, which unites players such as Canada's Automotive Parts Manufacturing Association, the Society of Indian Automobile Manufacturers and the Automotive Component Manufacturers Association of India.

The automotive sector, the "industry of industries" according to Peter Drucker's formula, constitutes the perfect illustration of the continental

---

24. HOWLETT, K. and Keenan, G. "McGuinty to Bring Sales Pitch to Fiat HQ", *The Globe and Mail*, May 6th 2008.

integration of Ontario's economy at the triple level of investment, production and market. Six top automakers are installed in the so-called auto corridor, which stretches from Windsor to Oshawa, southwest of the province. Added to that are 12 assembly plants and the biggest of the field's 450 subcontractors. That imposing array which essentially finds its market opportunities in the U.S. was significantly strengthened by the 1965 signature of the Canada-United States Automotive Products Agreement. A long period of growth for Ontario's industry followed, contributing to the province's wealth. It became the first car-making region in North America, ahead of Michigan and Mexico! That first rank was lost in 2010. In the midst of crisis spasms, Ontario slid to the third rank, behind the United States and Mexico.

The Ontarian car industry's record before the crisis deserves to be briefly reminded. An annual production of 2.5 million vehicles, that is 1 out of every 6 made on the continent, 85 per cent of which are exported. Added to the picture are recurring annual investments, with $30 billion going to subcontracting, $7 billion to research and $3.5 for plant maintenance and equipment upgrades. Furthermore, according to the 2009 Ontario Budget, the sector generates 125 000 direct jobs, out of 400 000 that are somehow linked to the industry. Thirty research centres dedicated to the automotive industry benefit from the support of companies in the field and of the Ontarian and Canadian governments under different types of partnerships. These centres cover the entire production process, as illustrated by the wide-ranging Initiative for Automotive Manufacturing and Innovation at McMaster and Waterloo universities. They also do research on all the technologies and materials of the field: nanotechnology, surface technology and microcellular plastics (University of Toronto), robotics (Ryerson University), catalysis and photonics (Ottawa University) as well as lightweight materials (Windsor University).

In 2008, the crisis devastated the industry. In the course of one year, more than 60,000 direct and indirect jobs were lost, exports fell by 22.8 per cent and their share of GDP went from 6.1 per cent to 3.7 per cent. One can then add to the market's collapse the Obama administration's policy of financial support to firms in the industry that repatriated jobs. Faced with the magnitude of the disaster, the federal and provincial governments have agreed to invest strongly in support of the sector's firms. Furthermore, Ottawa endowed Southern Ontario with an economic development agency, which was provided $1 billion over five years.

Since the mid-90s, the United States no longer leads the production
and market of the industry. Globalization also transformed the automotive industry: plant installations in Latin America, Eastern Europe and
Asia, multiplication of mergers between the industry's multinational
corporations and accelerated development of capacities, especially in
China and India. Asia now takes the leading role in terms of production
and global market for the automotive industry. According to a study by
auditing firm PricewaterhouseCoopers of October 2011,[25] the number of
vehicles made in emerging countries in 2011 will exceed that of so-called
mature countries which, at best, are in an replacement economy when
it comes to automobiles. According to the study, the sector's significant
growth stems from the production expansion in emerging Asian countries and from the considerable demand from BRIC countries, especially
China. According to then Director of Corporate Strategy at Ford Motor
Company, Matt O'Leary, "China is closer to being able to supply the
developed market products than most people think".[26] That feeling is
shared by *The Economist*, who wrote in 2011 that "eventually, Chinese
cars will flood into American and European markets".[27]

What is the future of the automotive industry in Ontario?

Many of our interlocutors have shown pessimism in that regard for reasons already mentioned above. The President of the Ontario Chamber of
Commerce, Len Crispino, does not believe in the return of a situation ante
for many sectors, "including the automotive industry". Only the Conference
Board believes that:

> The auto industry remains a dominant force for the
> province going forward... Over the next few years,
> the most significant gains for Ontario will come from
> the continued recovery in export demand—partic-
> ularly of autos and parts, which typically account for
> about 30 per cent of the province's total international
> exports. Although U.S. demand for new motor vehicles
> is expected to pick up steam, it will remain below his-

25. PRICEWATERHOUSECOOPERS, *La production mondiale automobile dopée par les pays émergents*, October 5, 2011.

26. *Idem*, p.6.

27. "Danger ahead. The car industry's crisis is over. Its long-term problems are not", *The Economist*,
January 13, 2011.

torical scrappage rates until 2012. After that, demand will grow at a more normal pace and will remain there through the medium term.[28]

But in the same paper, the research organization notes that "due to recent union renegotiations among the Big Three producers and the financial restructuring of General Motors (GM) and Chrysler Canada, Canada's comparative advantage in auto production has been severely eroded. Although job gains in auto assembly and parts production will persist through the medium term as production returns to capacity levels, employment in this sector will trend well below historical levels".[29]

Very few industrial sectors equivalent in significance and size will be submitted to such a large range of challenges in the coming years. The first of these challenges is about the ability to remain competitive in front of the usual players as well as those, in China and India notably; who are biting at the heels of the industry's big players and already produce the engines of the vehicles assembles in the United States. How many will survive that addition? Will alliances unite these players and if so, how? Which designs, new materials, technological and eco-friendly inventions will seduce consumers without forgetting the prices asked and the services offered? Which labour force and robots will make these 21st century vehicles? Finally, what places are able to offer competitive production conditions?

The financial sector

Maintaining and developing the important Ontarian financial sector, with its 222,000 jobs, is of major importance for Toronto, for the province and for the country. That sector is well-positioned to cultivate its competencies, innovate and remain a player on the global scale. That is not to say that such maintenance will be easy to accomplish. In that field too, the "shifting wealth" was felt in the last decade, as shown by the compared evolution in capitalization of American and Asian markets.

According to data by the World Federation of Exchanges, market capitalization in the Americas and in Asia represented $4,228,385,000 and $3,056,465,400 respectively in 1990. Twenty years later Asia's market capitalization took flight to reach $19,303,389,200 compared to $22,172,888,200 for the Americas. A new global financial geography is visibly shaping up;

---

28. The Conference Board of Canada, *Provincial Outlook, op.cit.*, p. *ii* and 51.

29. *Ibid*, p.56

this will have big effects on the world's financial centres and most likely on the regulation of the sector.[30]

A study ordered by the Ontarian government and presented in 2009, the *Partnership and Action: Mobilizing Toronto's Financial Sector for Global Advantage*[31] aimed at increasing Toronto's competitiveness as a an international financial centre, at placing it second in North America and maintaining it in the world's top ten. Defined as the "heart of Canada's financial services (FS) engine", the GTA saw 12 per cent of its jobs and 20 per cent of its GDP depend on the sector in 2008. For the Boston analysts in charge of that action plan, the assets of the GTA are numerous and include:

> access to a diverse, multi-lingual and educated FS talent base, excellent international accessibility, proximity to U.S. markets, a highly stable and well-regarded banking system and regulatory framework, and an existing cluster of large, respected players across multiple FS sectors.

Still according to these experts, Toronto's competitiveness also suffers from a few notable gaps compared to other major international financial centres:

> the city lacks the global profile that comes with being recognized as a world-leader in any specific area [and a] shared purpose and spirit of partnership between government and industry has been lacking for the Toronto financial services industry [while it has made the strength] of other major international financial centres.

Three themes are suggested in order to strengthen the status of Toronto's stock exchange: creating world-class hubs, fostering partnership between government and industry and lastly, guaranteeing the competitiveness of the sector. These themes include significant proposals such as the establishment of a global institute for integrative risk management that will recognize, analyze and manage these risks; the entrenchment of the TMX Group's position as the leading global hub for mining, metals and energy

30. OLSEN, E.; PLASCHKE, F. & STELTER, D. (2010) *Threading the Needle: Value Creation in a Low-Growth Economy.* Boston: Boston Consulting Group, September 2010.

31. BOSTON CONSULTING GROUP (2009), *Partnership and Action: Mobilizing Toronto's Financial Sector for Global Advantage*, report prepared for The Toronto Financial Services Working Group, November 2009.

financing;[32] leadership in retirement financing solutions by establishing a working group that would include the private and public sectors in order to come up with innovative formulas at the Canadian and international levels.

According to the Consulting Group's evaluation, the implementation of that action plan has the potential of creating a hike of "25,000-40,000 jobs and $4-5 billion in annual GDP over a five-year horizon". But the value-added lies elsewhere. In maintaining and developing a great sector of activities that supports more than 220,000 jobs, contributed to Ontario's growth and keeps important financial services in this country. Strengthened, developed and promoted, that great sector could serve as a lever to investment, research and exports of services throughout the world.

THE WORLD MOST INTELLIGENT INNOVATION POLICY

The idea of transforming the economy is part of the great objectives of Ontarian policy. It was suggested and detailed in important public policy statements, of which the Reaching Higher Plan and Move Ontario 2020. That economic transformation idea is not unique to Ontario. The province's think tanks, advisory boards and government have not invented the new knowledge economy paradigm. One could even say they adopted the idea tardily. It haunted all the governments of the first generation of OECD and European Union (EU) countries when they were faced with the success of the American model in the last decade of the 20th century.[33] It still haunts all the governments of the Atlantic area, including that of the United States, when faced with the new financial, economic, commercial and technological competition from the so-called emerging states.

ROGER L. MARTIN

In the community of thinkers about economic management and public policies, Roger L. Martin, Dean of the Rotman School of Management at the University of Toronto, is a global celebrity. His books and interventions are always the subject of great expectations, numerous commentaries and high appreciation. They can be found in China, India, Great Britain, continental Europe, Africa, the United Sates and of course in Canada. The

---

32. *"A target of achieving 70% market share of global energy, mining and metals listings by 2015 is proposed, up from 43% (energy) and 55% (mining) today."* Source: *Idem*, p.8.

33. OCDE (1997) *The World in 2020:Towards a New Global Age*. Paris: OCDE. ; (1998) *Growth and Competition in the New Global Economy*, Paris: OCDE. ; (2000) *The Creative Society of the 21st Century*. Paris: OCDE.

BBC and PBS reserve important columns about them, Fareed Zakaria comments them while Paul Volcker, former chairman of the Federal Reserve, commends them. Business magazines and reference newspapers such as *The New York Times* run features on that exceptional Ontarian and multiply the analyses of the doctrine that made him famous.[34] In 2005, *Business Week* included him in its short list of 7 innovation gurus and in 2007, the same publication placed him in its top ten list of the world's best business professors. Finally, in 2009, he was ranked 32nd by *The Times* of London and Forbes. com among the 50 top management thinkers in the world. These represent some of the acknowledgments granted the head of the Rotman School of Management school at the heart of the university of Toronto campus.

The glass house on St. George Street is eerily calm on that moody August day of 2011. A few students from China are deliberating in the great hall that opens up on archways and mezzanines accessible through wide stairways. A consequence of the continued and important growth of the school, considerable works are underway in order to double its size. Eco-friendly, transparent and illustrative of all forms of connectivity, the new architectural work envelops the Heritage House, an old red brick manor that links both buildings of the famed institution. The funding came from public authorities, especially the Ontario government, as a complement to significant private sector contributions and those of benefactors whose names are niched right next to the hall: Marcel Desautels, Sandra and Joseph Rotman and Michael Lee-Chin top that list due to their millionaire contributions.

The dean welcomes us in his relatively modest workplace where files just seem to pile up. Welcome to the realm of integrative thinking, whose reach today extends to numerous management schools in America and around the world. The doctrine lies in a significant proposition: substitute the analytical thinking, which recycles acquired knowledge and only produces little improvements to the status quo, with a new way of thinking called *design thinking*. To enter this universe of innovation and its implementation, we need no longer to ask one what he thinks but how he thinks. It is also important to master a three-step method that is likely to produce new knowledge.

The first step is intuitive in nature and hard to explain in part because of its unconcealed ties with "mystery". The second is heuristic, allowing us to get a little closer to a solution and the third leads to an algorithm

34. WALLACE, L. "Multicultural Critical Theory. At B-School?" *The New York Times*, January 9th 2010.

and to a kind of structure that is critical for implementation. Once that exercise is completed, one probably finds oneself far enough from known understandings to be able to adopt a new paradigm conducive to innovation and destined to procure comparative advantages. Martin has shown that societies inspired by that doctrine have gained considerable advantages. Its demonstration has seduced a great many people and today, Dean Martin's theory defines the curricula, partly or entirely, of a growing number of management and business schools.

The Rotman School of Management is considered by many as the nonofficial and nonpartisan think tank of the Ontario government. Political party leaders, the Liberal McGuinty as much as the Conservative Tin Hudak, are familiar with its work.

The Dean heads the Task Force on Competitiveness, Productivity and Economic Progress since its creation in 2001 by the Ontarian government. How does he assess its accomplishments after a decade of work?

> We have progressed in terms of corporate taxation in order to allow firms to accomplish what they have to accomplish. The stakes are better understood and instead of the old categories dividing the left and right about less or more taxes, we progressively substituted a renewed conception of smart or dumb taxes. Corporate tax rates can be very high and smart, as is the case in Sweden, or real high and dumb, as was the case in Ontario and Canada when we started our work. In 2012, we will have gone from worst to average. Ontario harmonized its sales tax with Ottawa's and reduced its corporate income tax; these are the transformations of a Liberal government, need I remind you.
>
> In the field of education, the Task Force has for the first time shown the real situation as it prevailed only a few years back in the country's richest province. If Ontario had comparable numbers of undergraduate students with the Canadian and OECD averages, it falls behind considerably at other levels of the education system. Nobody had analyzed these troubling data before. How can you develop a knowledge economy in such catastrophic context? We've been heard and some additional resources have

been allocated to change what must be changed. There has been real progress in that field too.

With regard to the resources, behaviours and support necessary to encourage innovation, we are progressing slowly. We still lack a true innovation policy. Our culture focuses on invention rather than innovation, it still supports science rather than the enrichment of the goods and services we produce.[35] For more than a century, the Canadian policy has been infantilizing companies, which felt little incentive to innovate, that is to say invest in the qualitative transformation of the goods and services they marketed. My objective for this country is to contribute to the implementation of the world's most intelligent innovation policy.

Invention or innovation? The former deals with exploring the unknown, the latter, with enriching what already exists with value added. The passage from one to the other implies deep changes in public policy and in the mentalities of those who manage or work in R&D labs. The stated ambition is considerable: get the world's most intelligent innovation policy.

JOSH SOOKMAN

Lodged in a renovated building along Spadina Avenue, Guardly is one of these new tech firms at the core of Ontario's economic reconstruction. These companies are multiplying in the regions of Kitchener-Waterloo and Ottawa, as well as in Toronto. A hospitality room, a couple of closed spaces and two bigger rooms; the first brings members of the team together, all working at their station, the other, serving another purpose, has a ping pong table as its main draw. In both cases you feel the notion of a quick and precise back and forth. The place is modest, unlike the ambition that drives it.

Josh Sookman welcomes us in that electronic lab dedicated to the development of personal safety systems. Josh has the attitude of a serious student obsessed with finishing his master's thesis. Focused and friendly, he tells us about the history of the company he created and which wants to "conquer the world". Our new friend gave it its technological DNA, his partners have the mandate of ensure its commercial and financial future starting with

---

35. For a clarification of the terms innovation and invention, see: MARTIN, Roger L. "Key to productivity is innovation, not invention", *Toronto Star*, May 31, 2011.

local markets and working their way, in concentric circles, towards every possible market. This adventure's central idea is relatively simple. Transfer personal safety services on the whole range of mobile devices and, in emergency situations, reach up to 15 people instantly in the click of a button: neighbours, family members, doctor, social worker, 911 and any other person or service selected by the client. The sick, the elderly, people in insecure situations, groups such as students on university campuses that today rely on security booths, would all be better served by Sookman's invention.

If Guardly is his baby, it is also a product of the MaRS Discovery District. Josh was working there when he developed his hypotheses and decided to implement them. MaRS's "free" services—access to research reports, location, marketing and distribution strategies, networking and other advisory sessions—"were very useful". He evokes other MaRS services: commercial missions, opportunity to show one's products, references on social networks, assessment of ideas or meetings with potential investors. Sookman also appreciated the direct, practical and useful dimension of these services, which managed to resist the mermaid's bureaucratic call.

He also evokes the funding difficulties of businesses such as his. Many are created in Toronto, that city of all diversities only to be drawn away in Boston, New York or California. The difficulty in getting Canadian funding explains this exodus towards the U.S. were funds are more accessible. Management teams are then invited to move and in the end, the whole firm packs up and settles elsewhere. Our host wonders:

> Are we condemned to this offshoring that deprives the country of its companies at the stage when they finally know growth and success? Americans have a risk culture that lacks here! We have an exceptional quality of life, a culture of liberty, an abundance of fresh air, clear water and an exceptional proximity with nature. In a city which ranks third as a technological urban pole in America, that culture of risk cruelly lacks.

Thinking the future differently

The changes in the nature of global finance, economics and commerce are well known. In a few decisive decades, the engine of growth and development has moved and keeps moving irreversibly. The affected fields constitute the second generation of vast transfers at the heart of globalization's current phase. If, at first, attention was mostly focused on the volume and direction of foreign direct investments, on offshoring and on technological transfers, the current movements are of a different nature. That second phase of globalization is about the production capacities of science and advanced technological products,[36] the access to strategic natural resources and the security of their means of transportation and finally, the control and use of financial reserves.

Beyond R&D, that new configuration will have to include the following elements: spectacular rise in patent applications from Northeast and Southeast Asia;[37] emerging countries participation in the production of advanced technological goods in industries that range from spatial to nuclear, aeronautics to new materials, pharmacology to ICTs, for instance; China's ambition to develop national standards that can replace current global norms;[38] the rise of powerful multinational corporations in emerging countries and their deployment in the world, including in Canada; the shifts in commercial balances, especially favouring China, the growth of South-South trade and investment, marked by the preponderance of southern economic actors in all the southern markets;[39] new financial reserves under the form of sovereign wealth funds, especially in China and the Gulf states, whose growth and influence potential is explosive. These funds' assets totaled $2,500 billion in 2007; it could reach $12,000 billion in 2015.

Investment in the human resource contributes to these advances. Former New Brunswick Premier Frank McKenna reminded us of that fact at the 2005 Ontario Economic Summit, in striking terms:

---

36. THURSBY, J. and THURSBY, M. (2006) *Here or There? A Survey of Factors in Multinational R&D Location.* Washington D.C.: The National Academies Press.

37. WORLD INTELLECTUAL PROPERTY ORGANIZATION (2007), *WIPO Patent Report: Statistics on Worldwide Patent Activities.* Geneva: World Intellectual Property Organization.

38. If successful, that Chinese crusade within the International Organization for Standardization and other international certifying bodies will pave a royal way to global markets for advanced Chinese technological products. That policy is said to be implemented and currently gathering "fire-power". One needs only think of the new Chinese standards for HD DVD players and 3G cellular telephony, of the new national Wi-Fi norm launched for the Beijing Olympics, the new Internet Protocol and the common standard for the Chinese automakers of electric cars. If, from the vast national market, these norms are applied to the world, China will gain significant industrial advantages and, by reversing a situation that was very costly before, will draw considerable revenues from the exploitation of these patents.

39. WESSEL, D. "The Rise of South-South Trade", *The Wall Street Journal,* January 3, 2008, p.2.

Here's a stat in my view that should give all of us a night-
mare in North America. China last year produced 367,000
engineers. The United States grew only 50,000. And
China's not alone. We shouldn't forget about India with its
billion people and 38 per cent a year growth in the information technology sector alone.

At the very same summit the following year, Jonathon Fischer reminded
the audience that in India, state governments operate 4,650 industrial training institutes with the capacity to train 678,000 students.[40] All the theses
on higher learning, especially those concerning engineering, were contradicted, sometimes strongly, by some European and American institutions
that challenge both the validity of these numbers and the quality of teaching in Asia. Fareed Zakaria has shared such critics.[41]

Thinking differently about the world also means taking stock of the
effervescence and expansions that are to come. Compared with today's 4.2
billion, Asia will hold 5.7 billion people in 2050; 2.15 billion will live in
Africa compared to 2011's 1.05 billion; and 850 million will populate Latin
America and the Caribbean, up from the 595 million they were in 2011.
The combined population of Europe and North America will reach 1.1 billion at that time. According to median projections, almost as many people
will live in cities by 2050 as there are living on the planet today.

At the junction of these complementary evolutions, one unavoidable
question needs to be asked: how can we think the future differently? Ontario
is working resolutely to answer that question, as can be seen through its
public policies in education or innovation, for example, and through the
number of think tanks that contribute to that renewal of the province's
vision of the world and have an impact on its policies.

The most precious of resources

As we were reminded by the Dean of the Rotman School, Ontario's
"considerable gap" in terms of graduation rates and funding of its education
system has been closed, in part at least, by the infusion of fresh resources, in
the billions, since the middle of the previous decade, an annual $1.6 billion

---

40. FISCHER, J. (2006) *Human Capital Panel Discussion*. Toronto: Ontario Economic Summit,
Ontario Chamber of Commerce.

41. ZAKARIA, F. "The Future of American Power: How America Can Survive the Rise of the Rest",
Foreign Affairs, May–June 2008, p.30.

of which was dedicated to postsecondary education between 2006 and 2010. Our interlocutors in that field have each acknowledged the importance and repercussions of those investments, which translated in significant increases in the number of professors, in financial help to the students, in the number of places available in academic programs, in innovative research activities and in a wider range of possibilities for Neo-Ontarians.

In the fall of 2011, *The Economist* published a briefing about global education in which it commends the systems of Poland, of Saxony, a German state, and of Ontario.[42]

> Ontario really is impressive. The Canadian province has a high proportion of immigrants, many without English as a first language, yet it now has one of the world's best-performing schools systems, after bringing in what one of its architects calls "reform without rancour." The Ontario reformers made a special point of gaining full public support. Every school—even in the remotest "fly-in" places—had to be improved by the reforms, and had to show in regular inspections that it was making progress. These efforts were not cheap—since 2004, total funding for education has gone up by 30 per cent.

IBRAHIM HAYANI

Here we are, north of Toronto, in Markham, at one of Seneca College's six campuses. Opened in 2005, it is vast and its main building is impressive, with its clean architecture. Professor Ibrahim Hayani warmly welcomes us. A common friend put us in touch. I know little about this economist, a Middle-East specialist, apart from his beautiful text *"Chronicles of passage: On becoming an immigrant without really trying"*. With obvious pride, he takes us on a tour of the place, shows us its large common areas and, from an overhead walkway with a view on the library, we gaze at a forest of computers and hundreds of students that type away on them. "Here you have it, says the Syrian-born professor who came to Canada in 1968, the intelligence revolution at work in this province. You have to multiply what you see here by 10 or 20; that's the expression of the true priority given to education". In the little conference room where he will answer our questions,

---

42. "Reforming education: The great schools revolution", *The Economist*, September 17, 2011.

he sets a plate of clementine at the middle of the table between us and dives with us in tales of the cultural diversity of his city of adoption.

> Globalisation has not yet produced all of its effects. For the first time in contemporary history, the dissociated development of the global economy and the American economy is appearing. The former remains robust enough and reaches high levels of growth in some places even if the latter is still in great difficulty. Such dissociation translates a loss of centrality and control from the United States.

Ontario's government is well aware of that dissociation. These past few years, specialized funds were dedicated to fields from life sciences and advanced health technology to innovation and emerging technologies—clean technologies, digital media, information technology—and from water technologies to support of aerospace and biopharmaceutical firms. Finally, major subsidies were granted to a whole range of research centres like the MaRS Discovery District, the McMaster Innovation Park in Hamilton, the Perimeter Institute for Theoretical Physics in Waterloo, whose facilities are the most advanced in the world, and the Institute for Quantum Computing at the University of Waterloo, among many others.

A forecasting laboratory

These policies are the result of Ontarian leaders' and public servants' analyses. They also come from the specific studies they themselves ordered and defined, such as the one former Premier Bob Rae steered in 2004 to examine the post-secondary education system in Ontario. Finally, they depend on the analyses and suggestions in a wide range of domains by numerous Ontarian think tanks installed within the government, universities and other private or civil society organizations. These past years, their teams have intervened in various fields important to the future of Ontario. We have met with the main players of some of these centres and learned more about their analyses and proposals.

That intellectual and political effervescence is a major element of Ontarian society at the beginning of the present century. In the years before the 2008 crisis, Ontario had become a real forecasting laboratory reminding some of the France of 6 decades ago, at the time of the Commissariat au Plan.

The idea of planning and preparing the future, of building it differently, is at the heart of the doctrine established by these think tanks, especially those affiliated with the ever-reliable Rotman School of Management. A few converging mantras—innovation, productivity, creativity, diversity and prosperity—give that idea its conceptual foundations and fix its horizon, one sufficiently wide to incorporate private and public management into a renewed political, economic and social vision. That doctrine is thus present in the works of many institutes and personalities that are part of the Rotman School. Roger L. Martin, Richard Florida, Mihnea Moldoveanu, and a few others are the advocates of that new doctrine. They are widely consulted, invited, read, quoted and their reputation shines beyond our borders. They all have a more or less distant timeframe, the famous 2020 Prosperity Agenda, and they all have Ontario as a reference.

During our meetings with Ontarians, we felt they were at ease with that effervescent vision, that bubbling of ideas that puts everything up for debate. During the first decade of the 21st century, before and after the crisis, the Ontarian society was animated by a feeling of optimism that strongly focused on the common desire to keep control of the province's future. Of course, the crisis shook some spirits and placed many people in considerable difficulties. Another reason to think and build the future differently, according to our interviewees. At work in their respective fields, they have often expressed their trust in the future as well as a feeling they had of participating and living in this rare moment when a given society seeks to deploy the entire range of its potentialities.

This intellectual and political effervescence contrasts with an apparent standstill at the federal level during the first mandates of the Harper government, seemingly uninterested and unwilling to understand and cope with the new internal and external requirements of a transformed world. That federal stance was obvious in the way the government dealt with the economic crisis. After having denied the crisis for a while, Ottawa finally presented a recovery plan, pressured as it was by a parliament that was about to withdraw its confidence in the government.

Many of our Ontarian interlocutors have insisted on the importance and significance of these considerable losses of will and capacity by Ottawa. For them, it means an abrupt stop in that continued exploration of Canadian internal and external interests which, since the Second World War, have powerfully contributed to the knowledge of Canadians' needs and federal and provincial public policies. Now a majority government and more integrated to the international economic discussion, the Harper government are giving signs of a certain aggiornamento that unfortunately does not include much needed federal and provincial consultations.

ONTARIO AND THE WORLD

A *Globe and Mail* article, June 11, 2010, expressed the new competition situation better than the most polished university thesis, through its title alone: "A breakthrough in China, another blow for Sudbury". That is why we must rethink the economic relationship with the world differently. The need to integrate the global dimension of markets constitute, for Canadian and Ontarian businesses, a complex and indispensable exercise. Easier said than done because that indeed implies companies reviewing their objectives, mastering new competition, searching for new clients, new service providers and new partners. That exercise also implies a command of new knowledge about the history, politics, institutions, laws and customs of the targeted countries. Lastly, it suggests new training for existing personnel as well as for their recent colleagues.

Thinking differently about the economic relationship with the world means significant financial, institutional, relational and cultural investments. In this unfolding mutation, Ontario can especially count on the diversity of its population as an innovation lever, an asset for transnational investment, research and production partnerships, as well as an entry point into networks all around the globe.[43] The province has unique advantages, especially with regard to China and India, due to the numbers of its citizens that come from these countries, to their high levels of education and to the vigour of their commercial initiatives towards their country of origin. In the mid to long run, these immigrant flows from all over the world will prove a precious asset for Ontario, and one the most powerful engines of its economy's transformation. In a sense, Ontario is and will remain a new world if these flows continue to enrich it demographically, culturally and economically.

If some dream of restoring or returning to the *status quo ante*, others plea for a recast, for bringing together sectors that still have promise with new ones that make up the paradigm of a knowledge society. What is at stake here is the selective production of advanced goods and services able to staunchly position Ontario in the global market.

In both instances, the American economy is a reference.

The former are convinced of its resilience and believe in its capacity to bounce back and again occupy the forefront of the global economy. For

---

43.. THE CONFERENCE BOARD OF CANADA (2010) *Immigrants as Innovators. Boosting Canada's Global Competitiveness, 2010 Report.* Toronto: The Conference Board of Canada.

them, despite current cyclical difficulties, the U.S. economy will remain unrivaled for many decades. Ontario, as a consequence, would find in its big neighbour the source of its own growth and development in the coming future. The first Harper government was not too far from that position.

Without denying the importance of the American market for the Ontarian economy, the latter place the relationship with the United States in the unprecedented context created by the new global competition. They think that the U.S. market is now part of the global market and that new paradigm requires a deep change in the perception, analysis and intervention of Ontario's economic public and private operators. "America's future seems limited now", former federal Finance Minister Donald Macdonald was reported as saying in a February 2010 *Globe and Mail* article. "We in North America have passed away from really having a dominant position in world economic trade ... the rise of China is no fleeting thing. The country's trade levels with the United States maxed out a few years ago, started downward and will probably continue to move that way. The world in which we find ourselves is "less America-centric".[44]

To these systemic evaluations, defenders of that point add more circumstantial data such as a slow but continued drop in Canadian and Ontarian exports. Without adhering to the theses about the inescapable decline of the American system, supporters of that position worry about its political and economic dysfunctions and about the high level of its public debt. In short, they doubt or do not believe that Ontario's future growth and prosperity can depend on the American market in the same proportions as in the past decades. Pierre Pettigrew, the former Canadian international trade Minister declared that the "American consumer will no longer be the engine of growth, post-recession. This is a turning point in the world economy".[45] That assessment appeared largely shared by our new Ontarian friends.

Both visions are present in Ontarian society. But the idea of thinking the future differently has dominated the last decade's public debates, policy decisions and research. Ontario's economic summits have articulated that vision in remarkably consensual fashion and, year after year, brought

---

44. MARTIN, L. "The U.S. economy is in turmoil. How about a royal commission?" *The Globe and Mail*, February 11, 2010.

45. CARMICHAEL, K. "Canada plays catch-up in race for trade with China", *The Globe and Mail*, August 10, 2009.

together the province's main economic actors. Universities have multiplied the creation of research centres specialized in productivity, innovation and competitiveness. The private sector also contributed to validate this paradigm through many initiatives such as the creation, in Toronto, of the MaRS Discovery District. The Government of Ontario built its official policy around it. One needs only read the governmental plan of 2003 to be convinced; it set the tone for a decade of public interventions, programs and budgetary choices.

Dealing successfully with the American market constitutes the dominant aspect of Ontario's modern economic history. It was facilitated by the establishment of branches from numerous American firms in the province, by the exceptional protection awarded the Ontarian automotive industry following the Auto Pact from half a century ago and, lastly, by the Canada-US Free Trade Agreement of 1988. Ontario greatly benefited from the American financial, economic, scientific, technological and commercial supremacy since the Second World War. It drew considerable advantages from the situation: its main source of investment, its integration to the most important industrial complex on Earth, its access to the most creditworthy market, a significant part of its own growth and wealth. Well, for Ontario since World War II, the benefits stemming from the proximity with American markets were such that the province's economic relationship with the world was seamlessly connected to its economic relationship with the United States.

That "integration" for some and "dependency" for others have given rise, at the time, to different theses and initiatives. Based on political reasons such as the apprehended loss of the country's independence towards its powerful southern neighbour and the threats of protectionism periodically evoked in the republic, such theses have reached their peak in Ontario during the debates preceding adoption of the Canada-US Free Trade Agreement, and these initiatives have been most strongly voiced under the Trudeau government and its famous Third Option.

Current debates are of another nature. They no longer only concern the feelings of Canadians and Ontarians with regard to keeping their country's autonomy and identity. They also concern changes in the nature of the global economy, those we have evoked already and that affect the U.S., whose future concerns Canada's.

Have we become, or are we becoming, a country of the Pacific after having been, for 4 centuries, a country of the Atlantic? And if such is our position, what strategy can we adopt to make it a reality? If the provinces of central Canada have suggested and strongly supported the free trade project with the EU, the western provinces, and more recently even the central ones, have asked for the same negotiation with Asian powers. And we know that our interests in the Arctic also hang in the balance given the appetite of northern American, European and Asian states for the wealth of the vast region.

Perceived in the background are the needs for the reconstruction of global governance, stability and security. So is the fate of the 3 institutions which, for the past 60 years, have been at the basis of international political economy cooperation: the World Bank, the International Monetary Fund (IMF) and the World Trade Organization (WTO). In that last case, questions of agricultural subsidies, commercial intellectual property rights, access to markets for non-agricultural products, trade in services and public markets have all, for more than 10 years, blocked multilateral commercial negotiation. Shifting wealth, in short, means much more than a one-way transfer of resources. It marks the access of emerging countries to means of claiming and defending their interests and means of influencing policies defined by so-called advanced economies at the time when they were predominant. Hubert Vedrine, former French Foreign Affairs Minister, has defined the current phase in premonitory fashion. In it "nothing can be imposed upon us, but we can no longer impose anything".[46] Comes to mind Henry Kissinger's troubling diagnostic concerning America's state of mind at the time it held the unique and short-lived hyperpower status:

> At the apogee of its power, the United States finds itself in an ironic position. In the face of perhaps the most profound and widespread upheavals the world has ever seen, it has failed to develop concepts relevant to the emerging realities.[47]

We can see that the interests of Canadians and Ontarians lie at the junction of the world's great regions, and that defending these interests calls for a strategy and policy that makes their interventions convergent. Ontario cannot afford to lose interest in these negotiations.

---

46. VÉDRINE, H. (2007) *Rapport pour le président de la République sur la France et la mondialisation.* Paris : Fayard, p. 122.

47. KISSINGER, H. (2001) *Does America Need a Foreign Policy? Toward a Diplomacy for the 21st Century.* New York: Simon & Schuster, p. 19.

The province's extreme proximity with the United States, the flow of goods and people crossing the border in both directions and the volume of technological, economic and commercial exchanges between them are all conditional to Ontario's global growth. It is thus in Ontarians' considerable interest to secure their borders, ensure the fluidity of controls, which have multiplied since 9/11, and the steep decrease in the impediments they may generate for traffic, trips and goods crossing the border. If the border issue is essential for every Canadian province, it is vital for Ontario.

A former Canadian Ambassador to the U.S. and highly-respected diplomat, Allan Gotlieb thus summarizes the effects of American security policy on the Canadian economy:[48]

> If a Canadian manufactured product must, as a result of economic integration, cross our common boundary half a dozen times in order to be constructed, who has the comparative advantage, the country without a common border, such as South Korea or China, whose goods need entry only once, or Canada and Mexico, whose goods must cross a number of times?
>
> The security leviathan is now part of a triad of forces creating restrictions on access. To border security must be added the rise of protectionism and environmentalism. As a result, the question must be asked: Is proximity becoming our comparative disadvantage?

Allan Gotlieb continues his important analysis with two significant observations. If we are to keep our comparative advantage, we have to deepen the North American Free Trade Agreement (NAFTA), at least between Canada and the United States, with the objective of establishing a unique economic space and a common security perimeter. "Given today's realities, we are unlikely to achieve one without the other". The chances of succeeding in that endeavour are slim, however. The diplomat's second conclusion comes as a confirmation of requests that he is not the first to express.

> This is why Canada's strategic thinking must go beyond the bounds of North America. The decision of the Harper government to negotiate a free-trade agreement with the

48. GOTLIEB, A. "Proximity, reality, strategy, destiny. The forces of history are challenging Canada's relationship with the U.S. – It's time to make some choices", *The Globe and Mail,* June 27, 2009.

European Union is a welcome one. But as the economic centre of gravity moves inexorably toward the Far East, particularly China and India, Canada should be laying the groundwork for deepening our trade with these countries, where demand for our resources, unlike in the sclerotic economies of Europe, is likely to grow exponentially.

Failure to diversify can only weaken our bargaining strength and make us more vulnerable to protectionist and other restrictive measures from the south.

Ontarians also have a major stake in the American public policies that grant governmental aid to firms on the condition that these firms bring back jobs to America. These types of proposals constitute a grave danger to the Ontarian economy. The same goes for protectionist and non-tariff measures aiming at the trade in goods and services.

The commercial dependence of the past is no longer an option. To the idea that Ontario's prosperity depended on its great southern neighbour was added the notion that said neighbour could also trigger the province's misfortune. Gotlieb ends his Globe essay on the future of the Canada-U.S. relationship with a quote from economist Lester Thurow: "The greatest challenge in public policy is dealing with incremental decline".

For the whole country and for Ontario, it has become imperative to occupy the global market vigorously all the while preserving the greatest possible share of the American market which in 2010, according to Sherry Cooper, represented "4.2 times the sum of exports to the next 15 nations".[49] Unfortunately, the federal government stayed for many years insensitive to calls emanating from the country and asking for an ambitious policy of market conquest in emerging countries. That disastrous policy was obviously revisited by Prime Minister Harper and his government. John Ibbitson, *The Globe and Mail* Ottawa bureau chief, thinks that Harper's rising interest for Asia reflects his new political understanding that "our future (not to mention his) depends on it".[50]

For the predictable future Ontario's primary economic area will remain that Great Lakes region. But the lesson from the crisis is etched in people's minds.

---

49. COOPER, S. (2011) *Canada Must Diversify Its Exports Basket*, BMO Capital market, The Bottom Line, 2 mars 2011.

50. IBBITSON, J. "Rolling up the Pacific rim to win", *The Globe and Mail*, November 14th, 2009.

Ontario's economic relationship with the world can no longer be confused with its relationship with the U.S. "Go global", said Mark Carney, the former governor of the Bank of Canada, during a meeting with the Globe and Mail's editorial team.[51] After having evoked the emerging powers' increasing weight in the global economy, and qualifying that fact as a profound and permanent change, the country's top banker stated that:

> Canadian companies need to adapt ... the need for "decoupling" from the U.S. and other advanced economies provides a "tremendous opportunity" for Canadian firms—if they're ready and willing to take advantage ... However, succeeding in the new climate will "take a substantial reorientation for all Canadian business," and "everybody, from government to small business, has to think through what its potential implications are."

The weak penetration of emerging markets, like those of China and India, by Canadian firms has been the subject of numerous analyses. In the western provinces, except Alberta, Asia occupies a significant and growing place: it attracts almost 40 per cent of British Columbia's exports, 15 per cent from Saskatchewan and Manitoba. In the central and eastern provinces, exports to Asia make up less than 5 per cent, the last spot being shared by Ontario and New Brunswick. Other measurements confirm that absence from external markets. The case of small and medium-size businesses is particularly meaningful. Only 9 per cent of them are exporting and, according to some analyses, that proportion is diminishing.[52]

> Recent trends in Small- and Mid-Size Enterprises' (SME) trade activity and international comparisons suggest that Canadian SMEs have not responded to globalization in a way that optimizes their long-term growth potential and their contribution to the Canadian economy as a whole. Strong growth in emerging markets and increased opportunities to participate in global supply chains due to the greater export orientation of the US economy pro-

51. TOROBINO, J. "Go global, Carney tells business", *The Globe and Mail*, September 17th, 2010.

52. SHENFELD, A. and TAL, Benjamin (2011) *Canadian Business: Targeting the new mix.* Toronto: CIBC Special Report, March 30, p.6.

vide Canadian SMEs with an opportunity to remedy
this imbalance.

The consequences are known: in 2011, 1.3 per cent of the Canadian
GDP came from the country's commercial relationship with China and
that proportion would be considerably lower if we were to take away the
resources sector.

Ontario remains massively linked to the Atlantic zone's economy. Its
economy's fluctuations between growth, recession and recovery closely
match those of the southern neighbour. In 2009, its exports to the United
States totaled $119 billion, 44 per cent of all Canadian exports to the
US. That same year, Ontario exports to the European Union were worth
$13.1 billion and those to Great Britain totaled $7.8 billion; that is the
equivalent of 40 per cent and 25 per cent of Canada's total exports towards
the EU and Britain. Still for 2009, Ontarian exports to Mexico, China,
India and Brazil were respectively $2.3 billion, $1.5 billion, $423 million
and $369 million. Together, exports towards these so-called emerging econ-
omies are equivalent to half the province's exports to Great Britain and a
third of what it sends to the EU. There is room for expansion, to say the least.

Ontario within Canada

Measured against the ideals that define the aspirations of our contemporaries wherever they're from, whether we're talking about rights
and liberties, standards of living or advanced policies of social protection, Canadian accomplishments are impressive. With its partners in the
federation, Ontario has built that system and its citizens are the beneficiaries.[53] Will it persevere throughout the 21st century? Nothing that has
been acquired must be considered guaranteed. Consequently, the answer
to that question is not an obvious one and it depends on the capacity
of the authorities to mobilize all of the country's resources within a
cooperative and functional federal regime and on the selected and implemented strategies of development and growth. The task will be arduous
and long given the global mutations. Its success, we might as well say so
frankly, is not guaranteed. Neither is, consequently, the perpetuation of
all Canadian accomplishments.

---

53. The province has provided the country with some of its most striking leaders, the likes of
MACDONALD, John A. MACKENZIE, King and PEARSON, Lester B. It was governed by
quality politicians such as MOWAT, Oliver ; FROST, Leslie and ROBARTS, John .

Global needs in natural resources, especially oil and gas-related ones, have transformed the configuration and the production of wealth in the country. As was demonstrated by Jim Stanford, the Canadian economy has returned, at the beginning of the new millennium, to its dependence on unprocessed natural resources or partially processed resources.[54] They once more represent the most part of our exports; exported finished goods once again occupying a minority and declining part of our trade. In the long run, that situation is disastrous. As we have stated ourselves before, all the strengths of the country have to be harnessed, upgraded and developed with clout and boldness: its natural resources, including energy, the production of advanced industrial and technological goods such as those created by Research in Motion before its current reverse of fortune; the development of a high quality service sector, including international financial services; the consolidation of education and of the economy as well as a culture and entertainment economy, whose markets on the world scene keep expanding.

Cause or effect of these mutations, the rise in regionalisms in the country probably constitutes one of the most significant evolutions of the past years. It is illustrated by the establishment of commercial agreements among western provinces on the one hand, between Quebec and Ontario, desirous to create a common economic area in central Canada, on the other, and also among Atlantic Provinces. These agreements reveal much more than a mere logic of neighbourliness between political entities responsible for societies living on contiguous territories. They reflect the fact that, according to the words of the Premier of Saskatchewan, "the regions of Canada are becoming ever more disparate in interests, our economy more diversified by sector and by region".[55] Such agreements thus stem from contrasted perceptions about the new growth conditions that rest on different assets and offers: exploitation of vast energy, mineral and agricultural resources in the West as an answer to current and future global demand; erosion of the industrial apparatus and investments in new fields of production emanating from the knowledge-based and services society in central provinces confronted with unprecedented global competition and development of their northern regions; demographic stagnation and a will to modernize the traditional sectors of the Atlantic

---

54. STANFORD, J. (2008) *Canada's economic structure: back to the future, in Canada in 2020*. Toronto: Key Porter, p.139.

55. WALL, B. "Welcome the new strength in Canada's regions" *The Toronto Star*, February 7th, 2011

provinces' economies. Newfoundland is in a peculiar situation due to its petroleum production. But its reserves are limited.

These agreements thus reflect strong aspirations that are likely to replace the systems built by Canadians in the second half of the last century with a new reference order or even a new architecture for the federation. That rise in regionalisms is due to Canada's constitutional and institutional rigidity; it is much like the pragmatic upgrade of a system that remains frozen in a time of great mutations. It fills the void created by the absence of any significant federal initiative or of any debate on the better functioning of the federation and the lack of interest displayed by the early Harper government in positioning the country internationally. Jeffrey Simpson observed, in 2009, that such absence of dialogue was creating formidable challenges for the country. "It is as if the country is on autopilot—a very comfortable place to be sometimes, but not good enough with the looming challenges at home and abroad".[56]

All the provinces, to varying degrees, adopt that regionalist stance and act as if a structural modification to the Canadian federation was already accomplished or becoming so. In 2008, the Canada West Foundation declared that "evidence suggests that most Canadian provinces are behaving in ways similar to member states of the European Union.[57]All exaggerations hide some truth.

The rise in regionalism within Canada is not only a construct of the political class, whose motives can sometimes be suspect. Some, among them Roger L. Martin, believe that "regions, here and abroad, will dominate in the future." Endowed with a concentration in human, institutional and financial resources, with a convergence of research facilities and complementary services, often hubs where locations are not limited by borders, regions often benefit from a whole range of means that support economic growth and development. In Canada, these factors are emphasized by the diversity of regional economies and, consequently, by their particular interests.

Some readers will say this author is biased, or that he sees the country through his Quebecois glasses. It may be so! But other witnesses also consider this country a mosaic of regions.

Evoking his cross-Canada journey in 2010, which brought him to all 10 of the federation's provinces, David Jacobson, the new U.S. Ambassador

---

56. SIMPSON, J. "Welcome to the no-go zone of Canadian Discourse", *The Globe and Mail*, December 29th , 2009.

57. CANADA WEST FOUNDATION (2008) National *Stabilization Policy and its Implications for Western Canada*. Calgary: Canada West Foundation, August 2008.

to Canada, shares his thoughts with *Maclean's* about the differences between his country and ours:

> There were a couple I didn't expect. There seems to be a greater allegiance that Canadians have to their provinces than typically Americans do to their states. It may be because provinces are bigger, or because of the nature of the governments, or because the provinces own their resources, or because provincial Crown corporations provide certain services that in the U.S. are provided by private companies. I think Canadians define their identity to a larger degree by the province they live in than Americans do.[58]

John Wright is senior vice president at Ipsos Reid, the most important market research firm in Canada. As a preview of a book of his soon to be published, he in turn shares his understanding of the country's diversity with *Maclean's* readers.

> In the United States, everyone expects that a Texan has different views than a Californian. But in Canada, there's this idea that we're more homogenous, partly because there's a really narrow media concentration. We don't have a lot of newspapers or television stations; there are only three or four chains that most people get their information from, so you can start to believe that Canadians think pretty much the same way about all sorts of things. But after 20 years of polling, I don't think there are many common Canadian views. We're very distinct in terms of regions and other factors [59]

Only time will tell if that evolution is to grow in the long run. Some question the authenticity and thus durability of these rapprochements between provinces on a regional basis. John Ibbitson operated a devastating

---

58. "The new US ambassador to Canada, David Jacobson, on the oil land, border tensions and the stereotype of the nice Canadians. A conversation with Luiza Ch. Savage.", *Maclean's Magazine*, January 18, 2010.

59. WRIGHT, J. & BRICKER, D. (2009) *We know what you're thinking: From Dollars to Donuts-Canada's Premiere Pollsters Reveal What Canadians Think and Why*. Toronto: Toronto Harper Collins.

autopsy of the notion, challenging the idea that western provinces shared any significant converging interests.[60]

A NEW VISION OF CANADA

If the provinces and regions of the country are revisiting their function and their politics, the federal branch is also submitted to profound transformations. After having dominated the federal political scene since World War II, significantly contributed to the redefinition of the country and ensured the deployment of its policies for more than three quarters of a century, the Liberal Party of Canada was relegated, in May of 2011, to the third rank of political families within the federal parliament. The party of Laurier, Mackenzie King, Saint-Laurent, Pearson, Trudeau, Chrétien and Martin is but a mere shadow of its former self. Does that decline foretell the progressive dissolution of the conceptions of country and federalism that were issued from the political culture of central Canada? Revisited by Trudeau, that conception aimed primarily at strengthening national unity. Little sensitive to regional specificities, it was rather interested in national standards and the guardian of a long-sought and finally acquired constitutional architecture, though without Quebec's assent. The heritage is far-reaching, but its heirs appear poorly prepared to defend and perpetuate it.

Inspired by the Calgary school of thought, which regroups intellectuals from that city's university, another vision and conception of the Canadian state, or just the state, of federalism and of public policies, has developed in the last couple of decades of the 20th century. It in turn inspires, in part at least, the current holders of power in Ottawa, following their electoral victories most notably their May 2010 decisive victory.[61]

That vision and conception reflects a political culture that is rooted in western Canada, and more precisely in Alberta. It feeds off its own historical experience, specific interests and philosophical references, often derived from important American lines of thought. It also feeds off accumulated Western Canadians' frustrations, today compensated by "the feeling that their national government will not lose sight of their interests and aspirations"[62] and by their

60. IBBITSON, J. (2005) *The Polite Revolution*. Toronto: McClelland & Stewart, p.56.

61. BOILY, F. (2007) *Stephen Harper : De l'École de Calgary au Parti conservateur : les nouveaux visages du conservatisme canadien*. Québec : Presse de l'Université Laval.

62. GIBBINS, R. "De l'indifférence : De plus en plus, les Canadiens de l'Ouest ont tourné la page et se désintéressent de la question du Québec." *La Presse*, december 16th 2007.

weight in the Canadian economy. Due to the wealth generated by the oil boom, some do not hesitate to see Alberta as the virtual engine of the country's economy, stripping Ontario of the status it held heretofore. However, that resources-derived wealth spills over the western provincial borders to such an extent that recent developments have seen Saskatchewan propelled to the first rank in terms of growth and development in the country.

From these observations and in prospective/fictive fashion, Roger Gibbins has shown both the strengths of a Canada "led by the western provinces" and the tensions that could, in a world thus foreseen, lead to a referendum on Alberta's independence.[63] For his part, Gordon Pitts has drawn the cultural, intellectual, economic and political extensions of these observations in *Stampede,* an explosive book.[64] So here come the end of the supremacy of the tacit and determining agreement between Ontario and Quebec, and the entry of the country in unprecedented times. From now on, the Canadian agenda will be set by new elite that come from the great region of the West. "Are the black tar sands and the BlackBerry compatible?" asks the Globe and Mail columnist.

Certain philosophical and political concepts at the heart of the Canadian psyche about individuals and about the state are shaken. First, concepts of equality and equal opportunity, of universal social programs and of the equalization policy. In the judgment of the Calgary School, these choices have led to a loss of capacity and initiative for individuals living in the provinces that benefit from these policies. Those that adhere to that school of thought also believe that the concept of state responsibility was broadened to include too vast a field of activities. They think this constitutes a fearsome takeover by the central government. They also questioned the validity of certain institutions: the Senate, deemed archaic in its current form, the Supreme Court that pushed the limits of the judiciary[65] and the representation of Canadians in the House of Commons deemed unfair. They also question the regional disequilibrium of investments granted by the federal government and the use of spending powers that allow the central state to intervene in provincial jurisdictions while it should keep strictly to the powers it is granted by the Constitution. Lastly, they question the place that

---

63. GIBBINS, R. "The Curse of Alberta", in *Canada in 2020, op. cit.,* p.67.

64. PITTS, G. (2008) *Stampede! The Rise of the West and Canada's New Power Elite.* Toronto: Key Porter Books, p. 11.

65. BOIVERT, N. "L'École de Calgary et le pouvoir judiciaire", in Boily, *op.cit.* p.99.

Canada occupies on the international scene and propose to change it substantially. For them, such a movement requires stronger ties with the United States.[66] These observations are linked in part to the political environment, but they are also rooted in a long tradition of protest and dissent.[67]

That doctrine is far from insignificant. Some of its components resonate beyond the western provinces' borders and well into parts of Ontario, as the May 2011 federal elections showed. Furthermore, said it benefits from the fact that it faces no other doctrine unless the NDP and its new leader, Thomas Mulcair, propose a new synthesis and sell it to a majority of Canadians. For the moment, the way is clear for Stephen Harper, as it was, in other times, for Pierre-Elliott Trudeau.

That vision lies on ethical references largely inspired by the concept of economic freedom as the matrix of all liberties. It is being politically implemented in Canada so individual liberties will be restored and false values that we call Canadian values, like subsidies to unemployed individuals and subsidies to unsuccessful provinces, will be abandoned.

These formulas are drawn from a May 2011 Montreal intervention by Danielle Smith, leader of the Albertan Wildrose Party.[68] Some consider her a radical provincialist. Unless she only has the courage to say loudly what others think, without saying it as frankly, with regard to provincial repatriation of powers held by Ottawa, such as management of income and corporate taxes, pension plans, immigrant selection and police forces. With regards also to the wastes engendered by economic stimulus plans to curb the effects of the 2008 crisis. Equalization policy and global warming theories are criticized as well. In his description forecasting Canada's 153rd anniversary, Andrew Cohen predicts the collapse of central Canada in 2014.[69] In short, a Canadian version of the Washington consensus is creeping in as a serious alternative that could shape the future. Its ultimate aim is to reach, by revisiting public policies, a new equilibrium between state and market, profiting the latter. If the Trudeau era was political through and through, the Harper

66. BOERGER, A. "Rendre au Canada sa puissance, La politique étrangère de défense canadienne vue de l'Ouest." in Boily, *op.cit.* p. 121.

67. MIOUSSE, B. "The West wants in: les revendications de l'Ouest comme vecteur de renouvellement de la droite canadienne ", in Boily, *op.cit.* p. 9.

68. REYNOLDS, N. "Wildrose plea to Quebec: Get off your dependence", *The Globe and Mail,* 2 mai 2011.

69. COHEN, A. "Imagining Canada's 153rd birthday", in *Canada in 2020,* op.cit, p.19.

era could be economic, through and through, with a common determination to redraw the fundamentals of the federation.

Uncompleted, Canada's mutations and those of its political system, affect all of the country's components, among them Ontario. In these times of change, some would even say rupture, what policy should the province adopt to ensure its growth, defend its interests and become the country's political heart and economic engine again? What to do, also, to renew with budgetary equilibrium, succeed in transforming its economy, implement its development plan and rank high in the global competition?

Despite the crisis, Ontario's government has sought to maintain a consequential level of public investment. It geared the implementation of its economic recovery plan towards more adaptability, innovation and creativity, as well as towards the production of advanced economic goods and an increasingly sophisticated and globalized supply of services. Without abandoning its ambitions, the Ontario government was forced to adopt, in 2012, rigorous budgetary measures due to the high level of its deficit and the low return of the Ontarian economy. Those situations call for the protection and control of resources as never before in contemporary history. John Ibbitson speaks of a perpetual conflict.

In Loyal No More, his hard-hitting essay, the journalist and essayist portrays the relationship between the Ontarian and federal governments and targets many preconceived notions; the idea for instance that both capitals have shared, and still share the same vision of the country. His book's subtitle sheds light, in his opinion, on the current and coming phases of Canadian federalism, both marked by Ontario's struggle for a separate destiny.

> From the time of Confederation until the 1940s, successive Ontario governments struggled to limit the power of the federal government to encroach on the province's freedom of action. Ontario, as well as Quebec, demanded the right to be left alone. After the Second World War, however, Queen's Park and Ottawa collaborated to ensure that the rest of the federation served the interests of the economic heartland. That symbiosis dissolved in the 1980s and 1990s, dissipated by federal deficits, provincial intransigence, and Ottawa's blinkered obsession with Quebec. And other even more important forces were at work: free trade, which both

invigorated and reoriented Ontario's economy, the increasing irrelevance of interprovincial commerce, and the internal contradictions of the national taxation system.

Today, a federal government that depends for its existence on extracting the wealth of Ontario—and to a lesser extent of Alberta and British Columbia—and redistributing it to poorer parts of Canada finds itself in perpetual conflict with an Ontario government determined to assert its people's interests, protect their taxes, and rule within its own house. A federation so constructed cannot endure.

The challenge to Confederation lies not simply in accommodating Quebec's ancient and frustrated nationhood, the Maritimes' sense of enforced dependence, or the west's geographical and political alienation. The biggest and most powerful region of all now demands: first you must account for me.

Accounting for Ontario will become the greatest and most intractable challenge to Confederation, one that will change the federation, incrementally but inexorably, over the coming years. No one should say with confidence that the federation as we know it will survive. Everyone should presume that, whatever the outcome, Ontario will have its way.[70]

Ten years after it was published, and given Ontarians, Canadian and international evolutions, what remains of that fascinating book, resembling a would-be Quebec manifest of the 80s with its historical reminders, criticism of the federal regime and arguments for that regime's radical review? Ibbitson answers that the contents of his book still express the Ontarian political trajectory, but he admits he was wrong in the timing of that review's implementation calendar.[71]

Accommodating Ontario

The idea of specific Ontarian interests appears reinforced by provincial, national and international evolutions as well as by the 2008 crisis. Indeed, if the central province's economic needs share similarities with those of Quebec, they have little in common with those of the West and the Maritimes. Ontario's stakes and challenges include the modernization of

---

70. IBBITSON, Loyal *no more, op. cit.,*p.5.

71. Interview with John Ibbitson, Ottawa, August 29[th,] 2011.

the industrial apparatus, a strategy to strengthen the automotive industry, investment in R&D and in workforce training, upkeep of a great financial sector, renewal of the Ontarian government's financial capacities and further developing the green economy and alternative energies.

To that list, one can add requests regarding ongoing policies and programs, some of which have received a favourable response from the federal government: level of funding for health services that is deemed unfair for the province, level of average federal unemployment benefits received by Ontarians being below those of other Canadian unemployed and lastly, the control by Ontario's government of the matching funds, corresponding to the federal infrastructure investment, in answer to the province's priorities.

More significant because of the sums involved, Ontarian demands regarding fairer fiscal arrangements have become, following the 2008 crisis, major requests. At the Ontario Economic Summit, in November of that same year, former Premier McGuinty pursued his campaign for equity:

> We're generating all the wealth that we need to succeed and flourish [in Ontario], but the truth is that Ottawa takes $20 billion out of Ontario and distributes it elsewhere. If we could keep more of that money, we could go further faster.

On the provinces' agenda for a long time, and especially since 2006, that file has not evolved and no solution is in sight. The question of fiscal equity was being asked before the crisis, but its significance was renewed due to the decline of the Ontarian industrial sector, the public finance deficit, the fact it passed from a contributing province to a receiving one in the equalization scheme. The province needs its resources in order to recover from the storm that hit it. It needs them to accomplish the transformation of its economy and invest in the development of levers critical to that. The stakes are high. They are about Ontario's political weight within Canada and its capacity to remain a vibrant society, one that is able to offer its citizens high standards of living and social policies that match. In sum, avoid the break with a modern history undeniably marked by economic success.

In the immediate aftermath of the crisis, the province is treated offhandedly by the Harper government. At the time, it went as far as denying the existence of a crisis. Federal officials blamed Queen's Park for the degraded state of the Ontario economy and invited the provincial government to lower corporate taxes as a recovery tool. The Canadian Finance Minister, Jim

Flaherty, even declared in early 2008, that Ontario was "the last place" one would go "to make a new business investment in Canada". "Blind ideology", answers Dwight Duncan, his Ontarian counterpart. Federal ministers ended up grasping the scope of the mess that is unfolding and the calamitous effects on Canadians of the storm that gathered south, blew north, and threatened their own political future if they maintained that denial at a time when the international community was mobilizing to try and stem the effects of the biggest financial crisis since the Great Depression of 1929. The federal government then launched a Canada-wide economic stimulus plan, came to the rescue of the Ontarian automotive industry and created the Southern Ontario Economic Development Agency to help that region, hardly hit by the crisis.

Ibbitson is partly right: the federal government could not ignore the needs and interests "of the most powerful and important" region of the country. However, the context of crisis is critical here. Questions regarding the equilibrium of the Canadian economy such as the issues of equalization, federal transfers to provinces and many more, have gained a new dimension. They are critical to the future of Ontario. Their settlement or not in the coming years will tell if the needs and interests of Ontario will be recognized in the federal capital. [72]

Don Drummond summarized Ontario's situation in clear and exhaustive fashion:

> For 2005, Statistics Canada estimates that the federal government extracted $20.1 billion more in taxes from Ontario taxpayers than it spent in the province. That amounted to a fiscal drag of 3.8 per cent of Ontario's economy, whereas, excluding Alberta, the other provinces had a net federal fiscal injection of 4 per cent. The point is not that federal governments should run deficits. Rather, it is to ponder how much redistribution the taxpayers of provinces with above-average incomes can finance when they need to be competitive not only with other jurisdictions in Canada but with the rest of the world as well. The current situation also makes it difficult for the Ontario government to finance the services its residents and businesses need at competitive tax

---

72. For fiscal year 2010-2011, the equalization totaled $ 14.4 billion, broken down as follows: Ile-du-Prince-Édouard, $ 330 million; Ontario, $ 972 million; Nova Scotia, $ 1.1 billion; New Brunswick, $ 1.58 billion; Manitoba, $ 1.82 billion; Quebec, $ 8,550,000,000.

rates. In 2005, Ontario received $1,235 per capita less in federal transfers than the median of all provinces. Its own source revenues were virtually bang on the median … The balancing item was that Ontario spent $1,109 less than the provincial median, putting it in tenth, or last, place among provinces. Education was one of the components that ended up in that last place standing, compromising the province's ability to meet its competitiveness challenges.[73]

Who will take charge?

Who will be in charge of that considerable and urgent priority? The federal or the provincial government? Or both? In that case, who will fix the objectives, determine the programs, control the fiscal resources and guarantee implementation?

The McGuinty government aligned its position on those of its immediate predecessors and, these past years often presented itself as the defender of citizens' interests, the protector of their taxes and the master of its own house. In these tumultuous times, he took public stands to drive in these points, to convince and mobilize his public opinion, to gain support from the economic and academic communities.[74] At the 2008 Ontario Economic Summit, the head of the Ontarian government noted that Ontarians regroup to better assert themselves in the face of the injustice stemming with their arrangements with Ottawa. Used again many times, that refrain refers to a specific Ontarian political entity, and interests in the Canadian whole. Before and after the crisis, Queen's Park requests have proven insistent and persistent with regard to the need for correcting the "unequal treatment", which the province suffered, and for its rectification in the name of fairness. During the federal campaign leading to the election of May 2011, the Ontarian Premier's critics towards Ottawa became sharper.

That policy is admittedly part of the period's difficult circumstances. But it also stems from more fundamental positions related to Canadian federalism and its dysfunctions, to some of its formulas guiding the relations between the federal government and the provinces and territories and to some of the new stakes that reflect the interior and exterior changes affecting the country.

---

73. DRUMMOND, D. "Whither the Canadian economy?" In *Canada in 2020*, op cit, p.56.

74. Dalton McGuinty's speech at the Canadian Club in Toronto, February 2009.

JEAN-LOUIS ROY

Do the practices of federalism exclude interprovincial consensus? Year after year, for example, the Council of the Federation has insisted for the need to "refocus Canada's international trade priorities", [to conclude] the Foreign Investment Protection and Promotion Agreement with China, and [to undertake] a review of economic opportunities with the European Union and India".[75] Since, the Harper government moved in thoses directions but with costly delays.

Many in Ontario are also worried about the dismemberment by the Harper government of the Canadian diplomatic apparatus and the political and economic effects this could have. In October 2010, two important and respected Canadian foreign policy actors, Allan Gotlieb and Colin Robertson, respectively former ambassador to the United States and former president of the Professional Association of Foreign Service Officers, coauthored an impactful opinion column in *The Globe and Mail*.[76] The title and spirit of their intervention pled for the reconstruction of the country's diplomatic resources through significant investments, for the strengthening of our network of missions abroad and for the revitalization of our foreign ministry as the focal point for coordination. Their plea was not heard.

In that context, the Ontario government supported the creation of the Mowat Centre for Policy Innovation. In a few short years, this centre, with relatively modest resources, has contributed significantly to the federal frameworks and strategies likely to have a strong impact on Ontario's prosperity and quality of life in this century.

The Mowat Centre

As presented by its director, Matthew Mendelsohn, the mission statement of the Centre captures the reflections of many regarding the state of the country and the need for clarification, renovation and orientation in its functioning and policies, including the fiscal ones. After stating that "Canada is one of the most successful national communities in human history" in his welcoming message on the Centre's website, Mendelsohn reminds readers of the extraordinary economic and social changes affecting the world and notes that "the policy frameworks which served Canadians so well in the latter half of the 20th century may not be right for the 21st century". His arguments are plentiful.

75. DOBSON'S, W. (2011) *Does Canada Have an India Strategy? Why it Should and What Both Sides Can Gain from Comprehensive Talks.* Toronto: C.D. Howe Institute Backgrounder.

76. GOTLIEB, A. and ROBERTSON, C. "Canada must rebuild its diplomatic resources", *The Globe and Mail*, October 13th 2010.

Many of the key elements of Canada's social contract and institutional infrastructure have broken down. In some cases our public policies are based on assumptions that are no longer valid; in others, the assumptions are valid but the programs that gave them life have been tinkered with so much that they no longer achieve their intended purpose. The time has come for reviewing and revitalizing Canada's policy strategies. Especially since, in addition to the new international realities, federal public policy has been slow to respond to the new challenges faced by Canadians at a time when demographic changes, including an aging population, are putting enormous fiscal pressure on social programs.

All Canadian provinces face these same challenges, but each province has its own unique reality and interests. Ontario is Canada's most urban and ethnically diverse province and the Canadian steward of our Great Lakes. Many of our communities are highly integrated with the United States. It is confronted with economic transformation that will see our future tied to our ability to innovate. Moving forward, it will be essential to re-imagine the Canadian social contract with an understanding of Ontario's new realities.

Ontario's new realities! Many of our interlocutors would adopt that expression.

Of federal leadership

How did we get here? Mendelsohn doesn't ask the question that bluntly, but he doesn't avoid it either. He reminds us that in the past, the federal public service was developing new political positions, sometimes with the support of independent commissions. In 1998 already, Graham Fraser was evoking the "intellectual and creative weakening of the federal government".[77] The situation has not improved since the election of a succession of minority governments, which reduced the central state's ability to undertake the long-term political analyses that are essential to the revitalization of Canadian strategies. Given the governing style of Prime

---

77. FRASER, G. (2001) *Vous m'intéressez*. Montréal : Boréal, p.76.

Minister Harper, it is not very likely that the situation will evolve, even if he now has a majority in Parliament. Consequently, federal political leadership is not involved in the substantive debates regarding the long-term stakes that will determine Canada's fortunes…all the while such debates are undertaken everywhere else in the world.

From that absence of federal leadership, Mendelsohn draws a surprising conclusion. One could have expected a pressing request for Ottawa to reverse such wait-and-see policy. No such thing. The Mowat Centre's director sees an opportunity in that situation for Canadians and their provincial and municipal governments, for private civil society organizations, for researchers in public policy, for social innovators. An opportunity to build networks, create partnerships and engage in new endeavours that are likely to successfully shape the policy agenda. "Although government remains the crucial player, others no longer have to wait." Such are the ambitions and practices of the Centre, which wants to "suggest new ways to reconstruct outdated policy architecture in order to strengthen Canada, its regions and its citizens…while ensuring that all of us continue to share a sense of common citizenship and benefit from equality of opportunity".

Generally conducted on a comparative basis, often submitted to public discussion and undertaken with partners from the private or public sectors, the Mowat Centre's ongoing or past work already constitutes a significant thesaurus; significant for the themes it contemplates as well as for the conclusions and recommendations it shares.[78]

The range of topics is vast: issues relative to political representation within institutions; detailed proposals for a more economically viable, effective and transparent federalism; analyses regarding regional differentiation in implementing labour force training and in unemployment insurance; the extension in the age at which one is eligible to retirement insurance and the functions of subnational authorities with regard to immigration.

It is too early to draw a political or constitutional doctrine out of this considerable range of proposals. Emanating from them, however, is an often harsh and systematically documented critique of the federal regime's structures, of its current policies and practices. A choice also stems from these proposals, one that gives special weight to provincial autonomy, Ontario's included, the province normally being at the heart of the Mowat Centre's analyses and recommendations. Mendelsohn has told us, after

---

78. All these works can be found on the Mowat Centre's website: http://www.mowatcentre.ca.

all, that "it will be essential to re-imagine the Canadian social contract with an understanding of Ontario's new realities".

The Centre's vocation is to contribute to the substance of coming debates about the often-entangled public policies of Ontario and Canada. In so doing, it acts as a counterweight to the works and orientations of other entities because, among other reasons, of its thoroughness, its empiricism and the importance it obviously places on certain values that are the best of this country's heritage since World War II. Even if it is difficult to gauge the Centre's influence, it is certain that its work is leaving its marks on the spirits of many within the Ontarian public administration, in the province's institutions and in the circle of commentators and pundits that make up a significant portion of our interlocutors. This was evidenced by their spontaneous and frequent references to hypotheses and suggestions borrowed from the Mowat Centre.

Ontarians and/or Canadians?

The question was asked to almost every one of our interviewees, in many cases provoking unease. In Toronto, the link to the city is often valued or even felt as the cornerstone of one's identity. Along with others, Karen Sun has evoked the "Toronto bubble" in which she lives. Lisa Rochon may also belong to that category. The director of the Centro Scuola e Cultura Italiana showed a preference towards the expression "Ontarian society" rather than "identity", reserving that feeling for Canada. Ajit Jain, publisher of India Abroad is more comfortable with his dual allegiance, Canadian and Ontarian.

In the imagination of Canadians, in the political literature and in numerous survey results, the notion of an Ontarian identity appears quite blurredly. The idea that Ontarians feel Canadian first dominates, as opposed to all other Canadians whose allegiance is constantly regional or provincial, national in the case of Quebecers. Asserted and reasserted, that assessment, which makes the Ontarian identity a by-product of the Canadian one, has for some the weight of obviousness. Others have pled for the double allegiance and double identity: « Canadian first and Ontarian second ».[79]

Have all the debates of the last few years, all that political rhetoric used by successive Ontarian governments and that string of injunctions— perpetual conflict, unfair treatment, fiscal iniquity, specific Ontarian interests, Ontarian agenda, absence of federal leadership—had an effect on the con-

---

79. PAIKIN, S. (2006) *Public triumph private tragedy, the double life of John P. Robarts.* Toronto: Penguin Books Canada.

ceptions Ontarians have about their identity and allegiance? Ontarians and/ or Canadians? Shall we have to get used to the new formula: "Ontarians first and Canadians second"?

The Mowat Centre has published a document titled: The New Ontario. *The Shifting Attitudes of Ontarians towards the Federation* , a snapshot aiming to verify if "Canadians in Ontario continue to have the lowest level of regional dissatisfaction in the federation".[80]

In January 2010, Mendelsohn's team used all the questions from the Centre for Research and Information in Canada surveys between 1996 and 2005. It interrogated 2,697 Canadians, of which 1,482 were Ontarians. The questions concerned Ontarians' feelings about the respect their province was getting from the rest of the federation, about Ontario's influence on national politics, about the fairness of federal spending in Ontario and their Ontarian or Canadian sense of identity. The findings of this inquiry reveal what the authors call "Ontarians' evolving attitudes toward the federation".

In 2010, 51 per cent of Ontarians don't believe their province is treated with the respect it deserves in Canada, compared to 31 per cent in 1998 and 27 per cent in 2004. That's close to a 100 per cent rise in just a few years. For the rest, around 60 per cent of Quebecers and Westerners, and 76 per cent of Maritimers, believe their province is not treated with the respect it deserves. Compared to Ontarians' shifting feelings, these other proportions are stable enough.

Furthermore, 32 per cent of Ontarians feel their province enjoys "less than its fair share" of influence on significant federal decisions, compared to 21 per cent in 1998 and in 2004. "When asked if their province's 'influence on important national decisions' is 'increasing, decreasing or staying about the same,' 50 per cent answer that it is 'decreasing,' and just 8 per cent think the province's influence is 'increasing,' a lower figure than in any other region." Other interrogated Canadians answered that their province enjoyed less than their fair share of influence in the following proportions: around 50 per cent for Quebec, 68 per cent for western provinces and 75 per cent for Atlantic Provinces. The authors of the report note that citizens from both central provinces have the feeling that their influence is diminishing. "This makes it more likely that Ontario and Quebec will attempt to exercise the considerable power that they retain in order to protect their interests."[81]

---

80. MATTHEWS, J. Scott and MENDELSOHN, M. (2010) *The New Ontario: The Shifting Attitudes of Ontarians towards the Federation*. Toronto: Mowat Centre for Policy Innovation, p.2.

81. *Idem*, p.4.

With regard to fiscal transfers and other federal spending in provinces, more specifically the perception of equity in the share their province gets, 63 per cent of Ontarians think that it receives less than its fair share, compared to 37 per cent who felt that in 1998. This constitutes another considerable rise in Ontarians' dissatisfaction, which is above the national average of 59 per cent. For Quebec, the western provinces and the Maritimes, the proportion of people answering that their province got less than its fair share are 45 per cent, 64 per cent and 66 per cent respectively.

Finally, when it comes to Ontarians' sense of identification with Canada, the Mowat Centre's answer is categorical: despite their sense of regional discontent concerning the fair treatment and the respect their province gets, the influence it wields and the fairness of fiscal transfers it receives, Ontarians still massively identify with Canada. Only 4 per cent of respondents identify with their province more than with Canada. Respectively 52 per cent, 11 per cent and 13 per cent of respondents in Quebec, the western provinces and the Maritimes identify with their province more than with Canada. The authors of the research draw an important lesson from all this:

> The fact that Ontarians continue to demonstrate the highest level of Canadian identity and the lowest level of provincial identity in the country represents a challenge for Ontario political leaders interested in mobilizing the Ontario public on issues of federal treatment. Ontarians have more negative judgements of federal treatment than in the past, but continue to lack the high level of provincial identity found in some other provinces. It is this provincial identity that can turn a sense of unfair treatment into a combustive political issue.[82]

What are we to conclude from such data, which draw a picture of varying Ontarian feelings toward the country and some of its major policies? 3 conclusions are unavoidable.

The first involves Ontarians' durable and undeniable attachment to Canada. That feeling is deeply entrenched and doesn't contradict their specific experience as Ontarians.

The second involves Ontarians perceptions about the treatment their province gets in the rest of the country. Most of them do not believe Ontario

---

82. *Ibidem*, p. 6.

is fairly treated as part of the federation. They think, as do most Canadians, that the current iniquities have to be fixed. The researchers see in that fact a significant political consequence. "The implications for our national politics may soon be apparent. The Ontario public may no longer be supportive of its provincial government playing its traditional role as a consensus-builder among competing provincial interests."[83] So at that level apparently, provincialism and regionalism do have a grip on minds.

The third conclusion involves the high level of dissatisfaction of all Canadians towards federalism as it is experienced today with regard to the vast federal programs and the fiscal and financial arrangements that stem from them. These $50 billion transfers generate a high level of dissatisfaction in the whole country for different reasons in different regions. Such unease calls for a major review, which could greatly affect the fundamentals of Canadian federalism.

What methods are we to adopt for that review? Can we renegotiate major programs such as fiscal and financial transfers in piecemeal fashion? How are we to make room in those negotiations for a positive agenda for Ontario as well as for the western provinces, Quebec and the Maritimes? Which of today's factors of unity and prosperity are likely to be shared by the partners in this federation? In our new environment, which needs and services should be handed to the federal government and which ones would benefit from a coordination or harmonization between the provinces and/ or regions of the country?

Living together is a vast operation that depends on the shared will, over the long run, to invent and implement convergent visions of a shared destiny. Is the federation's internal diplomacy, as it is evolving since Harper's decisive victory in 2011, able to change what must be changed, which the Mowat Centre is describing with precision and competence? Far from it.

Due in part to the work of the Centre, Ontario will have access to solid references when it sits at the federation's negotiating table. Authorities will have to take Ontarians' convictions into account: their Canadian allegiance as well as their demands about the equity of federal policies that affect them.

In any event, the last quarter century saw Ontario resume its early tradition of self-assertion within Canada, calling for the respect of its jurisdictions, for equity in its relationship with the federal government and for a larger margin of initiative as a reflection of its will to define solutions

---

83. *Ibidem*, p.1.

that are first and foremost adapted to its reality. It is engaged, according to Ibbitsons's expression, "in a struggle to return to its former self".[84] Of course, Ontarians haven't turned their backs on Canada, although they have a perception of it that contrasts with the new state of things. In short, they concluded it was necessary again to bend the country's course, which was leaving them deeply dissatisfied.

MATTHEW MENDELSOHN

Welcome to the Frank, the Art Gallery of Ontario's excellent restaurant; thus named to honour famous architect Frank Gehry, who enveloped the old institution with a sublime glass cloak. Even on that cloudy day, everything in here is luminous, the great space whose elevated centre is dominated by a warm dome, the paintings of Joyce Wieland, Paterson Ewen and Frank Stella's installation.

Our guest is a few minutes late to the restaurant and maybe a few years in advance in the country. Matthew Mendelsohn has been at the helm of the Mowat Centre for Public Policy since its foundation in 2009. In his different careers as a senior public servant at the federal and provincial levels, as an academic at Queen's University, and especially at its influential Institute of Intergovernmental Relations Center for federal provincial relations, he acquired some significant convictions. He believes for instance that the Canadian political agenda has been blocked for some years and that many federal programs rest on outdated postulates. Furthermore, the world's social and economic changes are challenging a political architecture that served the country quite well in the second half of the 20th century but may be are not adequate in this new century.

Let's take an example, invites our Montreal-educated, bilingual friend, who received his B.A. from McGill and his M.A. and Ph.D. from the Université de Montréal.

> Ontario is currently negotiating an agreement with Ottawa to recuperate the competence of labour force training, as Quebec did in 1998-99. The Ontarian government is held accountable for the current imbalances between pressing labour force needs and current labour force levels. However, in the current system, programs and resources are in Ottawa. That doesn't work. Such import-

---

84. IBBITSON, *Loyal no more, op.cit.* p. 4.

ant responsibility can no longer be centralized in the country. Because what do they know about real regional needs, about Thunder Bay's needs? We have entered a time of transition; big political decisions in the future will be taken at the provincial and municipal levels and will make entire portions of the federal public sector without real use.

Will the future fit Matthew Mendelsohn's ideas? His work certainly has the great merit of shedding light on the stakes and challenges of that future.

Ontario and Quebec

Political partners for almost 175 years, probably the continent's oldest such partnership, Quebec and Ontario have partaken in the same federal structure for close to a century and a half in an uninterrupted back and forth of alliance and divergence typical between members of such a system. Both governments have maintained permanent bilateral relations, as is quite normal for two contiguous states with such a historical connection and reciprocal interests. Furthermore, the constant migration of Quebecers to Ontario and the installation of branches from many of Quebec Inc's most recognized firms in the neighbour province have contributed, along with many other civil society initiatives, to create links between both societies.

So where are we today? What are Ontario's perspectives on the relationship between the two central provinces in the Canadian federation?

These perspectives are very contrasted. Part of Ontario's intellectuals judge Quebec's society quite severely and do not hesitate to evoke a decline, especially demographically, and consequently, in terms of political weight within Canada. In their opinion, these evolutions mark the end of a period of excessive attention awarded to the Quebec issue and allow English Canada to reclaim its values and ambitions, finally free from Quebec's strong influence. For them, the Quebec relationship is no longer significant or strategic.

Proponents of another line of thought are rather interested in the various forms of asymmetry in the federal system that were demanded by—and granted to—Quebec. They see in that experience some possible evolutions of federalism in the foreseeable future and thus remain aware of events in Quebec because they still believe in potential alliances between both provinces.

In addition, the governments of Ontario and Quebec have taken important steps towards updating their relationship after the negotiation, signature and implementation of the demanding and innovating Trade and

Cooperation Agreement between them. In astonishingly regular fashion, many of the Ontarians we interviewed, whether in the public or private sectors, have referred to that "essential" policy and showed their commitment to its full realization. Reversing the roles, some asked us about the interest engendered in Quebec by this Agreement which aims at setting up a common economic space between the two provinces. In another context, Ibbitson reminds us that "Ontario has compelling bilateral relations with Quebec...the provinces enjoy the most important interprovincial trade relationship in the country, even if that relationship, in both cases, is dwarfed by trade with the United States".[85]

Before we analyze the contents of that new bilateral policy, let us dwell a little longer on the theses brought forth by some Ontarian thinkers. With a few notable exceptions, the political literature in "English Canada", that inadequate but useful expression again, seems to insist on the exaggerated place taken by Quebec in the country's recent history and it focuses on the influence, also excessive, of Quebec's value system to the detriment of that which prevails in the rest of Canada. Such thinkers come to the same conclusions when reflecting on the Quebec-Canada relationship of the past half-century. They see a succession of uninterrupted tensions: referendums, failed constitutional negotiations, asymmetric federalism and too many concessions made to benefit the francophone province, an important one being the policy of bilingualism.

Many of these authors suggest a redefinition of the country, which would finally be rid of Quebec's weight, rid of what they see as a costly tribute in terms of values, references and public policies that come from that province. Contrary to the experience of the country, that tribute is said to have perverted its spirit and even its history. The redefinition mentioned above would be like a return to the Canadian spirit, to a culture of pioneers, with a vision of the state that is less imperial, a conception of individual responsibility that is more dynamic and a more restrained idea of social policies.

These visions are far remote, to say the least, from the policies of Ontario's government, which is committed to the deepening of its relationship with Quebec with the support, on both sides of the border, of numerous economic, commercial, professional and scientific partners. So, what is that policy?

---

85. *Idem*, p.199.

The 4ᵗʰ economic region of the continent

A common economic space between Quebec and Ontario would make that area the 4ᵗʰ such space on the continent behind California, Texas and the state of New York; and the 1ˢᵗ in Canada. Its implementation was decided by the governments of both provinces, and made official with the signature, in September 2009, of the Ontario-Quebec Trade and Cooperation Agreement (the Agreement).

That construct is also present in general or specialized studies like those of the Martin Prosperity Institute, whose specialists have analyzed, in 2009, the possibilities offered by greater economic cooperation between Ontario and Quebec. The argumentation of the influential institute rests on converging evidence. "Considered as one, Ontario and Quebec are among the largest economic regions in North America".[86] It represents the second largest destination for immigrants, the third largest in terms of population and the fourth in terms of wealth creation in North America. It also has one of the largest high tech industries on the continent. All of these assets are considerable. But so are some of the liabilities. Indeed, despite these formidable levers, GDP per capita and competitiveness in both provinces are lower than in many other North American regions. Lastly, regional density and connectivity between them will need to be enhanced. How are we to bridge that gap?

First, by recognizing the reality of the mega-region, "stretching from Quebec City through Montreal, Ottawa, Toronto, central Ontario, the Golden Horseshoe and including Upstate New York".[87] Also, by sizing up the prosperous industrial clusters in sectors that are based on the knowledge and creativity in both provinces and which constitute significant forces that could become common to Ontario and Quebec. Finally, by creating the conditions for greater collaboration between them.

These objectives aim at bridging the prosperity gap affecting central Canada's economy and the living standards of its inhabitants as well as at significantly raising the number of creative jobs, which are the best paid ones. It is obvious that in preparing the 2009 Agreement, both governments were directly inspired by the works of the Prosperity Institute as well as by the work led by their own public administrations.

---

86. MARTIN PROSPERITY INSTITUTE (2009), *Capitalizing on the Opportunity for Greater Economic Cooperation between Ontario and Quebec*. Toronto: Martin Prosperity Institute, September 2009, p.5.

87. *Idem*, p.4.

That Agreement is not the first such arrangement between Canada's two central provinces. It is the most ambitious, however, and the most exhaustive; maybe also the best prepared one in terms of its content, its support in both societies and its programmed follow-ups. The way it was prepared, negotiated, signed and implemented can be explained by the new global and national environments mentioned already. Indeed, in both capitals, the same explanations were given for its necessity.

First, an acute consciousness in Quebec City and Toronto of the fierceness of that new global competition, especially in both provinces' biggest market, that of the US, followed by the realization that they were losing their market shares, considered solid not long ago and the possibility of an even more dire erosion of these shares given the financial, scientific and technological capabilities of emerging economies, the list of which is ever-growing. Given also the new abilities of firms in these countries to produce advanced technological goods and specialized services that were imported barely a few decades ago and that are now happily exported throughout the world.

That Agreement is also part of a recent phase of provincial and territorial assertion illustrated by the organization of regional conferences of heads of governments from these political entities. Such provincialism/regionalism plunges its roots deeply in Canadian tradition and is taking an unprecedented turn these days, with provinces setting up regional blocs, all of them facing Ottawa. In western Canada, the Conference of Western Premiers was inaugurated in 1998 and in 2006, British Columbia and Alberta signed the Trade, Investment and Labour Mobility Agreement (TILMA). In the East, the Conference of Atlantic Premiers was inaugurated in 2000 and, 10 years later, the governments of Nova Scotia and New Brunswick have concluded an economic and regulatory agreement. This new assertiveness by Canadian regional economies reflects their political ambitions as well as their specific character.

In this context, it appears essential for the central provinces to open their markets and search for lines of convergence likely to increase exchanges with each other and sharpen their competitiveness as well as their political capacity during negotiations with the rest of the country. Together, Ontario and Quebec account for 65 per cent of Canada's population; they represent a market of 21 million people, a joint GDP of $900 billion, or 58 per cent of Canada's GDP at the time the Trade and Cooperation Agreement was signed. Furthermore, they are each other's most important trading partner behind the United States. Sixty one per cent of Quebec exports to Canada are headed to Ontario and the reverse is also true with 69 per cent of Ontarian exports to Canada ending up in Quebec, for a trade volume of over $40 billion, a sum which exceeds the total value of yearly Canadian exports to the European Union. The central provinces can, as their counterparts did in the country's other regions, join an integrated economic area with a lot of potential.[88] Finally, some important similarities between both economies appeared in the preparatory phases of the agreement, along with a great level of integration, as is demonstrated by the investment strategies of many Ontario and Quebec firms.[89]

The Agreement[90] expresses a shared will by Canada's two main economies to increase their level of exchanges with each other through the lifting of existing trade impediments and the harmonization of future regulation "in every domain and not only the sectors covered by the Agreement". Furthermore, both provinces "agreed to apply the rule of reciprocal non-discrimination, also called the principle of national treatment. As a consequence, each government will accord the other province's directly competitive or substitutable goods, businesses, services and investments a treatment no less favourable than the best treatment it accords to its own or to a third party's". Lastly, the agreement is supposed to harmonize a set of rules meant to control trade between the provinces and a reciprocal access to each other's procurements.

The Agreement confirms a common decision to establish and develop cross-border innovation hubs modeled on the European "BioValley" in life sciences, optics-photonics and green technologies. Other strategic sectors with high value added could also be the object of cooperation in the hope that their pooling would produce impacts superior to those they would have obtained by acting separately. Setting up an innovation corridor would link these innovation hubs. Qualified as a world-class biocluster, the Québec-Ontario Life Sciences Corridor was the object of a substantial 2011 analysis.[91]

---

88. These regional arrangements stem from the Agreement on Internal Trade signed by the provinces and territories in 1994 and which includes the possibility of bilateral or multilateral trade between signatories.

89. Almost every *Quebec Inc.* corporation today has installations in Ontario. Symbolically, the deal that was truck between *Groupe Transcontinental* and *The Globe & Mail* and planning for the latter to be printed by the Montreal group for 18 years illustrates the scope of the phenomenon. The transaction reached $1.7 billion.

90. http://www.mdeie.gouv.qc.ca/fileadmin/contenu/documents_soutien/apropos/strategies/accord_quebec_ontario.pdf, p. 8 and 15.

91. PwC, *Combining Strengths, Maximizing Impact: The Québec-Ontario Life Sciences Corridor*, 2011.

The Agreement plans to reduce and eliminate barriers to the movement of persons, goods and labour through joint or reciprocal certification formulas for 43 professions and 26 trades. It also aims at harmonizing financial services, especially in the fields of insurance, mortgages, securities and credit unions. Parties to the Agreement also committed to implement work plans on energy cooperation,[92] the manufacturing sector,[93] infrastructure[94] and access to public procurements.[95] Among the rare projects identified specifically, the two governments pledged to work in common and give priority to the high-speed rail link between Québec City and Windsor. That's an old promise!

Finally, the Agreement defines a major cooperation area with regard to the environment and sustainable development: strengthening their common environmental leadership in North America and an environmental assessment for Ontario-Quebec projects which have a significant trans boundary impact.

A strategic place in North America

Not as clearly expressed in this agreement between Ontario and Quebec but underlying it is the recognition of their partners' evolution within the federation, especially the undeniable momentum of western Canada. In this federalism of regional blocks, the 2 central provinces are facing the new capacities and demands coming from the governments of western provinces, whose policies are convergent in many fields, including reform of the federal regime. The topic is a delicate one and is never mentioned clearly by the signatories of the Agreement. Quebec former premier Jean Charest stretched it when he evoked the "confirmation of the strategic place in the

---

92. With regard to energy cooperation, the work plan agreed upon by Quebec and Ontario is articulated around 5 themes: energy efficiency, an improved demand management, policy development for emerging and renewable energy technologies, the enhancement of interconnectedness between the electricity systems of both provinces and the intensification of cooperation during energy emergencies.

93. With regard to the manufacturing sector, the work plan agreed upon by Quebec and Ontario involves a boost to the sector along with the enhancement of its brand image, particularly among the young workforce. It also aims at more collaboration between their respective sectors.

94. The work plan agreed upon by Quebec and Ontario plans the development of infrastructure, including joint services, systems and facilities, in a spirit of enhanced cohesion and complementarity.

95. With regard to public procurement, the work plan agreed upon by Quebec and Ontario ensures, in the short term, equal access by all Ontario and Quebec suppliers to the public and parapublic procurement process for goods and services.

Quebec-Ontario region in North America". In that context, it is not surprising that the Ontario-Quebec Trade and Cooperation Agreement plans for consultations and converging positions when facing the federal government.

To ensure the Agreement's implementation, three institutions were set up: the Ministerial Council (with the delegation of the Minister responsible for economic development), a joint Secretariat and a Private Sector Advisory Committee as well as a mechanism to resolve eventual disputes that the operation of this Agreement could engender.

Since the signature of the Agreement, the cabinets of Ontario and Quebec have met twice to review the advances in their joint projects and settle on new fields of cooperation. A Quebec-Ontario forum was set up with the purpose of informing both governments on new avenues of cooperation. The first such forum, held in Quebec City in February 2011 brought together more than 150 business leaders and people from the postsecondary and non-profit sectors of both provinces.

Will this "common market", as it was called by Jean Charest, survive political change in both provinces? Is it nothing more than a situational or incidental product? Or does it represent, on the contrary, a strategic lever that is likely to guarantee to Canada's central region a quicker and more profitable insertion in the new global economy and a more vigorous defense of its continental interests? Or a lever that could strengthen the region's capacity to have an impact on the orientation of the country as it is becoming? The accession to power by the Parti québécois in 2012 and the minority status of both governments in Québec and Toronto could impact the relations between the two provinces and in consequence, the implementation of the 2009 Agreement.

CONCLUSION

The idea of transforming the economy has dominated debates, initiatives and investments in Ontario before and after the 2007-08 crisis, the effects of which are felt ever since. The view that a status quo means regression of employment and of personal and government incomes is widely shared. Consequently, that transformation is felt as an urgent necessity to ensure Ontario's economic good fortune in the coming decades. The province could then continue to offer its citizens the good living standards they have known since the Second World War and maintain the projected immigration flows. It could also keep its status as the federation's biggest economy and maintain its reputation as one of the world's most advanced subregional economies.

Ontarians have rightly assessed the world's ongoing changes and those the 2008 crisis has unfurled on the continent. The discourses of the province's main private and public leaders, the analyses and propositions of its many think tanks, the results of the discussion platforms it sets up, like its Economic Summit, all converge. These global and continental changes also mean reviewing the province's relationships with the world's most creditworthy markets, the United States', which remains vital for Ontario, but coupled with the markets of the great southern economies that now control an ever growing part of international commerce and investment. Furthermore, these global and continental changes require major investments in human resources, in productivity and innovation along with investments in the infrastructure of a new generation. Finally, they mean strengthening the "Brand Toronto" movement, of which we will speak more later, given the Ontarian capital's representativeness of the Ontarian society's signature and their indivisible reputation. That strengthening is underway, as we have wanted to demonstrate in this chapter and as we will again in the next chapter dedicated to culture.

To conduct these major works successfully, the Ontarian society can rely on considerable resources that we have identified and evaluated. A vision that appeared to us as having the advantage of being shared by many; a political will that was deployed in policies of great scope but plagued by the economic situation and the minority status of the Ontario's government; a network of universities, research centres and institutions such as the MaRS Discovery District, unequaled in the country; a human diversity constituting a vast doorway on the most significant emerging powers; a vibrant civil society that can and did mobilize. The Ontarian society can also count on impressive assets like its status as an international financial centre, its reputation as one of the continent's major medical research hub and its rise as a bridge linking global cultures, as is illustrated by TIFF's success story. Is that configuration of wills and resources surrounding renewed priorities likely to entrench Ontario's solid economic performance in the long run?

It sure commends a good dose of confidence. But that good feeling does not diffuse another worried one, clearly expressed by the former Senior Vice President and Chief Economist at TD Bank Financial Group, Don Drummond, at the 2008 Ontario Economic Summit: "I'm worried about Ontario's future, and I think you should be too".

The Ontarian economy remains relatively prosperous when compared with other societies on the continent and in the world.[96] And it essential transformation has started. That it wishes to undergo that transformation in partnership with Quebec reflects a necessity: the creation of an integrated economic area, northeast of the continent, which will produce better results in a global competition that is expected to keep growing in the coming decades. That choice contains difficulties, according to Roger Martin. It constitutes, however, strategically and for both societies, an insurance policy for the future. But its own future also depends on important unknowns.

The first regards the Atlantic countries' economic evolution. This text is being written in January 2012, a time of light recovery in the US, fearful in the face of all the social and economic cracks revealed by the crisis and a time also marked by the deepening of structural difficulties for European economies. In short, the important sectors in Ontario are seriously weakened and could fall in their own cracks if the crises were to go on and amplify. The Ontarian government will need significant fiscal yields and investments, along with prosperous private sector partners and an active jobs market in order to be successful in transforming its economy, maintaining its policies and significant projects as well as rebalancing its public finances.

The second regards the internal evolution of Ontario's economy. What will the private sector actors do in order to increase their firms' productivity and finally install them in a culture of innovation? What will they do to significantly increase their investments in R&D and conquer new markets around the world? Will they fully benefit from that extraordinary capital embodied by Ontario's population diversity?

The province is blessed with a culturally diverse population that singles it out globally and that brings it what David Livermore called "The Cultural Intelligence Difference".[97] Following many studies and analyses, a special 2010 report by the Conference Board of Canada showed beyond doubt that in any given society, immigrants improve innovation capacities.[98] Such is the consequence of their high graduation levels, their knowledge of foreign markets, their ability to communicate in multiple

---

96. MARTIN PROSPERITY INSTITUTE (2009) *Ontario in the creative age*, Martin Prosperity Institute p.3.

97. LIVERMORE, D. (2011) *The Cultural Intelligence Difference*. New York: Amacom.

98. THE CONFERENCE BOARD OF CANADA (2010) Immigrants *as Innovators Boosting Canada's Global Competitiveness*. Toronto: The Conference Board of Canada.

languages and their unique perspectives in assessing stakes and challenges. In Canada, more than 25 per cent of patents result from the work of immigrants, 35 per cent of the 2,000 prestigious Canada Research Chairs meant to support innovation are presided by foreign-born Canadians, who merely constitute 20 per cent of the population. Twenty nine per cent of Giller Prize recipients are also Canadians from abroad.

Another unknown consists of the new political and fiscal margins at Ontario's disposal for it to complete the vast economic transformation it has undertaken. Our interlocutors have generally pleaded in favour of transfers in terms of responsibilities and financial resources allowing the province to conduct policies adapted to its labour force, immigration and regional development needs. They have also pleaded for fiscal equity for Ontario. Many of them also stated that in order to accomplish what must be done, the province must define and implement a new "Canadian social contract that would recognize Ontario's new realities", to quote the director of the Mowat Centre again. Finally, federal policy orientations with regard to Canada's place in the world also constitute a decisive factor in the success of provincial policies, or lack thereof.

All those challenges are perceived as interconnected and lighten by a common sense of urgency.

If the transformation of its economy is to be accomplished, Ontario will stand on human and financial foundations to lead the great works it announced these past few years: an accelerated development of its education sector, from kindergartens to university, an integrated transportation scheme for the greater Toronto and Hamilton region, including 1,200 kilometres of public transit fast lanes and a development plan for the Great North to revitalize this vast region of natural resources and protected areas.[99] One also thinks of the ambitious and controversial energy strategy calling for investments of up to $80 billion between 2011 and 2030. Lastly, to accomplish the transformation of its economy, Ontario has to maintain and accelerate the development of a cultural sector which, as we will demonstrate in the following chapter, has known a formidable expansion in the past couple of decades.

---

99. GOVERNMENT OF ONTARIO (2011), Ministry of Northern Development, Mines and Forestry, *Growth Plan for Northern Ontario*. Toronto: Government of Ontario, 2011.

CHAPTER 3
A CULTURAL SOCIETY

IN 2009-10, THE ENTERTAINMENT AND CULTURAL sectors in Ontario generated $15 billion in recipes and accounted for $12.2 billion of the province's GDP. That contribution is the equivalent of 2/3 of the automotive industry and a bigger take than the fields of energy, forestry and agriculture combined. The President and CEO of the Ontario Media Development Corporation (OMDC), Karen Thorne-Stone, in her organization's annual report for that year, reminds us that:

> In 2009-10, Ontario's cultural media industries continued to outpace the provincial economy as a whole in terms of both job and revenue growth. OMDC's Tax Credits department issued more than 1,300 certificates with a value of $268 million for projects valued at $2 7 billion.[1]

These sectors, entertainment and cultural creation, account for 295,000 jobs in the province, close to one out of two jobs in the field in Canada. The cultural industries—film, television, publishing, music and interactive digital media—represent a little more than 50 per cent of this domain and contribute to $6.7 of Ontario's GDP.[2] More recent numbers cited by the Greater Toronto Civic Action Alliance, evoke a contribution to the Greater Toronto Area's GDP that is closer to $9 billion. And the said GTA accounts for 8,500 cultural organizations.[3]

---

1. *2009-2010 Annual Report*, the Development Corporation of the media industry in Ontario , p.3.
2. Government Expenditures on Culture (May 4 2011):
http://www.statcan.gc.ca/pub/87f0001x/87f0001x2011001-eng.pdf.
3. CIVICACTION, *Breaking Boundaries : Time to Think and Act Like a Region*, Toronto, CivicAction, July 2011.

The data do not take into account the part played by the Ontarian cultural offer as a component of the tourism industry, whose contribution to Ontario's economy reaches $22.1 billion. The Ontarian government aims at doubling these economic benefits by 2020 with a policy of being present on the markets of Brazil, China, India, Mexico … and Quebec.

These statistics are impressive in and of themselves. They become even more so when submitted to their appreciation by Ontarians. In March 2010, the Ontario Arts Council (OAC) has tasked a survey company with measuring the opinion of Ontarians regarding the links between culture and life quality, or rather the quality of their lives.[4]

Of those interrogated, 95 per cent declared that arts enrich their lives and 89 per cent consider that, in these times of economic uncertainty, a reduction in the cultural offer would be a real loss. So 81 per cent of them believe that governments should continue to invest in culture and that such investments contribute to economic growth. This survey also demonstrates that a majority of Ontarians from every region and age group have a positive attitude towards arts and their importance for people and communities.

Of those interrogated, 95 per cent of respondents say they wish for more cultural activities, with 60 per cent, 55 per cent and 51 per cent of them attending musical concerts, plays and visiting museums respectively. And among other interesting data, let us note that 75 per cent of Ontarians aged 18 to 34 download music and that this age group is the one that is the most personally engaged in cultural activities of various nature. This makes it easier to understand the success of Ontario's Culture Days, launched in 2010 and based on the *Journées de la culture québécoise*.

Those are remarkable data, brought to our attention towards the end of our research. They brought answers to interrogations that kept coming up: how are we to explain the high volume of public and private investments, including by local governments, in culture in Ontario this past couple of decades? How are we to interpret the manifest and continued commitment of a great number of Ontarians in support of their society's cultural institutions? 4 out of 5 Ontarians think culture contributes to both their quality of life and to economic growth. In 2009-10, 16.2 million people have attended artistic activities presented by the 509 cultural bodies that received grants

---

4. ONTARIO ARTS COUNCIL (2011), *Ontario Arts Engagement Study – Summary*. Toronto: Ontario Arts Council, September 2011.

from the OAC and 4.5 million have participated in activities of artistic education offered by these bodies.[5]

BETWEEN GLASSHOUSES

At 305 King street West in Toronto, a glass façade, immense and luminous, takes up all the space between John and Widmer streets. Welcome to the TIFF Bell Lightbox, the new house of the TIFF, a name now known all over the world. An address that is visited quite a lot, with 600,000 people crossing its doorstep before it even celebrated its first anniversary.

Created 35 years ago, this non-competitive film festival imposed itself as one of the planet's most coveted rendezvous. People come to TIFF from Bollywood, Hollywood and Nollywood. Here, all the feelings of the world are shown on screen. Ephemeral, their trappings change, from black and white to the wonders of the digital era. Here, the traditional and experimental, occidental and oriental all discover some of their common DNA. Some of their shared preoccupations, also, with regard to the future of the industry and its international funding; one of the topics at a very popular forum organized at every TIFF edition.

Bill Marshall, Henk Vander Kolk and Dusty Cohl are the pioneers of this unique adventure: imposing a city in the great game of world cinema and an international rendezvous in a circuit that already has a great number of old and prestigious ones. A quixotic adventure! A remarkable success! It alone represents Toronto's potential as a global cultural meeting point.

Other images, also viewable in Ontario but much more ancient, evoke stories of animal kingdoms and the lives of men, their links and their human and natural environments. These images are sheltered in another glass house, that one bearing the comforting name of protective building. Since 2002, it protects the largest collection of such images in Canada against the inclemency of weather or man. These images are not printed on film but carved in white marble and there are 900 of them. These petroglyphs were discovered close to Peterborough in 1954, into what the First Nations people of Ontario call "the Teaching Rocks". Instead of seeing them in their natural environment, one can admire them in a movie that inventories and explains them. Other sites also testify about the physical and metaphysical representations of Native Peoples, the first to have mastered and developed Ontarian terri-

---

5. ONTARIO ARTS COUNCIL (2011), *Annual Report and Grants Listings, 2009-2010*. Toronto: Ontario Arts Council, p. 26.

tory and to have magnified it symbolically and superbly. London's Museum of Ontario Archeology, traces them, shows them and dates them. The most ancient are 12,000 years old.

Between these images and stories, fixed in stone for millennia, and those shown by TIFF, human presence has marked the material and immaterial territory of the central Canadian province. Ontarian culture was forged in that long run. Individuals, groups and associations have mobilized around culture. Apart from writers and painters of the 19th century, there's Egerton Ryerson, who founded the Educational Museum of Upper Canada in 1857 and others, who founded the Ontario Society of Artists, the Royal Canadian Academy of Arts in Ottawa and Toronto's Arts and Letters Club; the Group of Seven, which exhibited the work of its members for the first time in 1920, as a prologue of a constant involvement of Ontarians in the cultural domain.

As is the case for every society, Ontario's culture was built via successive waves: Indigenous, French, British, American, European, Caribbean and more recently, African, Arab and Asian. These contributions do not all share the same depth in time and in the spirits, but Ontarian culture would be incomplete without each of them. It was filled, like Ontario's Great Lakes, via multiple sources, tiny or abundant, tumultuous or imperceptible.

Ontarian culture, in its modern form, first registered in the continuity of its link with Great Britain coloured by its proximity to the United States. After the Second World War, it entered in a quest for its autonomy which helps define it today as independent from its origins but close to the US. It now sheds its own light on its unique landscapes and experiences. That story is well known by now. Among others, W. J. Keith told its literary version,[6] Douglas Daymond and Leslie Monkman did so for essays, editorials and manifestos,[7] Dudek and Gnarowski for poetry,[8] Wagner for dramatic arts,[9] Reid for painting,[10] and Lisa Rochon for architecture.[11]

---

6. KEITH, W. J. (2006) *Canadian Literature in English, volumes one and two.* Erin: The Porcupine's Quill.

7. DOUGLAS, Daymond and MONKMAN Leslie, (1984-1986) *Towards a Canadian literature, Essays, Editorials and Manifestos.* Ottawa: Tecumseh, vols. 1 and 2..

8. LOUIS, D. and GNAROWSKI, M. (1967) *The Making of Modern Poetry in Canada.* Toronto: Ryerson Press.

9. WAGNERS, A. (1980) The *Brock Bibliography of Published Canadian Plays in English, 1766-1978.* Toronto: Playwrights Press.

10. Reid, D. (1989) A *Concise History of Canadian Painting.* London: Oxford University Press, 3rd Edition.

11. ROCHON, L. op.cit.

From these waves thus came the metaphysics, the cosmologies and the languages of Native Peoples whose words are widely found in today's Ontarian toponymy with those left by the French. From them came the norms and values of European powers, especially the British, who colonized, peopled and modeled the territory and transmitted its rules, symbols and institutions. From them also, the experiences of other regions of the country, among them the unique case of Quebec; regions which supplied the central province many of its creators. From them, still, came the energy, the shapes and the rhythms of American culture which represents a chance and a challenge for Ontarian creators.

From them, finally, came an immense capital of references held in the suitcases and spirits of millions of immigrants hailing from every civilizational areas of the planet, virtually forming a majority in Ontarian society. W.J. Keith asserts that Jewish authors have injected in it a true dose of independence of thought and originality in language,[12] just as other authors instilled in it their specific spiritual and cultural references, depending on their origin. They thus contributed to install diversity at the heart of Ontarian modernity.

This set of references defies any attempt at typology. Today, it links Ontarian culture with all the cultures of the world. It powerfully innervates Ontarian cultural production, as can be seen with the works of creators, many of them having been cited in this book so far already. In short, the Ontarian cultural mirror reflects diversity as a time horizon and as current evidence. In Ontario, one sees more than Ontario. The formula is from Alexis de Tocqueville, who coined it for American society and culture. We felt it all along our stays in the province.

CAMERON BAILEY

Moviemaker, writer, television host, curator of important cinematographic events and, since 2008, Co-Director of TIFF, Cameron Bailey came to Canada in 1971, from London, where he was born of Barbadian parents. Our host is waiting for us at the back of LUMA restaurant, in the Lightbox. In this vast sanctuary of every noise, image and special effect, the restaurant is noticeably sober, with its large dark leather seats and walnut walls, from the tree which fittingly, like the movies shown here, can be found on every continent. The furniture blends in that pure décor. The menu is simple and the dishes unpretentious. The whole space looks like a

---

12. KEITH, op.cit., volume 1, p. 24.

monastery's dining room designed by a minimalist artist and the conversation, immediate, seems facilitated by the intimate atmosphere.

Involved in a myriad of social, educational and cultural projects, such as Civic Action's Art & Culture Working Group in Toronto and the Creative Capital group which prepared a report on culture for the new municipal administration in 2011 and a member of the board of Tourism Toronto, Bailey is deeply respected. Many of the people we met have encouraged us to have a conversation with that laid-back and elegant man, as knowledgeable about the Torontonian ethos as they get. If he is evidently cosmopolitan, he is also of that city which saw him grow in its streets. He mixes his personal experience with the adventure of the great festival he is in charge of, the evolution of Toronto's society as a preliminary and its ability to view the world and be seen by it.

> When I arrived in this city, everything was so different. It was a much smaller city, it felt like an almost entirely white city. I was I think the only black kid in my class for at least 5 or 6 years. You'd get chased around the yard, called names, you'd have awful encounters in the classrooms, sometimes the teachers as well. You know, the usual kind of petty racism. So when I see kids today of my age when I landed in Toronto, they're surrounded by people who are like them, no matter who you are. What I was taught is that "you have to be better because you're going to have prejudice directed against you." It shapes you. I have Jewish friends and for them I think it was the same...
>
> For almost two hundred years, the Orange order was such a dominant force in the culture of Toronto. What changed that was when Nathan Phillips was elected mayor in the 50s, first Jewish mayor, and he did so many things to change the sense of who led this city, that privileged group who held the reins of power in Toronto. That coincided with architectural changes in the city. City Hall was an example, not just the building itself, which was revolutionary at the time, but the open square in front of it, which we never had, where Torontonians could gather, interact, and bring the city to life. That was when, I think, the city began to change.
>
> In terms of the relative harmony within our diversity, I think a more liberal policy certainly contributed to the

country's transformation, especially under Trudeau. And also, you know, we had the example of the US, the civil rights struggle and the violence that we saw then, coming at us every day and the Canadian response to that, through the media, through the politicians, was so very different. People never wanted to have that here and they began to preach different policies. But I think what has been really extraordinary in Ontario, and I would say Toronto especially, has been the fact that people who are immigrants can actually attain positions of power. Even in places like Britain or France you don't see that, Bailey adds. People there have told me "You know Cameron, here, we would never have Black man in your job."

Diversity dominates Cameron's conversation, not as a problematic topic but as an obvious, normal state of things, a powerful lever that opens us to the world. In his perspective and in his words, the memory of that little Black kid, discriminated against, and today, the certainty that such a world is fading, as demonstrated by his prominent position in Ontarian society.

Cameron Bailey has a widespread knowledge of global cinema: that of Africa, which he discovered at the Pan-African Film Festival of Ouagadougou, that of Asia, which he enjoys in Mumbai, Hong Kong, Shanghai and Busan, as well as all the other cinemas, Canadian, American and European that he sees in Cannes, Berlin, Venice and all over the world. He's permanently on the lookout for all of them in order to establish TIFF's programming, his responsibility and obvious pleasure. With a touch of irony, he recalls the competition between the Montreal and Toronto festivals and the victory of Ontario's metropolis, which was well served by the exodus of many institutions and people who left Montreal for Toronto, with their wallets!

Since then, many films presented here went on to win international awards, including Oscars. The ripple effect was decisive. Now, American and Asian producers have taken the habit of launching their movies at the Toronto festival, certain to find an enthusiastic public here.

We show films from all over the world and there's always an audience locally for whom that's almost a home movie. And that's really made the big difference because you know, these films can show in Venice or in Cannes and they're essentially exotic, in a way. But they're not exotic here, where the audience embraces them because they know those films. That is true for cinema but also for the Opera or the Symphony Orchestra, when artists come from the countries of origin of many Torontonians.

On the closing night of the first edition of the Festival, in 1976, the pioneers congratulated each other for the 127 presented films, from 30 countries, and they profusely thanked the 30 000 Torontonians that filled the seats. In 2011, 268 feature films and 68 shorts, from 65 countries, were projected for the pleasure of the 400,000 moviegoers who enjoyed the Toronto International Film Festival's 34th edition. This name goes back to 1995 only. Before then, TIFF was known as the "Festival of Festivals", which it might well be in the process of becoming, with its strategic calendar, five months before the Oscars, with its selection of universally celebrated films, making room for cinemas from around the world, with a theme that is suggested rather than imposed; the smart theme of immigration and migrations for the 2011 edition was a hot topic not only in Western cinema but also in the African, Latin American and Asian ones. At that same 2011 edition, the correspondent for *Le Monde* observed that "as strong as it's ever been, TIFF managed to keep intact the surprising cocktail of glamour and conviviality on which it built its identity. Toronto is also the ideal place to take the pulse of cinema production for the year to come".[13] Her colleague from Montreal's *La Presse,* wrote the year before that the Toronto Festival was showing "true respect for cinema. Especially, contrary to what everyone believes, towards foreign films".[14]

The scale of the adventure is vast. Ten days of festivities that brings movie celebrities from around the world to Toronto. Actors—Indian, French, African, American, Chinese, Quebecers and British—and all other egos and beauties from faraway countries, producers, groupies, dream sellers and other fragments of that brotherhood of image makers can be glimpsed on red carpets and at A-list parties. All year long, the Festival offers abundant programming made possible by the TIFF Cinematheque's vast collection. Retrospectives, for instance, like those dedicated in 2011 to the work of Henri-Georges Clouzot and Nicholas Ray. Or conferences, workshops,

---

13. REIGNIER, I. (2011) " Toronto, festival drôle et détendu. Un très bon cinéma loin des superproductions ", *Le Monde,* September 17th , 2011.

14. LUSSIER, M.A. "Ce que j'aime (et aime moins) du TIFF ", *La Presse,* September 10th , 2010.

meet and greets with Canadian and foreign moviemakers. There's also the possibility of creating movies that can be projected at the Lightbox. Specialized festivals are also offered, one of which is dedicated to children. As of 2011, TIFF inaugurated its new Nexus program, dedicated to digital media, games and the communities they bring together.

More than one million Torontonians are TIFF adherents, one way or another, each year. They come here seeking images, and they get a lot. They also hear stories, from the truest to the most far-fetched, from the immediate to the most far-flung.

The Festival of Festivals sits near the top of the global movie scene. In Toronto, its primacy is obvious, although it must share its public with the 75 other film festivals that year in year out, show images from all over the world.[15] This sharing of movie lovers spreads all across Ontario, where film festivals have gained in notoriety. Among others, welcome to the Peterborough International Film Festival, the Cinefest Sudbury International Film Festival and to the Kingston Canadian Film Festival.

For the first time on American soil, Toronto welcomed the International Indian Film Academy Awards and for three days, in June 2011, showcased the world's most prolific cinema, with more than a thousand movies produced every year. The festivities were, like the extravagant, colourful, choreographed and beautiful cinema being celebrated, excessive and magnificent. They included concerts, projections of tens of movies in Toronto, Brampton, Markham and Mississauga, covering the wide variety of Indian cinema; the organization by TIFF of a retrospective of Raj Kapoor, the great Indian filmmaker. There was a fashion show displaying the work of Indian designers and Torontonians of Indian origin, a ROM exhibit of artists' copies of movie posters seen in all of South and Southeast Asia, in Africa and by the Indian diaspora on every continent.

For a brief moment, Indian movie stars lived in Toronto-Bollywood and were joined by 40,000 fans that came from all over to that award ceremony, which took place at the Rogers Centre in front of 16,000 people, its broadcast followed by another 700 million in 60 countries. Local and global, the

---

15. For instance: Planet in Focus, International Environmental Film and Video Festival; Indigeneous Resistance Documentary Festival; Toronto Palestine Film Festival; Toronto Jewish Film Festival; CinéFranco; Toronto Asian International Film Festival; Toronto Indian Film Festival; Toronto African Film and Music Festival; Toronto Latino Film and Video Festival; Toronto Urban Film Festival; European Union Film Festival; Brazil Film Fest.

party made many in Ontario's Indian community feel especially good; it strengthened the networks of Indian and Torontonian creators involved in cinematographic co-productions, it proved our friends at OMNI Television right in their decision to give a real place to Indian cinema in the station's programming. Lastly, the festivities enriched Toronto's reputation as a relay for world cinema. The Ontarian government has spared no effort to attract the IIFA to its capital: former Premier McGuinty even going to India and his government strongly contributing to the event financially.

THE ONTARIAN CULTURAL SYSTEM

In some ways, the Ontarian cultural system resembles that of its big southern neighbour: importance of the private sector, patronage, foundations, local powers, volunteering. There's also the abundance of cultural institutions, associations and organizations all over its territory and an attachment to heritage. But the Ontarian cultural system also partly resembles that of European states with its "énoncés politiques," its numerous institutions, programs and public financing.

Of course, the seduction of American culture is potent, here and elsewhere given the territorial and linguistic continuity between both societies. But potent also are the desire and need to show the wider world, culturally. Ontario is carried by that seduction and that desire, both intensely cohabiting within it. "How to say both No, and Yes", asks the author of *Moving Targets*. True in Ontario, in the West and in the world.

Moreover, Ontario belongs to a political dynamic that has little in common with the one found in the United States. Since the famous 1941 Kingston Conference and the implementation of parts of the 1951 Royal Commission on National Development in the Arts, Letters & Sciences' recommendations, the federal state can intervene in the field of culture based on specific references. Canadian provinces for their part, Ontario as much as the others, have occupied that field for the past half century according to parameters that differ completely from the interventions of American states in their own federation.

Ontario's cultural system is forcefully supported by the provincial government and the municipal authorities. Their respective contributions in 2008-09 reached $887 million and $1,162 billion in support of cultural production. American competition is permanently overshadowing, with 300,000 titles published every year in the United States against the 16,000 *Canadian publications and the volumes of television and cinematic productions of the two simply being incomparable.* Pierre-Elliott Trudeau's fable of the elephant and the mouse comes immediately to mind. Some, such as Pierre Berton, with his 50 books, his 100 in-depth special reports for *Maclean's* and his 1,000 *Toronto Star* chronicles have barely tilted the disequilibrium of the scale.[16] Such disparity does not prevent the production of culture or the national and international acknowledgement of a great number of Ontarian creators. In literature, for instance, the list of authors whose work is always expected and whose signature is respected in the world has countless names on it: Alice Munro, André Alexis, NourbeSe Philip, Margaret Laurence, Margaret Atwood, Michael Ondaatje, Rohinton Mistry, Shyam Selvadurai, Austin Clarke, Vincent Lam, Richard B. Wright, Lawrence Hill and many more. As shown by a 2008 survey, the great Canadian authors are celebrated abroad and little known in their country.[17]

Culture in Ontario! Is it possible in a society that first defines its identity as part of its Canadian experience rather than its Ontarian one? In a biting text published in the October 2007 edition of *Maclean's*, Andrew Potter answered with a resounding no![18] Is it sufficient "as a subproduct of American culture, to dedicate a few months of research on the topic and, ultimately, a few pages in very large print" an Ontarian friend asked me, skeptically but interestedly? "Mission impossible", whispers a senior federal public servant, mandarin of times past, who mixes up subsidy and creation and who forgets that Ottawa's time is not the country's real time.

We met a lot of those creators of the Ontarian cultural offer. John Ibbitson, the novelist hidden behind his brilliant political chronicles in *The Globe & Mail*, Cameron Bailey, the audacious manager at TIFF, who thinks of himself first as a writer, Howard Aster, publisher of diversity, and part time immigrant to Burgundy, John Ralston Saul, vice-royal consort as well as essayist exhuming the part of our DNA we received from our Indigenous people and the other part stemming from the convergent thinking of LaFontaine and Baldwin, Alberto Di Giovanni, the joyful curator of the Centro Scuola e Cultura Italiana. Without forgetting of course our witnesses Rahul Bhardwaj, Madeline Ziniak, Mihnea C. Moldoveanu and Lisa Rochon, and many more. We've observed them in Toronto and all across Ontario, in museums, cultural centres, libraries, the big festivals, playhouses and other places of culture. And

---

16. McKillop, A. B. (2008) *Pierre Berton: A Biography*. Toronto: McClelland & Stewart.
17. "Celebrated abroad, misspelled at home", *The Globe and Mail*, December 31, 2008.
18. POTTER, A. "What's best for Ontario? Newsflash: who cares? The reason Ontario has no culture? It doesn't exist", *Maclean's*, October 1st 2007.

they are plenty, millions in fact, those who elect, through their continued choices, the cultural dimension of their society.

We've also met Ontarian cultural animators, managers of modest projects and some whose ambitions are larger. One of them can be found looking at Artscape which, in the heart of Toronto, has been working for 25 years on important renovation projects of buildings and entire neighbourhoods, aiming to install culture, in its different institutional, educational and experimental forms in communities that are deprived of them. Aiming as well to provide artists with living and creative quarters adapted to their needs and means. The hand of the market alone is not likely to encourage such initiatives linking cultural, social and economic development.

Transforming spaces, transforming people, transforming economies, the trilogy defines Artscape's ambition, visible in its team's impressive realizations and significant ongoing projects. One must see what Toronto's Distillery District has become and what Regent Park is becoming. Among the poorest neighbourhoods in the city, spreading over 69 acres in its eastern part, Regent Park is currently under reconstruction, at the cost of one billion dollars, around a new cultural centre that will include a performance hall, facilities for cultural associations, youth programs and an important space dedicated to social innovation. Another great Artscape project was the upgrading of the western edge of Queen Street, now a centre of Toronto's cultural creation with its workshops, experimental galleries, musical scene, restaurants and fashion stores that make it "one of the world's most dynamic cultural place". The organization has renovated the Drake and Gladstone hotels, the Museum of Contemporary Canadian Art. It is also leading residential projects there, significant with their 7,000 intended new residents, including the renovation of a vast 27-acre space around the Centre for Addiction and Mental Health. Thus, the city is being recreated, according to a vision that integrates culture as a source of life quality and a support to economic integration. Artscape also works in other Ontarian cities interested in the group's spirit and way of doing things: Hamilton, Kingston, Kitchener, London, Markham, Mississauga and others.

Finally, we tried to understand Ontario's cultural policy. We discovered an important and powerful conglomerate that links public authorities and resources, both provincial and local, to the capacities and resources of the private sector. We also witnessed a vision which makes of culture a lever for growth and development. "Ontario's entertainment and creative cluster is a cornerstone of the province's new innovative economy", said Ontario's minister of Finance in his 2008 budget. Some also see in it a component of societal cohesion, including the greeting and accompaniment of immigrants and the anchoring of a sense of belonging and pride about Ontarian togetherness. Hence Ontarians' continued and fruitful mobilization in support of the various forms of culture.

The province has a ministry of Tourism and Culture with its own programs and directly supporting the provincial network of bodies dedicated to art. It has an arts council created in 1963[19]. It has a large set of institutions: the Trillium Foundation, created in 1982 to support community organizations that work to achieve cohesion in terms of social services, sports, leisure, environment and culture;[20] the Ontario Heritage Trust, established in 1990 and in charge of preserving the province's architectural and environmental heritage and the recognition of historic sites, more than 1,225 since the Trust's creation; the Ontario Arts Foundation, born in 1991 and managing 275 endowments established by individuals, foundations, corporations and art organizations. There's also the Ontario Cultural Attractions Fund, started in 1999 and which supported 380 organizations in 2010-11. The Ontario Tourism Marketing Partnership Corporation, also of 1999, and the Ontario Media Development Corporation which, since 2000, supports media companies, as we will further demonstrate at the end of this chapter. This cluster of institutions is not only wide-ranging, it is also exhaustive and endowed with significant resources that were substantially increased these past years, despite the crisis, following the remarkably accomplishments of its components in terms of performance.

JOHN BROTMAN

The Executive Director of the Ontario Arts Council is an immigrant who came to Toronto from his distant South Africa, *"at the time the most racist society in the world"*, after detours through Great Britain, Belgium, Italy, Alberta and Ottawa. This nomadic man has a few places he calls home and which can be discovered through his words: music, which is his own professional and personal space; creation which keeps amazing him, and everything that the institution he served for 10 years taught him about the relationship man entertains with culture, about the eminent place the latter takes in human communities, from the most humble to the most sophisticated.

---

19. In 2009-2010, The Council has subsidized 1,697 artists and 1,013 organizations in 236 communities.
20. In 2008-2009, The Foundation has subsidized 1458 organizations.

Bloor Street in Toronto, John Brotman greets us in his office, offering fragmented views of the great city through its wide windows. His colleague Kathryn Townshend, the Director of Research, Policy and Evaluation, joins us. Both are manifestly proud of what they've accomplished at the OAC, which served as a laboratory for the ultraconservatives in Queen's Park from 1995 to 2002. Their main challenge has been to restore the Council's intellectual and financial resources, to integrate to its functions the useful elements of the Conservative experience and guarantee the institution's influence over the entire Ontarian territory.

Always deferent, John Brotman describes the 2 last phases of Ontarian public policy evolution with regard to culture.

> 15 years ago, more or less, the government decided to disengage from culture and create specific support funds for each cultural institution, funds that would be sustained by contributions from the private sector and that would then be matched by the government. Convinced of the formula's fruitfulness, the government reduced the OAC's budget by 40 per cent. That theory is viable only if the private sector agrees to invest in culture and in the precise way that was planned by the government. The theory is also viable only if the economy and stock exchanges are doing well. The policy's results ended up being modest. Plus, they revealed a clear disparity between the big cultural institutions that were able to mobilize important financial resources and numerous others without the size, networks and notoriety that could've garnered the necessary support. So, for a constant and fair development of every institution and all regions, the public resource is indispensable. Its reliability brings a level of assurance to administrators of cultural institutions and associations, especially since OAC's help, contrary to the great majority of public subsidies, goes to operational budgets.
>
> Our goal, ten years ago, was to restore a good level of governmental contributions to the Council, which we managed to do, transfers to the OAC having been multiplied by 3 since 2000. Of course, the current government is sensitive to culture and makes no mystery

of its convictions. It believes the quality of life of people and communities and the attraction of culture to draw in and keep the best human resources are critical to economic and technological development and also to education. A good example of that complementarity is the cultural initiatives taken by the Kitchener-Waterloo Prosperity Council.

We ask John Brotman about the impact of Ontarian diversity on the Council's policies. His answer comes immediately: "major and formidable. Diversity permanently brings us new ideas. It forces us to go towards the different communities to know them and be known by them. It helps us realize, also, that many Ontarians have come here to flee fear and live in peace. I strongly believe they love peace; they love living in peace and seeing others live in peace". Kathryn Townshend, who promised us a myriad of data, and kept that promise, seems surprised by the question. "The different communities and their members are simply there, an evidence, a reality. Our reality."

Our discussion ends with a last question on the Executive Director's overall impression, at the end of his fruitful mandates. It lies in "the importance culture acquired in Ontarian society and its continued growth in Toronto, and everywhere in the province and in every community".

BRAND TORONTO

With the exception of Quebec, whose cultural specificity is undeniable, and the Ottawa region, whose cultural institutions, important as they are, constitute an artificial and impressive display case built according to a political logic specific to the Canadian federal regime,[21] Toronto is obviously the country's cultural capital. It will remain so as far as we can see in the future. W.J. Keith notes that it took a long time for Ontario to realize it was no longer *Canada West*, as can be seen with even the briefest stay in Alberta and British Columbia, and that there are now many "Canadas". However, the capital that was accumulated over time in Ontario—institutional, human and financial resources resulting from an international network—places the province and its largest city in a separate category, unique in the English

---

21. Exception must be made of cultural institutions which depend on the constitutional responsibilities of the federal level of government, such as Library and Archives Canada, and those created by Ottawa's municipal government.

part of the country. Furthermore, the Canadian metropolis is home to almost every professional cultural association, which significantly adds to its influence.

Since its European origins, Toronto has interested artists, painters, engravers and writers.[22] Some poets, too, such as Raymond Souster, chose it as the object of their work. In *The City Called a Queen*, he describes it as strange and cold, but still the object of his celebration and love. In *Cabbagetown*, Hugh Garner depicts it as hard-working and orderly. Dionne Brand draws a spectacular profile at the very beginning of *What We All Long For*. Ins Choi, the Torontonian playwright of Korean origin portrayed it in two important plays: *Window of Toronto and Kim's Convenience*. Atom Egoyan depicts it, in his movie *Chloe*, as complex, diverse, stratified with, and by, time, a city of concrete so close to nature, trivial here and sublime in multiple places. Is the city becoming culturally competitive on the global scene, as TIFF tends to prove? Rita Davies, Toronto's "cultural czar"[23] has been seeing to it, intelligently and with conviction, for more than 20 years

RITA DAVIES

One has to behold the city and the great lake that rims it from the heights of City Hall to appreciate its exceptional location. On that luminous day, motionless and glassy skyscrapers are struck with a wide spectrum of undulating reflections in a magnificent and evanescent flow. The office we're in is small and the tall charcoal sketches that adorn it give it an improbable dimension. Toronto's Executive Director of Culture, Mrs. Davies greets us with great amiability.

Born in Shanghai of a Jewish father and Catholic mother, she exemplifies Ontarian diversity. In a soft voice, she tells of the fluctuating political wills that marked the past decades with regard to culture: times of confidence when the city was run and animated by David Crombie, and the "long tunnel-crossing" of Mike Harris' provincial rule. Despite this back and forth, progress was accomplished, tangibly and abundantly.

Thousands of people live in the Czar's universe who quit City Hall in 2012. Former colleagues from the publishing world, her first profession; friends from the days when she led and won a formidable battle to substantially increase

---

22. SYLVESTRE, P.F. (2007) *Toronto s'écrit : La ville Reine dans notre littérature.* Toronto: Éditions du Gref.

23. KNELMAN, M. "Rita Davies, Toronto Cultural Czar", *The Toronto Star*, February 20th 2006.

the Toronto Arts Council's budget, perennial associations, circumstantial groups, street committees, droves of creators, anonymous art lovers and rich philanthropists, permanent forces and ephemeral ones, contributors, all, to the mobilization she encourages. Under her apparent softness, her strong will, resilience and relentless determination still show. We left her office, our arms filled with all kinds of documents, of which the fascinating read did not teach us not much more than what she had forcefully shared with us.

> You have probably seen the considerable cultural realizations that have changed our city and altered Torontonians' perspective on culture… That buzz can only grow. We will see to that. It will grow here and abroad if we can keep the support and pride of our fellow citizens for all those wonderful events that are happening in our city. Then, Toronto will belong to the group of great global cultural cities, alongside Chicago, Milan, Montreal, Barcelona, London, San Francisco…

Rita Davies' cultural ambition for Toronto has been the inspiration behind the reflection and proposals of the past decade concerning the Ontarian capital's cultural plans, which bear her signature or are marked by her vision and influence. Examples are many: the 2003 plan,[24] the vast "Live with Culture" campaign of 2006-07 and, in 2006, the proposed strategies to make Toronto a "creative city"[25] and so on.

Relays and follow-ups will be abundant. Among them, the 2008 contribution of Andrew Bell and Kevin Stolarick of the Martin Prosperity Institute deserve mention[26] for what it suggests and as an illustration of the cultural theme's inclusion in the prospecting and forecasting work on the Ontarian capital's desired evolution.

After having demonstrated that the City of Toronto's funding of artistic and cultural organizations has not followed inflation or population growth, the authors develop six scenarios to change what must be. The first of these evokes the dreariness of the status quo. The last one speaks of an 89 per cent increase in cultural funding. Just some of the options offered to the leaders of the city's government.

---

24. CITY OF TORONTO (2003) Cultural *Plan for a Creative City*. Toronto: City of Toronto.

25. CITY OF TORONTO (2006) *Imagine a Toronto… Strategies for a Creative City*. Toronto: City of Toronto.

26. BELL, A. and Stolarick, K. (2008) *Funding to Arts and Cultural Organizations by the City of Toronto, 1990-2008*. Toronto: Martin Prosperity Institute.

The authors are more categorical when it comes to the need to assert the unique and specific character of Toronto. They thus support the idea that a "Brand Toronto" movement must develop as an identity if the city is to attract tourists, interest international buyers of cultural goods and services as well as investors and financiers and if it is to engender a form of pride and "increased morale" in Toronto's creators. Their conclusion will surprise many: "An important element of creating brand Toronto is distinguishing it from 'Brand Ontario' and 'Brand Canada'".[27] These other brands stem from a different logic and pursue other goals. These perspectives have the important support of financial institutions and civil society associations. In that field and so many others, the Ontarian society reaps the benefits of an important and tightly woven fabric of cultural associations. *Tissée serrée*, as we say in Quebec.

TONY COMPER

Past president and chief executive officer at BMO Financial Group, Tony Comper is a proud Torontonian. He attended some of its schools, of which the De La Salle College and the St. Michael's College and worked at many of its most important institutions, such as the Canadian Friends of Simon Wiesenthal Centre for Holocaust Studies, St. Michael's hospital's Li Ka Shing Knowledge Institute and the University of Toronto, whose board he chaired. He also headed a big fundraising campaign for the University. In June of 2008, Comper spoke to the members of the Toronto Board of Trade at their annual general meeting. Of all the available topics, he chose to evoke Toronto's Next Leap Forward, or, in his words still, Toronto's "cultural renaissance".[28]

> As someone who watched, with ever-growing pleasure, as Toronto evolved from a "provincial" city, and all that term implied, into a global capital, all in (roughly) the 40-year space of a biblical generation. ... In the opening moments of the 21st Century, we filed notice that along with Toronto's other credentials for global city-hood, we could now lay claim to being cultural leaders as well.
>
> Maybe it's true that it takes more than "physical plants" to make a city into a cultural leader, but I know I am not alone in saying it could not have happened without the building

---

27. *Idem*, p. 7.

28. COMPTER, T. "Everybody's City: Toronto's Next Leap Forward", *Notes for remark at the annual general meeting of the Toronto Board of Trade*, June 2008.

boom that has given us an all-new Four Seasons Centre for the Performing Arts and Ontario College of Art & Design, spectacular additions to the Royal Ontario Museum and the Art Gallery of Ontario, and the dazzling makeovers of the National Ballet School and the Royal Conservatory of Music.

With these "Big Six" (to borrow a description from the Star's Christopher Hume) we have achieved the kind of critical mass that makes it possible for us to do what a growing number of us believe we ought to be doing next... which is helping Toronto transform into a new kind of city altogether, not just "worldclass" or "global" but both of those and more. I'm talking about the "creative city" that today is well within both our reach and our grasp now that we've turned ourselves into a state-of-the-art 21st Century cultural capital.

... When it comes to creating the first creative city, we have another special advantage—unique, in fact, unto ourselves. You know what I mean. Diversity.

There is literally a whole world out there, within a few dozen kilometres of this room, where many hundreds of thousands of people speaking 100 languages and dialects and brimming with ideas, have voted their confidence in our special part of Canada. These newcomers and their children and their children's children are the future of Toronto. A half-century or so from now, they'll be the concerned people meeting in rooms like this, to talk about their beloved Toronto and (maybe) what they need to do to make their fellow citizens' lives more fulfilling.

Toronto has come a long way since Jane Jacobs came to town and set us on the path toward the creative city of Richard Florida's dreams and ambitions. If she made us what we are today, her legacy is now making us what we must and will become tomorrow.

"Brand Toronto" obviously gives rise to real commitments!

Cultural gateway

Elected Toronto's 64th mayor on October 25th, 2010, Rob Ford is the remote successor of William Lyon Mackenzie, the revolutionary leader that occupied the same position in 1834. His election generated deep concern in the cultural milieu of the city and the province. The mobilization is immediate and the strategy is efficient. How are we to preserve the assets it had acquired and maintain its momentum? How are we it to counter the contractionary tendencies of Toronto administration's new boss?

Between the existing policy, the teams of civil servants in place and the new administration, a gateway was created; the Creative Capital Advisory Council, charged with updating the city's cultural plan. Michael Thompson, Chair of the City of Toronto's Economic Development Committee, tabled its recommendations while reaffirming the links between culture and the economy, saying that the former is a catalyst of the latter, one that "we can and must maximize". These recommendations are likely, in his opinion, to "help strengthen Toronto's economy and enhance our competitive advantage on the world stage".[29]

Deft presentation of the synergy between the new administration's preoccupations, especially the importance it places on the economy, and the orientation of cultural actions for the past decade in Toronto, the Advisory Council's report aims at strengthening the latter. It bears the signatures of three respected personalities: Jim Prentice, former federal minister now Vice-Chair at CIBC, Karen Kain, Artistic Director of the National Ballet of Canada and Robert J. Foster, CEO of Capital Canada. The Council was advised by heavy weights in all things cultural in Toronto: Cameron Bailey, of TIFF, Nichole Anderson of Business for the Arts, Richard Florida of the Martin Prosperity Institute, among others. The report lays down its choices and recommendations in a clearly stated frame of reference. Creativity is inherent to men and women, and exercising that capacity is what animates this city, participates in the quality of life and contributes to its economic development and to quality human resources coming to Toronto.

For these reasons, the city must maintain its investments in the domain, even increase them; so must the business community, foundations, organizations and associations dedicated to culture. The city must do more, notably by coordinating all these assets in order to position Toronto as a cultural capital likely to take its place in global cultural competitiveness. That is especially sensible economically when one knows that creative industries are creates twice as many jobs as financial, medical and biotechnology industries and that "it employs six times more workers than Ontario's aero-

---

29. CITY OF TORONTO (2011) *Creative Capital Gains: An Action Plan for Toronto,* Report from the Creative Capital Advisory Council. Toronto: City of Toronto.

space industry"[30] and roughly as many as the automotive sector. For those who doubt these numbers, the Council reminds that for every dollar the city invested in culture in 2009, cultural organizations were able to leverage $17.75; in that wake, the private sector invests 5.5 times the amounts put in by the city, that is the equivalent of the cumulated contributions of the three levels of government. All in all, from 2000 to 2010, the public take in culture in Toronto reached $335 million while that of the private soared to one billion dollars. Any back-tracking from the public sector would provoke a proportional reduction from the private sector. Such is the true dimension of the city's cultural action. It laid the foundations of the impressive upgrade witnessed at Toronto's main cultural institutions these past years. The city's cultural policy is thus framed by the Advisory Council and apparently protected from those who consider it a senseless luxury.

JOHN RALSTON SAUL

In the spacious living room of his residence in the heart of Toronto, John Ralston Saul greets us with that mix of enthusiasm, originality and distance that characterizes him so well. If he expresses himself with assurance, he often does so in the interrogative way "intellectuals should adopt", he says. His week was long and busy. He's just back from Moncton where he received an honorary degree and he was, just before we met him that day, partaking in the International Festival of Authors. In the coming days, he will travel to Senegal where, as President of Pen International, he would meet African writers and members of the organization that promotes literature and defends freedom of expression.

He settles on a small right chair in front of a superb painting representing Louis Riel and his companion Gabriel Dumont, an extension of his book A Fair Country. To his great surprise, the book did not stir controversy when it was published, even if it unveils all the bushwah that has always coated the conventional Canadian discourse on Indigenous people. The book's thesis is known.

> We as a people drew a significant part of our inspiration
> from Indigenous civilizations, especially when it comes
> to peace, fairness and governance. Here's what really lies
> at the heart of our history, of the Canadian mythology,
> English and French alike. If we could use a language to

---

30. *Idem*, p.6.

embrace that history, we would feel something like a great relief. We'd discover a remarkable power to act and be true to ourselves.

John is a storyteller. And he tells real stories. He offers us a fine and complex analysis of Toronto's cultural evolution, although "it is not my hometown", he specifies. He is not one of those which splits time and points to a precise breaking point between colonial times and the moment of cultural assertion. John is a Bergsonian, mindful of what remains and what changes at the same time. That day, the story he shares with us is one of creative evolution.

> We come from a world where there was more culture than institutions to host that culture. Suddenly, we have institutions. Seven major physical elements, rather well conceived (except the ROM) popped up in the city in just a few years. Even Paris or London would be proud of that. The importance of culture has become visible for what it is in itself, for the economy, for jobs. It is a huge industry here.

> But we are also the heirs of Toronto's Arts & Letters Club, which was at the heart of creation for more than a century. In the beautiful St. George's Hall at 14 Elm Street, the institution is still very active. In the past, the Group of Seven has debated its hypotheses there; U of T academics have debated the modern theory of communication, bearing the signatures of Innis, Frye, Carpenter, McLuhan, and which since has taken the world by storm. They have shown, among other things, that western linear thinking could not represent the mutations of the world. Toronto is also the city of Glenn Gould.

> The city is becoming ever more exciting with the arrival of people from the world over. If the occidental notion of a nation founded on race ever existed here, and I believe it did exist in some minds, it was being contradicted by the existing diversity which was constantly reinforced by an increasingly diversified immigration. Of course there were bad periods and unfortunate episodes, but the basic idea here was not racist. It had little to do with the mentality

and the doctrine of empires that used to control the world in a way never before seen: five little countries full of superior feelings and imposing their norms to the entire planet, or almost.

When I look at our history, and without denying the atrocities that were committed, I believe that the idea and reality of diversity were in the end dominant. Between 1900 and 1920, we received more immigrants than today. Not proportionally but in absolute numbers! The settlement of western Canada accentuated the country's diversity and since the war, that movement and that quality have kept blossoming, especially in Ontario. Fact worth noting, the newcomers are widely greeted by Ontarians themselves issued from immigration. Suddenly, people are no longer scared. They began to enjoy that city of difference, that different city. They're proud of themselves.

Today, we greet the equivalent of 1 per cent of our population every year and 85% of newcomers become citizens in less than 5 years. Furthermore, in Toronto, we observe that 50% of professionals intermarry. That situation is unparalleled in the world. It doesn't stem from our British or French roots. This non-racial approach is very similar to the Indigenous ways of doing things. We freed ourselves from the domination of the Orange Order and from some Catholic factions, from the racism that Europe can't shake itself away from.

Finally, this city of proprietors is not centralized. It is really a city of neighbourhoods, to which these homeowners are attached. This situation feeds a powerful sense of belonging. We've witnessed that feeling in tense or critical situations such as the Spadina Expressway crisis, a moment when Torontonians refused to see their city destroyed. They were facing corrupted promoters and powerful interest groups, but the neighbourhood associations federated under the leadership of William Kilbourn, David Crombie and the likes. The project was abandoned by Premier Bill Davis and the revolutionaries finally brushed with power at City Hall. This episode of Toronto's history has given a better shape to neighbourhood associations.

Today, Toronto hosts, supports and benefits from great cultural activities whose international reach is certain. TIFF and the International Festival of Authors are just two examples. Plus, this city now is now the home of many internationally-recognized authors, many of them having come from elsewhere and quickly showcased their talent here and abroad. The first came from the Caribbean and then from all over the world. As a consequence of these evolutions Toronto also became a great literary city. Montreal, I feel, is in the same situation.

John is right to link culture and diversity and to declare that the idea and reality of the latter ended up being dominating forces. Such is, indeed, the glowing centre of the Ontarian society's historical experience. That experience is not only the sum of particular situations but also a place where things occur, where people meet, which opens up on a complete score that could not exist without them.

TORONTO AND THE OTHERS

Take 1: Audiovisual

Even if Toronto's leadership position can hardly be denied, Ontario's cultural scene is also well alive in all the regions of the great province. Our nomenclature "Toronto and the others" is more methodological than qualitative. It does nothing to offend our Ontarian friends living outside the GTA; quite the contrary. We thus use it as nomenclature for our argument as well as a way to best account for the distinct and often complementary realities between the cultural offer in the metropolis and that of other Ontarian cities and communities.

Ontario is unquestionably the country's admiral-ship in terms of TV and movie production, no matter the genre. These productions are in part guaranteed by the private producers, the telecommunications companies owned by the big media groups and the Canadian Broadcasting Corporation. They receive financial support from the Canada Media Fund and from the provincial government and the City of Toronto's support programs. All indicators converge. Headquarters of the main independent producers and the big audiovisual groups in the country,[31] Toronto accounted for 39 per cent of Canadian production in 2009-10, which represents a total of $5 billion. Since 2003, industries in that domain were regrouped by Film Ontario, a large consortium of 50,000 members from all branches of the field that promotes the province as a world-class movie and TV production centre. Film Ontario also has the mandate to influence public policies that affect the industry, including digital production. The body benefits in all these functions from the vast network of services and contacts of OMDC, a governmental agency that serves the interests of publishing, of interactive digital media, of the music industry and of movie and television.

With regard to TV production, Ontario ranks first with 45 per cent of Canadian production and 61 per cent of the internal production of television networks.

When it comes to movie productions and foreign ones that are made in Canada, one must look at a longer period due to the highly fluctuating situation between years. However, in the past years, the province has seen its share grow continuously. Hence, in 2007-08, 37 per cent of the total Canadian movie and TV production and 32 per cent of foreign work and services offered in the country were so in Ontario. This meant more than 40,000 people with directly or indirectly-related jobs and an economic activity of $1.9 billion.[32]

This position has historical reasons and current ones, of which an aggressive tax credit policy by Ontario's government that covers 35 per cent of spending on labour force hired in the province and 40 per cent in the cases of producers who are working on their first production. An additional 10 per cent are granted when the shoot takes place outside the GTA.

That policy bore fruit. In 20 years, from 1990 to 2010, Canadian and foreign productions in Ontario multiplied by 6 and 3 respectively. As of 1970, Canadian cinema, including Ontario's, slowly emerged. Federal funding

---

31. CBC Television, réseau public propriété de la Canadian Broadcasting Corporation; CTV et CTV Two, réseaux privés propriété de Bell Média, succursale de Bell Corporation qui opère depuis la capitale ontarienne même si son siège social est toujours officiellement situé au Québec; Global, réseau privé appartenant à Shaw Media; Citytv, un réseau privé appartenant à Rogers Communications et diffusant en Ontario et dans les trois provinces de l'Ouest; Omni Television, un groupe de cinq télévisions multiculturelles appartenant à Rogers Media; TVO-TFO, le réseau de télévision éducative de l'Ontario.

32. CANADIAN FILM AND TELEVISION PRODUCTION ASSOCIATION (2008) *Rapport économique sur la production cinématographique et télévisuelle au Canada*. Montréal : Canadian Film and Television Production Association, p.14.

and tax credit programs, to which were added provincial government interventions, allowed for the production of a growing number of movies. But
the absence of distribution and promotion networks weighs heavily on the
industry. However, despite these obstacles and with the American competition, Ontarian filmmakers managed to impose themselves and their
work, building a Canadian audience. Some gained international fame:
Norman Jewison, David Cronenberg, Atom Egoyan, Deepa Metha, Sturla
Gunnarsson and a few others.

The images are from Ontario, but so are the editorial policies, the scenarios,
the programming schedules, the executive jobs in that field and in others—
in the thousands—governance and budgets, the rumours and the audience
wars... And the critics, from its capital which hosts the country's most influential daily newspapers and 70 per cent of Canadian magazines in English.

The CBC is also from Toronto and, bound by its national mandate, has
regional antennas from Sea to Sea. As illustrated by its 2011-16 five-year
plan, it always redefines itself in order to be more Canadian, an admission it
may not be so as much as it should except with regard to the news, its main
quality and one of its rare genuine merits. The rest wobbles between mass
broadcasts of American productions and local ones which, even if they lack
an audience, apparently respect Canadian content quotas. Culture should
normally be at the heart of its programming, its original signature, its essential contribution. It is almost absent from its TV network but thankfully
still discernible on its radio programming.

Take II: Publishing

Ontario also dominates the field of Canadian publishing.[33] Indeed, the
province is home to more than 50 per cent of the country's publishers, an
industry that produces 16,000 books annually and generates $1 billion in
revenues while supporting close to 6,000 jobs. With close to a third of publishers present in its regions, the Ontarian industry remains mostly installed
in the GTA, which counts close to 50 publishing houses. Some are very
old, more than 100 years old in the cases of McClelland & Stewart and the
University of Toronto Press, whose catalogues are genuine thesauri on the
intellectual and cultural evolution of the country. Others are more recent
and successful, with a sure influence on the evolution of Ontario's society.
One thinks of the House of Anansi Press, where many Ontarian writers

33. *A Strategic Study for the Book Publishing Industry in Ontario.* Toronto: Castledale Inc,
11 September 2008, p.10.

got their first chance and where translations of Quebec works are regularly published. We also think, among many others, of Playwrights Canada Press, which highlighted the works of a great many Ontarian and Canadian playwrights; of Shumack Press, specialized in feminine and feminist literature and the numerous publishers of children's books, a niche Ontario specializes in, for its own market and for the international market. Some Torontonian houses specialize in the distribution of works from authors that immigrated to Canada; such is the case of Antonio Delfonso's Guernica, of the South Asian Review, which publishes a periodical and a few titles from Asian authors, of Groundwood Books, without forgetting *Mosaic Press* in Oakville. Finally, Toronto's community of publishers also includes the Éditions du GREF, 1 of 9 francophone publishing houses in Ontario.

CAROLYN WOOD

Brushing contradiction aside, the Executive Director of the Association of Canadian Publishers starts our interview by evoking the oldest publishing house in the world, the Cambridge University Press, whose model endures to this day. She then disserts for a while on the constant changes affecting the industry she's watching over in Canada. In a rejuvenated building at 174 Spadina Avenue in Toronto, Carolyn Wood wanders through the 16th century and returns calmly but surely to the requirements of the present.

Her association has 130 members across the country, a good half of those in Ontario. Mrs. Wood's message is clear. Canadian publishers control a 25 per cent slice of the market and their profit margins are extremely slim, not much more than the equivalent of financial support they get by Ottawa and Queen's Park. The lion's share goes to the multinationals of the industry, to Random House, controlled by German interests, or Penguin Canada, by British ones, as well as to the big American publishers that have invaded every sector, including educational publishing. They have considerable means to promote their product, even if it means mobilizing Oprah Winfrey or other great relay-readers. If there was a time at which these publishers were working with a few Canadian authors and integrating them in the publicity of all their titles, such is no longer the case. Canadian literary works have become very little visible except for a short period if they benefit from the promotion that comes with an award.

> The situation is not encouraging. Little publishers are disappearing and even medium-sized companies are fewer

and fewer. The capacity to self-publish and the requirements of the digital era increase their precariousness. Then, foreign domination and the concentration of distribution add to that fragility. Continued governmental support to the publishing sector constitutes rare good news. Without it, the industry would disappear without a doubt.

Carolyn Wood is a straight-talker and her worries are tangible. The situation she describes with passion and realism is even more troubling considering the fact that books occupy a real place in public space and that Ontario's libraries, such as Toronto's Public Library, are among the most visited in the world.

The book occupies a real place in Toronto's public space because of some recurring literary manifestations: the annual festival The Word on the Street, which mobilizes 250 exhibitors, about a same amount of authors and attracts 250,000 Torontonians; the International Festival of Authors which, in 2011, invited 190 writers on a tour of 17 Ontarian cities; the Toronto Book Fair and the Salon du livre francophone de Toronto, whose evocation reminds the long list of book fairs elsewhere in the province, particularly in Sudbury, Hearst, Brockville, Perth, London, Kingston, Elora and Norfolk, without forgetting the Ottawa Antiquarian Book Fair. Furthermore, Toronto is also home to a number of groups and associations in the field, like Access Copyright, the Association of Canadian Publishers of which we just spoke, the Canadian Children's Book Centre, the Writers' Union of Canada, Book Net Canada and the Canadian section of PEN International.

Take III: Libraries

Might as well admit it, meeting the people in charge of the Toronto Public Library, visiting its main branch and a few of its numerous other branches and conversing with its users were unforgettable experiences. So much for objectivity! As soon as he entered into office, the new ultraconservative mayor of the city, Rob Ford, suggested a 10 per cent reduction in the budget of that wonderful institution and the closing of some of its 99 branches. He even evoked its privatization! Seventy seven per cent of Torontonians surveyed were opposed to that measure. Writers such as Michael Ondaatje, Vincent Lam, Linwood Barclay and Susan Swan mobilized along with Margaret Atwood.[34] The famous novelist was joined by thousands of citizens, a good amount of them surely among her 290,000 Twitter followers at the time, and launched

---

34. LAM, V. "Modern citizens know a library's worth", *The Globe and Mail*, 31 août 2011.

a fierce offensive, like starving people blocking a food train. Not bad for a library. Like Napoleon's army in the Russian campaign, the mayor and his troops retreaded piteously.

For the moment, the most frequented public library network in the world for cities over two million immigrants is saved. In 2009, it received 17.5 million visitors, 8 million of them having stayed a while to use the facilities; it leant out 32 million books, CDs, DVDs, e-books, audio books and computers. Twenty three million people visited its website, 17 million consulted its database and close to 600,000 subscribed to its diverse programs; 300,000 kids and 7,000 elderly people listened to stories in twelve languages on telephone lines dedicated to that functions. Lastly, given the city's diversity, the library's collection has books in over 100 languages. Its cultural program is very significant, with 2,500 literary and artistic events taking place in 2010 and, that same year, 16,500 Torontonians attending meetings with Canadian and foreign writers such as Nino Ricci, Austin Clarke, Adrienne Clarkson, Jane Urquhart and Salman Rushdie.

In these harsh economic times, the library enriched its collection by 35,000 books on jobs and careers. According to these needs, it developed programs that were followed by 6,000 people, offered online services for that clientele and increased trainings to counter functional illiteracy.

The funding for this whole range of services essentially comes from the City of Toronto and, in a smaller share, the Ontarian and Canadian governments. The library can also count on the contribution of the Foundation that bears its name. Since its creation in 1998, that contribution totaled $57.8 million and the Toronto Public Library Foundation undertook a funding campaign, *Revitalize*, with the objective of investing an additional $10 million in the upkeep of the institution's facilities. Lisa Rochon, our great witness, visited some renovated branches and was simply seduced.[35]

Statistics undeniably show the strong link binding Torontonians to their library. That relationship is made richer by the multiple operations the institution is organizing each year: in April, Keep Toronto Reading, a full month of reading events in partnership with the Friends of Toronto Public Library collective—workshops, conferences, award ceremonies and the Book Lover's Ball at the Fairmont Royal York, attracting more than 500 people. A last example of its reach, since we can't name them all: when the Library asks for its users' opinions online, it can expect 5,000 answers in no time.

---

35. ROCHON, L. "New library architecture is a clear victory", *The Globe and Mail*, 14 avril 2009.

JANE PYPER

Everything seems light in the splendid house of knowledge, culture and social bonding that is the Reference Library, the network's main branch, at Yonge Street, just north of Bloor. All is white, from the high ceilings that look like the sculpted cells of a giant beehive to the vast storied spaces filled with abundant natural light. Designed by renowned architect Raymond Moriyama, the building is undergoing a makeover. $34 million are dedicated to that, the third of which is the result of a specific fundraiser. Despite the ongoing works, barely half an hour after it opened on that morning we visited, the great reading room is already half full and the computers are taken over by a clientele composed of youth and seniors, a crew hard and happy at work. This reference library also includes public services in genealogy, health, disability-related support and governmental information. For the past three years, Jane Pyper is at the head of that all-important public library network, in these atypical headquarters where aesthetics and functionality merge, where apparent calm and the wild requirements of such an organisation blend. She answers our curious interest with words that display self-assurance, satisfaction and precision.

> 55% of the citizens of this city are members of the library and 72% use the services it provides, a significant majority of them being young users. These numbers are 10 to 15% higher than the ones prevailing in America's big cities. You ask me why? There are many explanations.
>
> We have, in this country, a very ancient tradition of public libraries; it goes as far back as the 18th century. Furthermore, we encourage as much as possible immigrants and citizens that immigrated to visit the institution by reducing to the bare minimum the administrative paperwork for them to do so. They form a bigger share of our clientele than the Torontonian average. In our collections, services, programmes and all our activities, they find works, documents and tools to join the labour force, staff members that speak their languages and computer facilities at their disposal. We also celebrate their heritage and take great care to include them and their interests in our discussion groups. I would also add that our large number of branches means a greater access close to home or work for all Torontonians. Lastly, our library and its relays on all

the territory constitute one of the rare public institutions, if not the only one, that's open for everyone at all times and whose access is free due to the provisions of the Public Library Act. In great part anyways, these factors explain the loyalty of Toronto's citizens toward their public library, which is funded by the City of Toronto to the level of 93%.

In her big and unadorned office, Jane Pyper insists:

> We not only greet the new citizens who visit the library in big numbers. We also go and meet them in the communities. We have agents in our branches that work on that. We offer the classic services of a library but also access to cultural institutions thanks to the partnerships we developed with museums, the Opera, TIFF, playhouses... Some consider that a removal from what they consider our mandate. For us, these services are totally part of the cultural mission of our institution. The same goes for the transition toward the digital world and the support to creation it enables.

In that field, Toronto is no Ontarian exception. Four hundred twenty five municipalities, cities big and small, offer public library systems that they fund at a level of 95 per cent. We have seen and visited many and observed their importance for communities, neighbourhoods and their millions of users. We have witnessed the effervescence that animates them and the considerable effort put in to make them genuine houses of knowledge, culture, social cohesion and economic development as well as the advanced tools that are likely to strengthen their functions and mission.

We have chosen 10 of those establishments in so many cities, a non-scientific selection, to illustrate the vitality and modernity of this vast network.[36] Together, these 10 establishments had a budget that totaled $3 billion between 1998 and 2008. These important resources essentially come from local governments. In 2008-09, they welcomed 65 million visitors physically and 35 million via their websites. These visitors borrowed more than 85 million traditional or electronic documents.[37]

---

36. Besides the Toronto Public Library, we have selected libraries in Ottawa, Mississauga, Hamilton, Brampton, London, Windsor, Kitchener-Waterloo, Burlington and Sudbury.
37. FEDERATION OF ONTARIO PUBLIC LIBRARIES (2010) 2010 Annual Report. Toronto: Federation of Ontario Public Libraries.

Some of these establishments are quite old. The Windsor library is one of them, created in 1855 following a petition signed by 542 citizens. Ottawa's library is also more than centenary. Others are more recent, such as Mississauga's, which recently celebrated its twentieth anniversary. The buildings that house them are often beautiful, the ones we visited in Windsor, Mississauga and Hamilton among them. According to the strategic plan of the Ottawa library, a new central building is in the works...a welcome occasion to build something nice there as well! They share important preoccupation and act accordingly: they fight against illiteracy, they promote reading for the youth, offer adapted services to the elderly and serve the diverse Ontarian communities. Most of these establishments have multilingual collections, with French having its place. The website of the Mississauga library can be viewed in 52 languages and the institution promotes its World Language Collection; London's collection is available in 30 languages, plus a noteworthy French section.

Take IV: Museums

Considering the great number and quality of its museums and related institutions, Ontario ranks very first in Canada in that regard and also has an enviable situation when compared to the rest of the continent and the world for regions of the same age and size. Its most ancient museum institutions, real houses of memory, education and creation are barely a century-old, but some of them belong to the restricted circle of great global museums.

Everything that exists in that field in Ontario was built by 3 or 4 short generations. As was the case for TIFF, the expression "quixotic adventure" was often followed by another: "remarkable success". The 600 Ontario museums and related institutions are testament to that not only because of their numbers but also their qualities in Toronto and all over the province, as we have witnessed in London, Windsor, Hamilton, Kingston, Markham and Sudbury. Other proofs of that remarkable success are the scope and reliability of their initiatives, the strong support from public authorities, the private sector, foundations and citizens that constitute, after all, the growing number of their users. Finally, one last and significant testament to that success is the investment in the billions which, these past few years, contributed to the expansion and modernization of many Ontarian museums.

The Art Gallery of Hamilton

The Art Gallery of Hamilton (AGH) is born at the end of the 19th century thanks to a coalition of citizens from three associations: The Canadian Club, created in 1893, the City Art Association, in 1894, and the Art Students' League of Hamilton which dates back to 1895.[38] The museum will celebrate its 100th anniversary in 2014. After having moved many times, it settled definitely in its nice current location in 1997. In 2010, it welcomed 155,000 visitors in person and 57,000 more on its website; it offered education programs, conferences, creative workshops and showed art movies. These programs are similar to those offered in museums all over the provincial territory. The gallery has a budget of $10 million. As is the case for 275 other Ontarian institutions, the AGH has an endowment fund at the Ontario Arts Foundation which, since 1991, manages the assets granted by individuals, foundations, associations and private firms.

The gallery was enriched by numerous and significant gifts by will: the William Blair Bruce collection in 1906; that of W. A. Wood in 1928 and, among others, a selection of fine European paintings from the 19th century and assembled by Joey and Toby Tanenbaum. It organized great exhibits such as Jade, the Ultimate Treasure of Ancient China, which in 2001 drew more visitors in Hamilton than in Vancouver. There was Future Cities in 2004; Forging a Path: Quebec Women Artists 1900-1965 in a 2010 collaboration with the Montreal Museum of Fine Arts; The French Connection, the museum's 2011 theme that included exhibits such as Masters of French Realism and Passe-partout: A Century of Canadians in France. In the summer of 2010, the Art Gallery of Hamilton (AGH) exhibited the works of Jesse Boles, immense and luminous photographs of the Great Lakes. Impressive for a city of 500,000 that has 19 other museums and related institutions such as the respected McMaster Museum of Art.

These institutions are diverse in nature. They could be linked to heritage, as in the case of the Griffin house, modest in its wood trappings but vital in its function as a relay of the underground railroad used by African American slaves that were fleeing the neighbouring US at the end of the 19th century. There's also the superb Dundurn Castle, built by Allan MacNab, entrepreneur, board member, politician hostile to the 1837 Rebellion and Prime Minister of Canada from 1854 to 1856. They could also be linked to military tradition, like the Battlefield House and the Military Museum, rich in documents and artefacts linked to the War of 1812, the 1837 Rebellion and the American Civil War. Lastly, these institutions can be of an industrial nature, such as the

---

38. FOX, R. and INGLES, G. (1989) *The Art Gallery of Hamilton, Seventy Five Years (1914-1989)*. Hamilton: The Gallery.

Hamilton Museum of Steam and Technology, housed in an impressive stone building covering the country's most ancient water pumps.

This cultural detour via Hamilton calls for an explanation. We wanted to demonstrate with a precise example that culture in Ontario is not all contained in Toronto. It breathes abundantly on the entire territory. It finds solid institutional, political and associative support in the regions, as well consent and participation from Ontarians that live there and display deep attachment to their heritage and an interest for the cultural offer in their communities. We could have chosen other cities: Mississauga and its 6 museums, London which has 14, the remarkable London Regional Art and Historical Museums and an interesting archeology museum among them, Kleinburg and its famous Canadian Art Collection, Windsor and its beautiful Art Gallery, founded in 1943, along with its six other related institutions, Kitchener and Sudbury, which count 20 and 5 respectively.

THEMUSEUM, in the former, is dedicated to art and electronic technologies. Finally, we could have picked either Kingston, also known as the capital of museums with 22 such institutions or Ottawa, which unabashedly shows off its cultural overweight with 36 museums and related institutions, some with a deserved international reputation.

We could have introduced the Ontarian museums according to a different classification, choose thematically, for instance: museums dedicated to First Nations[39], to pioneers,[40] to diverse communities[41] and to science.[42] Due to their singularity, some are harder to categorize, like the Niagara Falls History Museum, which traces the history of that spectacular natural site which is Canada's most visited.

Toronto: 123 museums

Recounting only confirms it: Toronto indeed has 123 museums and related institutions! Superb, renowned, some preserve their treasures in pal-

---

39. Withney's Algonquin Logging Museum.
40. O'Hara's Mill Pioneer Village and Delhi's Windham Township Pioneer Museum.
41. Amherstburg's North American Black Historical Museum, North Buxton's Buxton National Historic Site and Museum, Richmond Hill's Canadian Museum of Hindu Civilization, Maple's Amici Museum & Italian Canadian Interpretive Centre and Scarborough's Chinese Cultural Centre.
42. Waterloo's Earth Sciences Museum, Guelph's Arboretum and Oshawa's Canadian Automotive Museum.

aces newly-expanded and reconfigured by famous architects. The other are often hidden in that vertical city. Together, they form memory links that trace the city's history, show its diversity, its relation to nature, science and art created here or elsewhere in the world. It also shows the way it belongs to the dramas and joys of the human family. A real window as well for creations and inventions of today such as digital art and installations.

Here we are at 82 Bond Street, facing the little house of William Lyon Mackenzie, head of the 1837 Rebellion after having been the first mayor of the city. There, in Toronto's north, you have Fort York, huge complex dedicated to the city's history, which can also be learned at the Market Gallery, the Black Creek Pioneer Village and in other places of recollection for its diverse communities, Jewish[43], Japanese,[44] African[45] and others.

And here is the other dimension of evolution, the one showing science and technology at work: the Allan Gardens Conservatory, the Textile Museum of Canada, the Redpath Sugar Museum, the Canadian Museum of Health and Medecine, the Canadian Air & Space Museum, the Bata Shoe Museum and the Ontario Science Centre, inaugurated 40 years ago. This last one greeted more than 40 million visitors, has 72,000 members and, in 2009, was visited by more than one million visitors physically and five million virtually. That same year, four of its exhibits were seen in China, Europe and the United States. The institution has a strong reputation here and abroad as was shown by its hosting in 2008 of the 5th Science Centre World Congress.[46] This reputation is also that of the two major art museums that add to Toronto's own reputation as a "cultural city".

The Royal Ontario Museum

At the very heart of the metropolis, the Royal Ontario Museum (ROM) shows the diversity of world cultures and that, complementary, of the planet's natural diversity: the dinosaurs' age and North Asia's archaeology, biodiversity and human ancestors, the wealth of planet Earth and those of China, Korea, Japan, India, Byzantium, Greece, Rome, the Middle East and much more. Welcome to one of North America's most important temples of the multiple pasts of mankind and of the little planet that has been, is

---

43. The Beth Tzedec's Reuben & Helene Dennis Museum.

44. The Japan Foundation.

45. The Underground Railroad Museum of Toronto.

46. ONTARIO SCIENCE CENTRE (2009), *At the Forefront, 2008/09 annual report*. Toronto: Ontario Science Centre.

and might be its habitat for a long time still. Monumental, literally, the Museum's galleries succeed each other and exhibit, as the streets of Toronto do, the multiple faces of our common humanity.

A paradox, this century-old museum is also a recent invention. The old baroque and Victorian building was expanded and completely reinvented in 2007 by celebrated architect Daniel Libeskind, which enveloped it in a steel, aluminium and glass ribbon, that famous crystal addition which, ever since its appearance in Toronto's sky, is sparking controversy. For some, it now belongs to the select group of the world's nicest museums. Others feel that addition is a great but failed endeavour. That reinvention cost $244 million, 30 of those a donation from Michael Lee Chin, this Canadian citizen who immigrated from Jamaica. One has to pinch oneself while reading the institution's 2009/10 annual report. Thirty seven foundations, firms and individuals supported the new ROM with contributions ranging from 1 to 5 million dollars; 48 more chipped in between $250,000 and $1 million; added to that comes a multitude of more modest donations.

Six million objects identified in French and English when they are on the exhibit floors, wonders of abundance such as the magnificent Chinese textiles, translucent Iranian china, refined African sculptures and jewelry worn by Inca chieftains. Footprints to follow, abundant as well, to go on a trip around the world by choosing the era you want to travel to, be it prehistoric, from Canada's past or Europe's modern times. Here you have other galleries, interactive this time, and remarkable exhibits such as the one that brought to Toronto the Dead Sea Scrolls: Words that Changed the World. Some, closer to today's reality, show Bollywood posters and memorabilia from the 50s to the 80s, or landscapes, subtle and beautiful, captured with iPhones or iPads. Prestigious partnerships: the Centre Pompidou, the Withney Museum of American Art, Egypt's Supreme Council of Antiquities, the National Museum of the American Indian, London's Victoria and Albert Museum and many more. Ontarian partnerships as well, with the province's museums intelligently relaying the offer of the great Toronto museum.[47]

More than a million people came to lay eyes on its wonders in 2009/10, to participate in workshops, attend conferences and meet artists and other celebrities. Thousands more follow its activities on social networks, the Twitters, Facebooks and Youtubes of the web. The ROM opens its doors

47. Data concerning the ROM come from the 2009/10 Annual Report.

when the city is in the midst of festivities, sometimes even initiating the celebrations. Caribana, Nuit Blanche and TIFF, among others, are now accustomed to collaborating with the ROM. New publics also get involved: youth, citizens that are less well-off, thanks to a partnership with the Toronto Public Library and United Way, immigrants also, benefiting from an intelligent program from the Institute for Canadian Citizenship (ICC), brought to life by Adrienne Clarkson and John Ralston Saul. In the October 4, 2011 edition of *The Globe and Mail*, Dawn Walton tells of the story of Darshan Harrinanan's family, happy beneficiary of that program headed by the former Governor General.[48]

In their native Trinidad, Darshan Harrinanan and his wife decide to immigrate to Canada with their three young children. Their project panned out and they settle in. Their challenge, to use Darshan's own words, "is not about losing your identity, but adding your identity to what is the fabric of Canada". That is no simple task and, as we've established at length earlier in this book, the adventure is filled with risks and hopes. All the gestures of the host country count in the eyes of newcomers that are going through a world of change and exploring their new societal environment. ICC's gesture toward new citizens is real and welcoming, innovative and meaningful. A gift, the simple gift of a yearly pass to a wide range of cultural treasures and parks; that is, an encouragement to explore, discover and deepen their knowledge of their new environment, to mingle with the crowds, to create common references and memories. That simple card opens multiple visible and invisible doors. Because of it, Harrinanan, now a commercial analyst at U of T, and his family visited some 20 places of culture for free, the ROM among them, in the first year after becoming Canadian citizens. "More than 1,000 of Canada's cultural institutions and parks from coast-to-coast-to-coast" thus freely open their doors to new Canadians. What a magical idea!

The Art Gallery of Ontario

Among the architectural attractions of Toronto's cultural district, the Art Gallery of Ontario (AGO), along with the ROM, occupy the very top. On Dundas Street West, between Spadina and University, it rises, imperial, dressed in its new theatrical garments by Frank Gehry. Less visible, two nonetheless important additions in the Weston Family Learning

---

48. WALTON, Dawn "Helping new Canadians feel at home: Popular program gives new Canadians free access to cultural institutions", *The Globe and Mail*, October 4th 2011.

Centre, which offers art initiation programs and a vast range of studios, and second, a new wing dedicated to contemporary art, completed the initial spaces of the Museum. Architecture buffs and national and international critics are unanimous: "Frank Gehry managed to do something exceptionally important in 2008". That was The New Yorker critique Paul Goldberger.[49] The Globe and Mail freed up 5 superbly-illustrated pages to the Museum's re-opening. That was the photography. Lisa Rochon took care of the radiography in a gem of a text. "Frank Gehry has an appetite for more. His architecture craves abundance... He has created an exhilarating work of architecture that honours the art it houses, gives new life to Toronto's downtown, and confirms Gehry's stature as one of the world's great creative geniuses".[50]

Started in 2000 and completed in 2008, the institution's transformation added a surface of 50 per cent for exhibits and created immense and sober niches for its geography collections from Africa, Oceania and South America. It also offered a statuesque gallery, the Galeria Italiana and gigantic arches that open up on baroque ribbons that conceal large suspended staircases inside and outside the building. All these beauties bathe in the skylight. Lastly, a spectacular glass façade, 183 metres long and 21 metre high reflects the urban life that surrounds it. It is impossible to remain indifferent to the changing beauty of the permanent spectacle offered by that gigantic mirror. The little colourful houses that face it and that, slightly misshapen, can be seen on the Museum's face. The hurried pedestrians and slower-paced groups, the natural and artificial lights that make it vary permanently. In its own right, this architectural masterpiece belongs to the Museum's vocation. It is a major piece of its collection, a kinetic art work that is permanently displayed.

Visitors to the AGO come for its collection made of 80,000 pieces, also identified bilingually, for its exhibits and other offered activities: educational programs, workshops, libraries, publications, resident artists and animations that are decided by the AGO Youth Council.

That remarkable work is first of all that of an architect from Toronto whose reputation is established the world over. It is also the work of the institution's leaders, its board and its fund-raising committee. It is last but not least the work of a significant number of Ontarians that contributed concretely. An excerpt of the AGO's 2008-09 annual report, the following quote reminds us

49. GOLDBERGER, Paul "Architecture's ten best of 2008", The New Yorker, December 2008.
50. ROCHON, L. "A monumental moment", The Globe and Mail, November 8th 2008.

of that fact and undeniably illustrates their commitment toward culture and its place in society. In a reference to the inauguration of the new Art Gallery of Ontario, the President of the Board and the institution's Director wrote:

> On that historic day in November, the Gallery also announced that the Transformation AGO Campaign had raised a total of $300 million, surpassing its goal of $76 million—an unprecedented success for the AGO and the community that supported it. And thousands did, including forty seven generous donors who contributed $1 million or more. The Thomson family also continued its remarkable support of the AGO. In addition to the extraordinary gift of the Thomson Collection, the family donated $100 million to the AGO's redesign.

Spectacular, these results are the consequences of numerous partnerships between the Museum, other Toronto institutions, important cultural events that enliven it and finally, Torontonians themselves. Among others, and we have mentioned some of them before in the case of the ROM , the Toronto Public Library, the Institute for Canadian Citizenship, the Luminato Festival, Black History Month and the big party that is Nuit Blanche, which alone brought 16,000 people to the Museum in 12 hours during the 2007-08 edition!

"Art matters", proclaim the institution's leaders. They can't be disappointed by the answer Torontonians and Ontarians give them. Part of Ontario's Ministry of Tourism and Culture, a third of AGO's funding comes from the provincial government and two thirds by private donations, by its own activities and by an endowment fund. Twenty one foundations have brought their financial support to the Museum in 2009-10.

900 volunteers and 875,500 visitors, twice as much as before its transformation, have all animated, supported and participated in some of the museum's activities in 2009-10. They have seen parts of its vast Canadian and European collections, that which was donated to the institution by Ken Thompson and the AGO's unique collection of photographs. They were able to contemplate the most important collection of works by Henry Moore, famed British sculptor. Finally, in the Toronto now gallery, they admired the work of Will Munro, as well as large exhibits like King Tut : The Golden King and the Great Pharaohs. In previous years, the AGO showed Andy Warhol/Supernova: Stars, Deaths and Disasters in 2006,

Emily Carr: New Perspectives on a Canadian Icon, in 2007 and Maharaja: The Splendour of India's Royal Courts in 2010.

Spectacular, these investments transform ancient museums in Toronto, participate in programming reviews and in the development of their links with citizens. For AGO Director, Matthew Teitelbaum, that "signals a palpable gravitational shift. Canada's most populous and cosmopolitan city now has a clearly defined campus of thought... redefining it as a city driven not principally by commerce but by culture and creativity. In this arena, we can be world-beaters".[51]

Take V: Performing arts and folk arts

From the great classical music of Mozart or Bartok to the Kompa Zouk Festival celebrating the world's créolité, from the theatre scene that shows Robert Lepage's *Lipsynch* in Toronto and Shakespeare in Stratford, from the three opera companies installed in Toronto[52] to the National Ballet of Canada; from both jazz festivals launched 25 years ago, in Toronto and in The Beaches to those that bring wind orchestra to Etobicoke, drummers to Mississauga and heritage lovers to London without forgetting the popular musicals which, between New York and London, make a stop in Toronto... Needless to repeat that Ontario's scene is proliferating.

Since the 80s, cultural activities have multiplied, their offer was strengthened and programming, like the audacious and cosmopolitan one at Toronto's Harbourfront centre, was enriched on all the Ontarian territory. It is impossible to give a good account of such abundance.

How are we indeed to assess the activities of each of the 125 theatres in the province, even if 61 of them are accounted for in the GTA? How are we to assess and fully report on the activities of more than 68 orchestras, 32 of which received OAC grants in 2011-12, among them the Toronto Symphony Orchestra, founded in 1922 by Luigi von Kunits, an Austrian immigrant?[53] How is one to evaluate and give a full account of the whopping 230 festivals supported by Celebrate Ontario and the 157 that were funded by the Arts Council for 2011-12? The same question applies to the 237 non-profit professional dance, music and theatre companies that received support from

---

51. MILROY, S. "Arts person of the year: Matthew Teitelbaum", *The Globe and Mail*, December 27th.
52. Canadian Opera Company, Opera Atelier et Opera in Concert.
53. The Toronto Symphony Orchestra had 225,000 subscribers in 2010. Since 2004, under Peter Oundjian, its current conductor, it inaugurated the *New Creations Festival* series, dedicated to contemporary orchestral music.

the OAC as well and whose performances were seen by 5 million spectators in 2010?[54] We had to make a choice.

Some of these cultural activities deserve a brief reminder due to their deep anchoring in Ontarian society or for what they teach us on Ontarians' relationship with culture.

First among these is the Canadian National Exhibition, difficult to categorize but certainly venerable. In 2011, it held its 133rd edition! Each year since 1879, on the shores of Lake Ontario, this event displays a galore of genres: fun fairs, blues, soul and pop music shows, circus, contests and tombola, fine cuisine, with the continent's best chefs used to attend. In 2011, the event offered 500 attractions, greeted 700 exhibitors to satisfy more than one million visitors that cross the great Hollywoodian archway to take pleasure in these elusive and fantastic worlds.

The Caribana parade also belongs to this category. First major public demonstration showing the diversity of Ontario, it deploys for the first time in 1967, as circumstantial contribution to the centenary celebrations of the country. Its success was immediate and considerable. The celebration strikes the imagination of Torontonians who discover a hidden part of themselves, exuberant, talented, colourful and noisy, all dance and music. Their city could therefore also be festive and Torontonians are spreading in the urban space in a friendly contagious! It owes its discovery to a minority who chose to be in their uniqueness and creativity. Toronto discovers diverse and happy to be. In the wake of Caribana, other ethnic communities out of the closet and open to all public performances of their original typical: Hispanic Fiesta in 1981; Hina Matsuri the following year; Afrofest in 1990; the Canadian Aboriginal festival in 1992; the Toronto International Dragon Boat Race Festival in 1999; the Brazilfest en 2002; the Diwali Fiesta in 2006 and many more still, such as the Sri Lankan Festival, the Franco-Fête and the Arab Canadian Heritage Festival.

For nearly half a century, Caribana is permanently inscribed on the agenda of cultural and festive Queen City. People come from everywhere and in the hundreds of thousands to attend the annual parade, applaud the 10,000 performers and participate in the largest North American festival celebrating the cultures of the Caribbean region.

In their particular niche, the new Harvest Festival in June, the Wines of Niagara in September and Icewine production in January celebrate secular modernization in the early 80s following the replacement of native vines

---

54. Meeting with the direction of the Ontario Arts Council and exchanges with Kathryn Townshend.

and vines imported by its impressive growth since. Today, vineyards cover 15,000 acres between the Niagara Escarpment and Lake Ontario. They feed over 100 producers and employ 6,000 workers. Gala evenings, concerts, visits to vineyards, seminars, lectures and tastings of course animate these festivals. We will say that it is disguised promotional campaigns, but they still attract 750,000 people: amateurs, collectors, and curious revelers who come to celebrate the wine in this beautiful region.

In the second category, major events more closely associated with culture deserve better than the few paragraphs that we pay.

Festivals

The Stratford Shakespeare Festival ranks first among these major events mainly because of the recognized and celebrated quality of its productions and its international reputation. People come for the natural beauty of the town of Stratford, for its tended parks and the rippling water that divides it, for its Victorian houses in an apparent barrier to the intrusion of ugliness in this haven of harmony. The poet James Reaney has celebrated its splendor in his *Twelve Letters to a Small Town*. People come here since 1953 to the continent's most famous theater festival, taking place in four rooms, totaling 3,466 seats that are always full from April to November.

The calm of the place is broken in these rooms by the fury of situations and words coined by Shakespeare half a millennium ago, words which constitute the substance of this festival. The English bard opened the Festival's first season with Richard III and, in 2012, the Festival showcased three of the English playwright's plays in its programming,[55] as well as works by Canadian authors Daniel MacIvor[56] and Paul Thompson[57] plus *Electra,* by Sophocle. There is also the acting, the festival having hosted the greatest names in the field since Alec Guinness, the first, has lent his considerable talents to the fledgling festival. One also comes to enjoy an often daring programming and staging, depending on the public, for this festival offers a variety of activities: master classes, lectures, and concerts. Finally, Stratford also has a significant component dedicated to classical music and, in this area also, it has become customary to receive the greatest: Glenn Gould, Claudio Arrau, Oscar Shumsky, repeatedly, but also Isaac Stern, Elisabeth Schwarzkopf, Lois Marshall, Benjamin Britten, Ella Fitzgerald, among many others.

---

55. Much Ado About Nothing; Henry V and Cyberline.
56. The Best Brothers.
57. Hirsch.

In the same vein of events primarily dedicated to the works of an established playwright, the Shaw Festival, created half a century ago in Niagara-on-the-Lake, shows primarily the works of George Bernard Shaw, of his contemporaries or of authors who situate their writings in the long period of his life (1856-1950). With 4 theaters totaling 1,724 seats, the festival produces 10 to 12 plays annually, offers nearly 800 performances in front of an audience which, in a single season, totals 300,000 people. Virginia Woolf, Pirandello, Oscar Wilde, Agatha Christie, Federico Garcia Lorca, Eugene O'Neill, Anton Chekhov, William Somerset Maugham, Georges Feydeau and Kurt Weill, among many others, were showcased, whether in their original versions or in adapted plays, next to their Canadian counterparts such as Michel Marc Bouchard and Michel Tremblay. A theater not without force, in accord with the spirit of Shaw; the man, in his time, having himself placed in his writings reformist and politically-incorrect ideas.

Both festivals have had to adjust to the diversity of Ontarian society. Stratford's took the initiative in 2005. Since then, its management has increased its orders for writers of diverse communities including those of the Black community, giving their due place to its playwrights and actors. Under pressure from famous authors, Shaw's had to answer a few challenging questions: "Does the festival actually have a policy to exclude people based on race?" Andrew Moodie, a prominent African-Canadian playwright and actor asked in 2008. The festival counters that even if the movement was slower than expected, the arrival of Jackie Maxwell to the post of artistic director in 2002 led to a policy of "redressing racial and gender imbalances".[58]

The International Festival of Authors and the Luminato Festival both belong to the category of great Ontarian cultural events.

The first celebrated its 32nd edition in 2011 by hosting 150 authors from 25 countries including India, Somalia, Denmark, Israel, the Democratic Republic of Congo, the Netherlands, France, Nigeria, Norway, the United States, Britain, Ireland, Scotland, Germany and Canada.[59] From HarbourFront where many of the festival's events are concentrated, these authors spread throughout the city to conduct workshops, readings, lectures, panel discussions, master classes. For two weeks, the city vibrates with the literatures of the world. Here, diversity is manifested in the writers' ori-

---

58. AJAIERA, J. "Shaw Festival urged to diversify lineup", *The Globe and Mail*, aout 13th 2008.
59. 90 Canadian authors participated in the 2011 edition of the *International Festival of Authors*.

gins, or in the dual nationality of many of them.[60] Those under 25 years of age have free access to the activities which, after its deployment in Toronto, moves its guests in 16 Ontarian cities.

Created more recently, Luminato is a wonderful cultural intrusion into urban life. Inaugurated in 2007, the festival has become a popular and original festivity. Luminato shows creations where you least expect them and preferably works in cultural encounters and reflect local diversity and the world. The 2011 edition has greeted such writers and actors in the Middle East and Chinese writers and artists, choreographers and dancers from India, celebrated the 150th anniversary of united Italy, showed the great works of Egyptian cinema, recreated the atmosphere of New York in the 50s and gave the floor to the craftsmen of *The New Yorker* magazine, presented K. D. Lang's first continental tour, displayed the sky through the works of famous photographers, presented an adaptation of *A Midsummer Night's Dream*, adapted by Tim Supple and performed by 30 actors from the Arab world and played Mahler's *5th symphony* by Toronto Symphony Orchestra. It put these creations in connection with each other in crossover performances often offered in public squares, large halls and other unpredictable places. Luminato has been called a cultural "tidal wave" unfurling on the city. Succeeding it is the Toronto Summer Music Festival, established in 2004, having since become an important meeting place of great music on the continent and in the world.

Belonging to a same intention, the Found in Translation festival illustrates, in an original way the diversity of the world and of Ontario. The invited authors have in common that they realized their works in a language other than their mother tongue. In 2010, the festival of authors having chosen French as their preferred language of expression over their own languages: Ying Chen, from China; Louis-Philippe Dalembert of Haiti, the Guinean Tierno Monénembo, Renaudot prize laureate, Laura Alcoba, of Argentina; Mustapha Kebir Ammi of Morocco and Russian Andrei Makine, Prix Goncourt and Medicis.

The CONTACT festival extends in images, these words festivals. In 2010, it brought together over a thousand photographers from here and abroad to exhibit their works in the cultural spaces of the city, 32 main exhibitions and 160 others. That year, artists explored the legacy of

---

60. Canada-Togo; Canada-Inde; Canada-États-Unis; Canada-Lettonie, Canada-Haïti, Canada-Royaume-Uni; Canada-Australie; Canada-Jamaïque; Canada-Thaïlande.

Marshall McLuhan and extended his views in three major installations, *The Mechanical Bride*, shown at the Museum of Contemporary Canadian Art, *The Brothel Without Walls* and *Through the Vanishing Point*, which have been shown at the University of Toronto Art Centre.

Finally, since we must choose, Nuit Blanche transforms the city, one October evening, into a large performance hall. Galleries, museums, libraries, theaters, public squares and halls of large buildings become places where we meet around works and original creations, modern and, necessarily, ephemeral. Lisa Rochon confessed her emotions every time during the Nuit Blanche.

Guy Mignault

It begins its 43rd edition, this 9 shows in 2011, against three in 2000, and sees his audience grow year after year. Here the French theater in Toronto! Molière, Gratien Gélinas, Marcel Dubé Michel Tremblay, are showing. Franco-Ontarians, Francophone recently moved here from Quebec and across the world, speaking Francophile or not the French language but who can follow the shows thanks to surtitles in English flock there, participating its financing and want more. Actors, playwrights and technicians from all sources. A show is in the process of writing and the feathers are held by three actresses of Haitian origin. Co-productions are negotiated with other theaters in Ontario and Quebec; tours in preparation.

Guy Mignault is a happy man. Came from Montreal 15 years ago, he has headed since this theater whose health is clearly thriving. He received us in the offices of the institution in the heart of Toronto. With eloquence, he recounts his adventures Toronto, two or three difficult years, escaped a threatened closure following a major intervention of French patrons of the city and entering a long cycle of consolidation and growth. The feeling also, and felt deeply, that Toronto's Francophones value their theater and show it unequivocally. "As soon as I got here, I felt this connection and it really touched me."

From French theatre, we widen the scope of our discussion to all of theatre. The answer comes right away:

> Toronto has become a phenomenal cultural city. There is a plethora of troops here, many theaters, major festivals such as Fringe, built on the model of the Edinburgh Festival of the same name, and Summer Works, more conventional and more stringent. There are also institutions that merely creations and showing the works of playwrights Ontario, take the Tarragon Theatre, for example. In this

area, Toronto is becoming one of the most exciting cities on the continent due course of the works shown but also the wider membership of a bigger crowd.

Take VI: Digital arts

They are five hundred, gathered for the fifth edition of the X-Summit organized by Interactive Ontario in late October 2011 to explore the emerging trends of new media linking generations and those who will prevail in the medium and long term. The organization brings together companies in the area annually and offers a platform for exchange, networking and partnership with Ontario's digital industries. Its partners include the Computer Animation Studios of Ontario CASO and OMDC. The language here is almost esoteric: interactive windows, interactive digital convergence, new applications for mobile platforms, trans-media invasions, transatlantic trans-media and other components of the current forms of digital world.

The sector is in major development. In a few short decades, the field has grown dramatically. Generations of the first users of the 70 remained faithful to this new medium of entertainment now mostly preferred by people in the age group 20-40 years. Accordingly, the video game market has reached global sales $56 billion in 2010, "more than twice the size of the recorded-music industry".[61]

Recognition of the field happened rather late in Toronto when compared to Montreal or Vancouver, but its recent development has been rapid and significant. In 2002-2003, companies specialized in the production of animation and digital special effects had 8,000 employees. They were 20,000, five years later.

Federated by Interactive Ontario, more than one hundred studios that just joined a big player, with the arrival in Toronto of the giant Ubisoft, ensuring the development of industry whose production reached $ 1.5 billion in 2008-2009. Of course, this movement primarily depends on entrepreneurs and creators of the field and their access to development capital that is rare for them. But it was also strongly supported by the Ontario government, directly or through its specialized agencies, including OMDC, has spared no effort to catch up: significant support to the summits in 2006 and again in 2008 bringing together all players in the field; generous policy

---

61. *The Economist*, "Video games: The serious business of fun", December 10th , 2011.

tax credit benefiting nearly 200 projects per year for ten years.[62] Finally, he benefited from the diversity of the city and its status as a crossroads of world cinema, the matters mentioned by Ubisoft executives to explain their decision to settle in the capital of Ontario.

Year after year, OMDC reports illustrate this progression. In 2008-09, we recall the existence of new instruments: the DocShop website accessed in less than a year by 8500 people, the program Assistance Initiative for the production of content display and the Fund for the export of interactive digital media content. The sector is too recent to draw some conclusions whatsoever about his future but to signify that it is for cultural and economic ambitions of Ontario.

CONCLUSION

How are we to measure the cultural dimension of a society at a particular time in its history? And in Ontarian society at the outset of the second decade of this 21st century?

The cultural offer is undoubtedly one of the preferred criteria; supply but also the response to this offer. However, as we have established throughout this chapter, the cultural offer is abundant, diversified and spread throughout the territory of the great province. If Toronto is undoubtedly the country's cultural capital and cultural showcase of Ontario, it is not, in this respect, a monopoly on the Ontario side. Other regions and cities in Ontario have also a significant cultural offer and are capable of quality initiatives, including through intelligent arrangements between institutions of the city and those of the province.

For 20 years, the cultural offer in Ontario has grown considerably in size and quality as a result of provincial and local governments' public policies and of private sector investment including corporations, foundations and associations of many kind dedicated to culture. Without an ambitious cultural policy, this enrichment would not have occurred. However, the Ontario government has established and funded at a good level that ambitious cultural policy, even in times of economic crisis, as we have shown, detailing the many levers it has established for its implementation. It did not hesitate to invest to reinforce some major initiatives in Ontario or attract major cultural events. This policy has led to the development of a true partnership public and private partnership, one based on specific

---

62. To favour Ubisoft's installation in Toronto, the provincial government spent $263 million.

goals, whose cross-investments are spectacular and transformed the cultural offer in Ontario.

This offer is also enriched as a result of major initiatives taken by individuals and groups discussed in this chapter and whose realized ambitions have had for effects the rebuilding of a large number of existing cultural institutions and the creation of new ones, to set up countless cultural events public, local, provincial or international. So are shown in full light and constantly, products and works of culture. In Ontario, culture is definitely out of its ghettos, were they the most prestigious, to spread in communities, to inspire and seduce them.

In the official literature, the promotion of the province and cities, development plans or redeployment of regions, districts and urban centers, the cultural dimension plays a significant and consistent role. This dimension is incorporated into the analysis, reflection, planning on society and its future, including economic. The trilogy gurus Ontario - innovation, creativity and productivity - includes culture as an essential element of their proposals. In short, culture has become a major component of Ontario's vision of growth and development. Born beliefs of some, this transition was facilitated by the success of their businesses that reveals in Toronto but also in parts of Ontario.

This passage is a considerable change in itself and because of the undeniable and strong support by Ontarians. Their massive participation, in millions, to cultural activities is well documented. But that which cannot be measured precisely is the deep commitment of Ontarians to this dimension of their collective life. In Toronto, the citizens rallied and forced the mayor to Ford postpone indefinitely his planned cuts in the budgets of the municipal library. This event is worth a few polls.

In our journey through the great province, many of our interlocutors in Toronto but also in London, Sudbury, Windsor, Niagara, Kingston and many other places mentioned their joy of living in a culturally vibrant community. They talked about as a major element of the quality of their lives.

The terms used by our partners deserve a clear reminder. For most of them "living in a culturally vibrant community" refers to the diversity of cultural offerings, that it shows the world's cultures, this mirror of reality in Ontario. Ontario's culture is defined by this reference.

The chemistry between the cultural offer and the response of Ontario has produced results. The Ontarian society is now at work with confidence and to realize his cultural project. In support of this ambition, it has quality human resources, designers, managers, publicists that bring together the same aspiration. It involves reinforcing existing cultural assets and to develop them and, in some cases, bring them to a high level of radiation as a successful TIFF.

The radiant center of Ontario's culture has a name, its identity and also creative horizon, and it is the same: diversity. In it are concentrated the idea of society, its constituent memories and shared hope. In it, is illuminated a large area for the deployment of all forms of cultural hybridization awaiting their realization and their exploration, painful or light. In this space, the concepts of majority and minority representation as a hierarchy and fade. Another representation of the common humanity emerges and there combine the personal destinies, the markers of various communities and the values shared by all Ontarians. Ontario's culture is its central object. Its creators have already begun to uncover it with his dreams, his fantasies, his truths and mirages. The Ontarian universal is inseparable from its constitutive diversity. It is its daily bread.

Show products and works of culture is one thing. Create them is another. The current state of culture in Ontario that we have traced throughout this chapter has shown that Ontario society became a society open to creation, a company that, in literature especially but not exclusively, countless designers from all walks of life, enjoying international exposure. The Quebec journalist Emilie Folie-Boivin evokes "the vibrant community of designers and artists who crash in Toronto's neighborhoods."[63] Lisa Rochon, Rita Davies, John Brotman have all our attention to this growing community and Guy Mignault told us about the Toronto theaters "that merely creations and show the works of playwrights Ontario".

I found a note jotted down while in Windsor in the beautiful museum of the city that had been devastated by the economic crisis. Its mayor, Eddie Francis has just summarized the calamitous consequences. The President of the Museum does not hide his concern, but insists that this house (the museum) is not a "patch" of community life and contribute to boosting the overall activity. I write in my notebook: "a cultural society." I'll write the same words again after my interview with Jane Pyper at the Toronto Public Library. She just won the battle of her life. The library system of the city, frequented by 72 per cent of Torontonians, will not be reduced. I note: "a cultural society." Such is the origin of the title of this chapter that our crossing of Ontario upheld at all times.

---

63. BOIVIN, É.F. " La surprise ou la découverte ", *Le Devoir*, december 4 th 2011.

EPILOGUE

THE IDEA OF CHANGE IS DOMINATING all societies in the world today, those whose power and influence are increasing, those who are seeing their historical position threatened by the current disruptions, and all the rest who are affected by the ongoing changes that are redefining the parameters of international relations. Ontarian society is no exception. It too is deeply involved in a major undertaking to reposition itself.

SOME HISTORICAL CHALLENGES

The success or failure of this undertaking will have an impact on Ontario's ability of maintaining a system of freedom, growth and solidarity that is one of the most accomplished in the world. Built over few generations, this system has attracted millions of men and women to join Ontarian society from all walks of life. Maintaining it would enable the influx of new citizens to continue in the coming years. It would also permit greater development of ways to manage diversity successfully, which has not been the case for many western societies deeply divided by their pluralism. And finally, it would allow better consolidation of a cultural life that has expanded tremendously in recent years.

These achievements were made possible by a sound economy, one of the most productive sub-national economies in the world. They were also made possible in recent years by an expansionist and active policy favouring investment in human resources, development of the education system at all levels, emphasis on research, innovation and creativity, establishment of an intelligent infrastructure, implementation of an ambitious, if controversial, green policy and support for cultural institutions and enterprises.

The success or failure of this undertaking also depends on the evolution of the Canadian political system as we know it and the policies that make it so unique. Not by maintaining the *status quo,* nor by clinging cautiously to the advances already made, but, based on solutions adapted to the needs of the times, by maintaining the equal opportunities for all Canadians made possible by creating and sharing wealth and focussing on the social dimensions of our collective and individual lives. Measured against the common ideals that define the aspirations of our fellow citizens—i.e., rights and freedoms, quality of life, advanced social net policies—the achievements of Ontarians and Canadians in general are impressive. It is well worth making a concerted, profound effort to safeguard these achievements.

A weaker Ontario would have a disastrous effect on these distinctive values, on Canada's economy, its role in the global economy and its negotiating power, and on the quality of life of Ontarians and all Canadians. In the present continental context, whether cross-Atlantic or global, our federation depends on strong regional economies. Advances made by one should not be made at the expense of the others! Ontario must be accommodated in the Canadian system, as some of its best thinkers assert: Ontario, Québec, the Western provinces and the Maritimes, nothing less, nothing more! This is the raison d'être of Canadian federalism, its original and current identity, its challenge and its promise.

The entities with whom we will have to negotiate in the coming years are all impressive in terms of their size and real or virtual economic strength: the European Union, India, China, Brazil, MERCOSUL, ASEAN, the United States and other countries such as Turkey and Indonesia. A war between the provinces due to a federal policy that is not committed to their collective success, ignoring their common interests and investing in one region to the detriment of the others, would lead inexorably to a weakening of the whole, on both levels, internally and externally. This is why we must hope for success in Ontario, which can and must parallel that of Western Canada, Québec and the Maritimes.

To succeed in passing from a player in the continental economy to a player in the global economy—a difficult and daunting transition—Ontario needs more leverage, which its successive governments have demanded for at least the past quarter-century. Current political conditions and opposing ideologies are creating tension between Ottawa and the provincial capitals. The work of the Mowat Centre is another matter. It demonstrates the obsolete nature of certain fundamental mechanisms of the federation still stuck in the 19th century and the harmful effects this can have on the growth and development of Ontarian society and more generally on the entire country today, at the beginning of the 21st century.

Without ideological blinkers limiting the vision of different ways of thinking and proposals, Ontario's efforts will first and foremost serve the interests of Ontario but will also be of major importance to its partners in the federation. Indeed, they are all faced with the same challenges and share, at least partly, the same needs. Finally, the nature of policies pursued by the federal government in its areas of jurisdiction may or may not conflict with the objectives of its federated members. The Harper government's lack of vision regarding Asia, which has improved only recently, illustrates this point. What can Ontario and the other provinces do to conquer markets in this new economic centre if the federal government does not include them in its vision? How can labour policy be redesigned to suit the new economic reality if Ottawa proceeds with a pan-Canadian vision that ignores the diversity of regional or provincial economies? How can federalism be practiced successfully in the face of all these pitfalls?

These are not theoretical questions.

The effort that Ontario and its partners in the federation must make to transform their economies is without precedent, given the cumulative effects of globalization and the current financial, economic and social crisis occurring in the United States.

The immediate future will be difficult. Globalization has seen the emergence of international competition that is expanding into new areas, including: the design and implementation of major projects on a planetary scale; the production of advanced technological goods; science in general and the mastery of space; health sciences; the development and application of artificial intelligence; the harnessing and use of new kinds of energy; global financial services; urban planning in this "Urban Millennium". The current crisis, for its part, has put an end to the kind of risk-free insurance that used to give Canadians privileged access to what used to be the world's top solvent market.

In light of world demand, the resources sector will play a primary role in the economic positioning of the country and certain provinces in the west will enjoy a privileged position in this new world. But, as we have shown previously, basing Canada's economic future solely on the natural resources sector would be a costly regression, both socially and economically. We must develop our natural resources but we must also maintain and develop a strong industrial sector, with the jobs and research it supports; we must encourage the development of an advanced technological products sector, an indispensable factor in this new century; and we must ensure a strong services sector, including financial services whose added value will allow us to sustain our international competitiveness. For Ontario, like the rest of Canada, these are historic challenges.

CONSIDERABLE RESOURCES

To tackle these major undertakings competitively and implement them successfully, Ontarian society has considerable resources to draw upon, which we have referred to throughout this work:

- A multiethnic, multicultural and multilingual diversity which is a microcosm of the world and gives access to valuable assets not only for all kinds of international undertakings in this era of diasporas but also for strengthening our capacity for innovation.

- A range of policies based on modern development objectives that the current Ontario government has maintained until 2012 throughout these uncertain times in pursuit of fundamental goals: maintaining a balance between social and economic needs and preparing for the future by maintaining public policies and targeted investments.

- A cultural positioning not yet fully achieved but whose recent development has made Ontario one of the most attractive societies in the continent and Toronto a centre of cultural influence. There is no question that culture is now an integral aspect of how Ontarians think of themselves and is a significant factor in their identity, ambitions and interests.

Ontario can also benefit from the impressive number of private and public think tanks focusing on innovation, creativity and productivity and committed to an essential objective: thinking differently about the future.

Ontarian society has finally found a balance between its traditional communities and those who, though not without roots in the past, have not yet been fully defined. Speaking of Toronto, Lisa Rochon observed that "here there is a lightness thanks to the absence of historical weight. Toronto is not imprisoned by or in its history". This assessment can be extended to all of Ontarian society. In a certain sense it is always a society of pioneers, a condition that perhaps accounts for such an uninterrupted influx of new citizens arriving from the four corners of the Earth.

Despite the current uncertainties, Ontarian society can draw from its recent history a justifiable optimism thanks to its remarkable accomplishments. Considerable though they may be, these resources will be of little use if the economies of the Atlantic zone, or the entire world, experience severe contractions in the years ahead. They will be of little use if the province's economy flaw by large public deficit and a too conservative private sector cannot reverberate again and produce development and wealth. Those are defiant challenges.

AN ADVANCED SOCIETY

How to conclude this long journey through Ontario and the countless hours of visit and interviews with Ontarians from all walks of life that we have undertaken over the past three years?

The diversity of the population amazed us throughout our journey; it was the most immediate impression of Ontarian society. As we have shown, it comes with some challenges. At the same time, the sheer number of new Ontarians is so great, and their economic, social and cultural influence so important, that trying to explain away their differences is literally unthinkable. This huge influence has led the provincial government, as well as those of large population centres, to provide multilingual information and services on a scale not seen elsewhere in Canada and perhaps in North America. There is also a sensitivity to diversity that places Ontario at the cutting edge of western society in the pragmatic management of the fresh challenges that arise from this pluralism. Finally, the multifaceted nature of this diversity shields the province from majority-minority showdowns and the acrimony that these can cause. Hence the atmosphere of normalcy rather than forced tolerance that arises from Ontarian coexistence.

These are not speculative findings: We have taken into account the work of many think-tanks and specialized institutions, including universities, concerning the diversity of Ontario. But we have also met with many diverse communities in Toronto and elsewhere in the province, and have directly engaged their leaders, their spokespeople and their artists. Our questions were received differently in different communities: some voiced complaints, particularly about their reception in the job market, access to professional organizations, advancement opportunities in private companies, and treatment in the media. But for the most part, their experiences were similar.

Ontario society is not ethnically segregated, nor does it want for accommodation among its diverse communities, although some are worried about the risk of ghettoization. Its diversity comes without apologies for differences and without the pressure to conform. How to interpret the role of minorities in a society where, taken together, they constitute a potential majority? If diversity is a patent fact of Ontarian society, it is also a shared value and one that is proudly worn. This is shown in public policy that actively seeks to engage a diverse population, in institutions that account for the diversity of their clientele, and in the ever-increasing public celebrations of cultural diversity. It is also revealed by a re-examination of historical discourse that embraces multifaceted memories of the past. The traditional main thread of the province's history—its British dimension—is not denied; however, it is substantially enriched by the experiences and contributions of diverse communities that make up Ontario society today. Without having sought or desired it, fully half of our respondents, generally those in positions of authority, were born outside Ontario.

The interviewees all expressed their views on the specific sites of integration: schools, first and foremost; workplaces and professional associations; the well-developed sense of civil society in this province; consumerism; shared successes and accomplishments; interethnic marriages and partnerships. But also, the universal rule of law and the freedoms it affords. No one knows precisely the result of this transformation. But a synthesis has developed in Ontario society in terms of its far-reaching roots, with enormous consequences for civilization. This post-multiculturalism belongs to Ontario as a constitutive reality, tangible and irreversible. The Ontarian identity has been reinvented as a unique balance between unity and diversity that promises to bring all Ontarians together around shared goals, tangible and intangible.

Examining the vast territory of the province, the acute interest of Ontarians in their shared past and future were also striking. This relatively young society is intensely faithful to its heritage, which is celebrated, protected, and promoted. This commitment is palpable not only in Toronto—after years of neglect—but also in London, Kingston, Oakville, Hamilton, Mississauga, Kitchener, Sudbury. It encompasses and enriches the entire province.

But as we have noted, this vast constellation of diverse groups, some united by community influence, others by business relationships, university ties, or shared social backgrounds, craves a way forward to a common future.

Our investigation into the future of the province clarifies the values that are present today in Ontario society: a sense of control of a shared destiny; a capacity for dialogue among diverse societal elements; a critical capacity that is exercised openly; a strong desire to find ways to maintain growth and development, living standards and investment that make Ontario's economic success "the fundamental metaphor in its history," in the words of John Ibbitson.

In our journey through Ontario, we also saw a society that, in a few critical decades, has embraced culture as a major element of its development, its cohesion, its identity. Our respondents agreed that this process is one of the most valuable in Ontario society, as a salutary counterweight to its materialism. The cultural self-affirmation we have observed and documented are go far beyond the institutional gains that, in Toronto and throughout the province, have transformed existing cultural hubs and created new ones where they were lacking. It also concerns the gradual rise of a cultural infrastructure in a society that was formerly known as a massive consumer of foreign cultural products. The true significance of this relates to Ontarians' collective realization of their shared destiny, and their support for the policies and initiatives that make this possible. Many of our respondents framed the development of Ontario diversity not as a simple cause-effect relationship, but rather as a progressive embrace of shared physical and cultural environments. For example, the Caribana Festival started as a big, noisy, colourful, but exclusive Caribbean party; but over time it has developed into an event that is shared by all elements of society. Culture is always hungry for diversity, and this is nowhere more evident than in Ontario.

Cultural events have become one of Ontario's most visible resources, and have gradually spread to all of its constituent cultures and their artists, in literature, photography, museums, music and cinema. The province's stated ambition of becoming a major nexus of world culture is certainly a work in progress, but by transforming and internationalizing its cultural offerings, Ontario and its capital are home to two complementary movements: one makes the world's cultures available to Ontarians; the other showcases Ontario, and especially its capital, throughout the world.

Three issues are at the heart of this book: the changing demographics of Ontario that make it one of the most diverse societies on the planet, and how to manage this diversity; the transformation of its economy as a result of the new world order; and the changing relationship between its society and culture.

JEAN-LOUIS ROY

Our dialogue with Ontarians gave us a glimpse of this new reality, but whatever answers we have found are of course incomplete and debatable; this is a story that is very much still being told.

This dialogue has allowed us to better understand a society that is among the world's most diverse and most advanced, in terms of freedom, material well-being, and quality of life. It also provided insight into Ontarians' collective push to consolidate this status. It allowed us to engage with people whose hard work and achievements reminded us over and over again of the words of Northrop Frye in *The Educated Imagination*, one of the great works of Ontarian literature:

> The world you want to live in is a human world, not an objective one: it's not an environment but a home; it's not the world you see but the world you build out of what you see.[1]

---

1. Frye, *The Educated Imagination, op. cit.,* p.5.

242

SELECTED BIBLIOGRAPHY

ABEL, K.M. (2006) *Changing places, History, Community, and Identity in North-Eastern Ontario*. Toronto: McGill-Queen's University Press.

ABELLA, I. & Troper, H. (2000) *None is Too Many, Canada and the Jews of Europe, 1933-1948*. Toronto: Key Porter.

ABU-LABAN, B. (1981) "The Canadian Muslim Community: The need for a new survival "*in The Muslim community in North America*. Edmonton: University of Alberta Press.

ALEXANDER, L. M. (2006) *Go to school, you're a little black boy*. Toronto: Dundurn Press.

ARCHIVES PUBLIQUES DE L'ONTARIO. (2003) *Documenting a Province. The Archives of Ontario at 100. Chronique d'une province. Le centenaire des Archives publiques de l'Ontario*. Toronto: Queen's Printer for Ontario.

ARTHUR, E. (2003) *Toronto, No mean city*. Toronto: University of Toronto Press.

ATWOOD, M. (2004) *Moving targets: Writing with Intent, 1982-2004*. Toronto: House of Anansi Press.
(1972) *Survival: A thematic guide to Canadian literature*. Toronto: House of Anansi Press.

BAROU, J. (2007) *La planète des migrants. Circulations migratoires et constitutions de diasporas à l'aube du XXIe siècle*. Grenoble: Presses Universitaires de Grenoble.

BENJAMIN, D. (1856) *A North-Side view of Slavery. The Refugee: or the Narratives of Fugitive Slave in Canada, related by Themselves, with an Account of the History and Conditions of the Colored Population of Upper Canada*. Boston: John P. Jewett and Company.

BODE, C. (1996) *La Nuit du rédacteur*. Ottawa : Éditions Le Nordir.

BOILY, F. (2007) *Stephen Harper : De l'École de Calgary au Parti conservateur : les nouveaux visages du conservatisme canadien*. Québec : Presse de l'Université Laval.

BOUDREAU, F. & als. (1995) *La francophonie ontarienne : bilan, perspective et recherche*. Hearst : le Nordir.

BOURAOUI, H. (1999) *Ainsi parle la Tour CN*. Ottawa : Éditions l'Interligne.

BOYDEN, J. (2008) *Là-haut vers le Nord*. Paris : Albin Michel.
(2009) *Born with a Tooth*. Toronto: Cormorant Books.

BRAND, D. (2005) *What we all long for*. Toronto: Knopf.

BROWN, R. (2007) *Unusual things to see in Ontario*. Erin: The Boston Mills Press.

BROWNE, K. (2007) *Bold visions: the architecture of the Royal Ontario Museum*. Toronto: ROM Media.

CALLAGAN, M. (1970) *Strange Fugitive*. Vermont & Tokyo: Charles E. Tuttle company Inc.
(2001) *The New Yorker stories*. Toronto: Exile Editions limited.
(2008) *A Literary life*. Holstein: Exile Editions Ltd.

CANADIAN PARENTS FOR FRENCH. (2008) *French second language education in Ontario, Report and recommendations to the Ontario minister of education*. Mississauga: Canadian parents for French.

CARPENTER, T. (1990) *Queen's. The First One Hundred and Fifty Years*. Newburg: Hedgehog Productions.

CENTRE FRANCOPHONE DE TORONTO. (2008) *Annuaire des ressources francophones*. Toronto : Centre francophone de Toronto.

CHAMBRE DE COMMERCE DU CANADA. (2009) *Perspectives économiques de 2010 : sur la voie de la relance*. Ottawa : Chambre de commerce du Canada.

CHINESE CANADIAN NATIONAL COUNCIL. (2007) *Upping the Antiracism: Chinese Canadian Youth against Racism*. Toronto: Chinese Canadian National Council.

CITOYENNETÉ ET IMMIGRATION CANADA, *Découvrir le Canada : Les droits et responsabilités liés à la citoyenneté*.

CIVICACTION. (2011) *Breaking Boundaries: Time to Think and Act Like a Region*. Toronto: CivicAction.

CLARKE, A. (2008) *More*. Toronto: Thomas Allen Publishers.

CLARKSON, A. (2008) *Heart Matters*. Toronto: Penguin Books.

COADY, L. (2007) *The Anansi Reader, Forty years of very good books*. Toronto: House of Anansi Press.

COHEN, A. (2007) *The Unfinished Canadian: the people we are*. Toronto: McClelland & Stewart Ltd.

COMMISSARIAT AUX SERVICES EN FRANÇAIS DE L'ONTARIO. (2008) *Premier Rapport annuel du Commissariat aux services en français,* Ontario : Ouvrir la voie.
(2009) *Rapport spécial sur la planification des services de santé en français*. Ontario : Imprimeur de la Reine pour l'Ontario.

COMMISSION ONTARIENNE DES DROITS DE LA PERSONNE. (2003) *Un prix trop élevé : les coûts humains du profilage racial*. Toronto : Commission ontarienne des droits de la personne.

CONSEIL DES ARTS DE L'ONTARIO. (2011) *Rapport annuel et liste des subventions*. Toronto : Conseil des Arts de l'Ontario.

CONSEIL DES SCIENCES, DE LA TECHNOLOGIE ET DE L'INNOVATION DU CANADA. (2011) *De l'imagination à l'innovation : le parcours du Canada vers la prospérité*. Ottawa : Gouvernement du Canada.

CORBEIL, J.P. & als. (2006) *Les minorités prennent la parole : résultats de l'Enquête sur la vitalité des minorités de langue officielle*. Ottawa : Statistiques Canada.

CORBEIL, J.P. & Christine, B. (2007) *Le portrait linguistique en évolution, recensement de 2006 : résultats.* Ottawa: Statistiques Canada.

COOK, R. (2005) *Watching Quebec, selected essays.* Kingston and Montreal: Mc Gill-Queen's University press.

COOPER, S. (2011) *Ride the wave, Taking control in a Turbulent Financial Age.* Toronto: Financial Times - Prentice Hall.

CREATIVE CAPITAL ADVISORY COUNCIL. (2011) *Creative Capital Gains: An Action Plan for Toronto.* Toronto: Creative Capital Advisory Council.

CROWLEY, B. L. (2009) *Fearful symmetry: the fall and rise of Canada's founding values.* Toronto: Key Porter Books.

DABYDEEN, C. (1987) *A shapely fire: Changing the Literacy Landscape.* Oakville: Mosaic Press.

DEAN, W.G. (1969) *Economic Atlas of Ontario - Atlas économique de l'Ontario.* Toronto: University of Toronto Press.

DEMARIA, Harney N. (1999) *Eh, Paesan! Being Italian in Toronto.* Toronto: University of Torronto Press.

DENNIS, R. (1989) *A Concise History of Canadian Painting.* London: Oxford University Press, 3rd Edition.

DI GIOVANNI, C.M. (2006) *Italian Canadian Voices: A Literary Anthology, 1946-2004,* Oakville: Mosaic Press.

DIVERSITY INSTITUTE (2011) *Diversity counts 3.* Toronto: Ryerson University Press.

EXPORTATION DÉVELOPPEMENT CANADA. (2011) *Les dividendes de la diversification, Prévisions à l'exportation.* Ottawa : Exportation Développement Canada.

FRAZER, G. (2001) *Vous m'intéressez.* Montréal : Boréal.

FROST, K.S., Bryan, W., Neary, H.B. & Frederick, H.A. (2009) *Ontario's African-Canadian Heritage.* Toronto: Dundurn Press.

FRYE, N. (1963) *The Educated Imagination.* Toronto: House of Anansi Press. (1980) *Across the River and out of the Trees in the Arts in Canada: the last Fifty Years.* Toronto: University of Toronto Press.

GERVAIS, G. (1999) *L'histoire de l'Ontario français (1610-1997), Francophonies minoritaires au Canada — L'état des lieux.* Moncton: Éditions d'Acadie.

GODARD, B. (2008) *Canadian Literature at the crossroads of language and Culture.* Edmonton: Newest press.

GOH, C.H. (2002) *Beyond the Dance, a Ballerina's Life.* Toronto: Tundra Book.

GOUVERNEMENT DE L'ONTARIO, ministère des finances. (2009) *Budget de l'Ontario 2009.* Toronto : Imprimeur de la Reine pour l'Ontario. (2002) *Loi sur les services en français, Lois refondues de l'Ontario de 1990.* Toronto : Imprimeur de la Reine pour l'Ontario.

GOUVERNEMENT DE L'ONTARIO ET FONDATION TRILLIUM. (2010) *Le profil de la communauté francophone de l'Ontario.* Toronto : Imprimeur de la Reine pour l'Ontario.

GREEN, N. (2007) *Les politiques de départ.* Paris: Éditions de l'Éhess.

GRIFFITHS, R. (2008) *Canada in 2020.* Toronto: Key Porter Books.

(2008) *American Myths: What Canadians think they know about the United States?* Toronto: Key Porter Books.

HARBER, R.J. (2010) *Go Canada, The Coming Boom in the Toronto Stock Market & How to profit from it.* Bolton: Feen Publishing Company limited.

HILLMER, N. & GRANATSTEIN, J. L. (2006) *The Land Newly Found: Eyewitness Accounts of the Canadian Immigrant Experience.* Toronto: Thomas Allen Publishers.

HOLDEN, M. (2010) *Activités de commerce et d'investissement du Canada. Le Canada et les États-Unis.* Ottawa : Bibliothèque du Parlement.

Hood, Mc. (1967) *Oshawa, Canada's Motor City.* Oshawa: McLaughlin Public Library.

IBBITSON, J. (2001) *Loyal no more: Ontario's Struggle for a Separate Destiny.* Toronto: Harper Collins.
(2005) *The Polite Revolution.* Toronto: McClelland & Stewart.

HOOLBOOM, M. (2009) *Practical Dreamers. Conversations with movie Artists.* Toronto: Coach House.

INNIS, H.A. (2007) *Empire and Communications.* Toronto: Dundurn press.

INSTITUTE FOR COMPETITIVENESS AND PROSPERITY. (2009) *Canada's innovation imperative, Report on Canada.* Toronto: Institute for Competitiveness and Prosperity.

JACOBS, J. (2008) " The ecstasy of Saint Jane subtitled: Toronto, in the midst of becoming, learns to embrace risk, variety and complexity ", in *Azure magazine.*

KEITH, W.J. (2006) *Canadian literature in English, volumes one and two.* Erin: The Porcupine's Quill.

KEITH, W.J. & SHEK, B.Z. (1980) *The Arts in Canada, the Last Fifty Years.* Toronto: University of Toronto Press.

KERRY, P. (2008) *The story of four Canadians tortured in the name of fighting terror.* Toronto: Viking Canada.

KETTANI, A.M. (1986) *Muslim Minorities in the World Today.* London: Mansell.

KILBOURN, W. & CHRIST, R. (1977) *Toronto.* Toronto: McClelland & Stewart.

KING, M. (Sans date) *Le Canada et la Guerre.* Montréal: Bernard Valiquette.

KNEEBONE, R. (2008) *National stabilization Policy and its implication for Western Canada.* Calgary: Canada West Foundation.

KNOWLES, V. (1997) *Strangers at our Gates: Canadian Immigration and Immigration Policy, 1540-1997.* Toronto: Dundurn press.

LABRIE, N. et Gilles, F. (1999) *L'enjeu de la langue en Ontario français*. Sudbury: Prises de paroles.

LANDON, F. (1951) *Ontario's African-Canadian heritage: collected writings*. London: London Free Press.

LAPIERRE, A. (1981) *Toponymie française en Ontario*. Montréal : Éditions Études vivantes.

LECLAIR, D. (2000) *Toronto, je t'aime*. Ottawa : Édition du Vermillion.

LOPES, S. (2011) *Charting prosperity: practical Ideas for a stronger Canada*. Toronto: Maytree.

LYOTARD, J.F. (1979) *La condition postmoderne*. Paris : Les Éditions de Minuit.

MACBRIDE, J. & Alana W. (2005) *Utopia towards a new Toronto*. Toronto: Coach House books.

MACGREGOR, R. (2007) *Canadians: a portrait of a country and its people*. Toronto: Penguin Canada.

MACLENNAN, H. (1961) *Seven Rivers of Canada*. Toronto: Macmillan Co.

MAHARAJ, R. (2010) *The Amazing Absorbing Boy*. Toronto: Knopf.

MAHBUBANI, K. (2008) *The New Asian Hemisphere*. New York: Public Affairs.

MATTHEW, M. & MATHIEWS, J. Scott. (2010) *The New Ontario. The Shifting Attitudes of Ontarians towards the Federation*. Toronto: Mowat Centre for Policy Innovation.

MARTEL, F. (2006) *De la culture en Amérique*. Paris : Gallimard.
(2010) *Mainstream, Enquête sur cette culture qui plaît à tout le monde*. Paris : Flammarion.

MARTIN PROSPERITY INSTITUTE. (2009) *Exploiter les possibilités offertes par une plus grande coopération économique entre l'Ontario et le Québec*. Toronto: Martin Prosperity Institute.

MARTIN, R.L. (2009) *Ontario in the creative age*. Toronto: Rotman School of Management, University of Toronto.
(2011) *Fixing the Game*. Boston: Harvard Business Press.

MCKILLOP, A. B. (2008) *Pierre Berton: A Biography*. Toronto: McClelland & Stewart.

MCCLELLAND, M. & Stewart G. (2007) *Concrete Toronto: a guidebook to concrete architecture from the fifties to the seventies*. Toronto: Coach House Books and E.R.A architects.

MCLUHAN, M. (2008) The *Gutenberg galaxy*. Toronto: University of Toronto press.

McQueen, R. (2010) *Blackberry*. Toronto: Key porter books.

MELNYK, G. (2008) *The Young, the Restless and the Dead: Interviews with Canadian Fimmakers*. Waterloo: Laurier University Press.

MIKA, N. & Elma. (1985) *The shaping of Ontario. From Exploration to Confederation.* Belleville: Mika Publishing Company.

MOFFETT, S. (1972) *The Americanization of Canada.* Toronto: University of Toronto Press.

MOLDOVEANU, M. & MARTIN, R.L. (2010) *Diaminds: Decoding the Mental Habits of Successful Thinkers.* Toronto: University of Toronto Press.

MONTIGNY, E.A. & Lori, C. (2000) *Ontario since confederation, A reader.* Toronto: University of Toronto press.

MORRIS, D. & KRAUTER, J.F. (1971) *The other Canadians, profiles of six minorities.* Toronto: Methuen publications.

NEIL, B. (1995) *Le marché aux illusions : la méprise du multiculturalisme.* Montréal : Boréal.

OCDE, (1997) *Le monde en 2020 : vers une nouvelle ère mondiale.* Paris : OCDE.
(1998) *La croissance et la compétitivité dans la nouvelle économie mondiale.* Paris : OCDE.
(2000) *La société créatrice du XXIe siècle.* Paris : OCDE.
(2010) *Perspectives du développement mondial 2010, Le basculement de la richesse.* Paris : OCDE.

ONDAATJE, M. (1995) *Canadian stories: FROM INK LAKE.* Toronto: Vintage.
(1996) *In the skin of a lion.* Toronto: Vintage.

ONTARIO HUMAN RIGHTS COMMISSION (2004) *Paying the Price: The human cost of Racial profiling.* Toronto: Inquiry Report.

PACI, F.G. (1978) *The Italians.* Toronto: Oberon Press.
(2003) *Essays on his works.* Toronto: Guernica Editions Inc.

PAIKIN, S. (2006) *Public triumph private tragedy, the double life of John P. Robarts.* Toronto: Penguin Books.

PARAMESWARAN, U. (1990) *The Door I Shut Behind Me, Selected Fiction, Poetry and Drama.* Madras: Affiliated East-West Press.

PETERBOROUGH. (1967) *Land of shining waters.* Peterborough: University of Toronto Press.

PITTS, G. (2008) *Stampede! The Rise of the West and Canada's New Power Elite.* Toronto: Key Porter Books.

PRICE WATERHOUSE COOPER. (2011) *La production mondiale automobile dopée par les pays émergents,* Price Waterhouse Cooper.

ROACH, R. (2010) *State of the West 2010: Western Canadian Demographic and Economic Trends.* Calgary: Canada West Foundation.

REDHILL, M. (2006) Consolation. Toronto: Doubleday Canada.

ROBERTS, J.M. (1999) *The Penguin History of the Twentieth Century.* New York: Penguin Books.

ROCHON, L. (2005) *Up North. Where Canada's Architecture Meets the Land.* Toronto: Key Porter Books Limited.

ROSENBLUM, R. (2008) *Once.* Toronto: Biblioasis.

ROY, J.L. (2003) *Technologies et géopolitique à l'aube du XXI* siècle.* Montréal : Hurtubise HMH.
(2008) *Quel avenir pour la langue française? Francophonie et concurrence culturelle au XXI* siècle.* Montréal : Hurtubise HMH.
(1978) *Le débat constitutionnel Québec-Canada, 1960-1976.* Montréal : Leméac.

RYERSON UNIVERSITY'S DIVERSITY INSTITUTE SCHOOL OF MANAGEMENT. (2010) *Diversecity Counts: A Snapshot of Diverse Leadership in the GTA,* Toronto: Ryerson University's Diversity Institute School of Management.

SAUL, J.R. (2009) *Mon pays métis.* Montréal : Boréal.

SAUL, J.R., Dubuc, A., Erasmus G. (2002) *The Lafontaine-Baldwin lectures: A dialogue on Democracy in Canada.* Toronto : Penguin Canada.

SANTUR, H.G. (2010) *Something remains.* Toronto: Dundurn.

SCHACHTER, D. (2011) *The Cultural Intelligence Difference.* New York: Amacom.

SCHLESINGER, A.M. (1993) *La désunion de l'Amérique.* Paris : Nouveaux Horizons.

SELVADURAI, S. (2004) *Story-wallah! A celebration of South Asian fiction.* Toronto: Thomas Allen Publishers.
(2005) *Story-Wallah:Short Fiction from South Asian Writers.* New York: Houghton Mifflin Company.

SIMPSON, J. (2000) *Star-spangled Canadians, Canadians living the American dream.* Toronto: Harper Collins.

SINGH, K. Narwar (2005) *The Argument for India.* The Inaugural India lecture: The News Service. Rhodes Islands: Brown University.

SMART, T. (1990) *The collection, London Canada.* London: London Regional Art and Historical Museum.

SUGUNASIRI, S. (1994) *the Whistling Thorn: an anthology of South Asian Canadian Fiction.* Oakville : Mosaic Press.

SYLVESTRE, P.F. (2005) : *L'Ontario français au jour le jour, 1 384* éphémérides de 1610 à nos jours. Toronto : éditions du Gref.
(2007) *Toronto s'écrit. La ville Reine dans notre littérature.* Toronto : Éditions du Gref.
(2010) *Cent ans de leadership Franco-Ontarien.* Ottawa : les éditions David.

THE BOSTON CONSULTING GROUP, Toronto Financial Services Working Group (2009) *Partnership and Action: Mobilizing Toronto's Financial Sector for Global Advantage, an Action Plan.* Toronto: The Boston Consulting Group, Inc.

THE CANADIAN ETHNIC JOURNALISTS' AND WRITERS' CLUB. (1986) *Mosaic in Media I, Selected Works of Ethnic Journalists and Writers.* Toronto: the Canadian Ethnic Journalists' and Writers' Club.

THE CANADIAN ETHNIC JOURNALISTS' AND WRITERS' CLUB. (2004) *Mosaic in Media II, An ethnic anthology, a fresh perspective.* Toronto: The Canadian Ethnic Journalists' and Writers' Club.

THE CONFERENCE BOARD OF CANADA. (2009) *How Canada Performs.* Toronto: The Conference Board of Canada.
(2011) *Provincial Outlook: Long term Economic Forecast.* Toronto: The Conference Board of Canada.
(2010) *Immigrants as Innovators. Boosting Canada's Global Competitiveness.* Toronto: The Conference Board of Canada.

THE UNITED EMPIRE LOYALISTS ASSOCIATON OF CANADA. (1934) *Loyal she remains: A pictorial history of Ontario.* Toronto: The United Empire Loyalists Associaton of Canada.

TRAD, K. (2007) *Les caractéristiques du migrant interprovincial au Canada*, Mémoire de maîtrise. Montréal : Université de Montréal.

TRUDEAU, P.E. (1967) *Le fédéralisme et la société canadienne française.* Montréal : Éditions HMH.

VACHON, A. ; CHABOT, V. & Desrosiers, A. (1982) *Rêves d'empire, le Canada avant1700.* Ottawa : Archives publiques Canada.

VÉDRINE, H. (2007) *Rapport pour le président de la République sur la France et la mondialisation.* Paris: Fayard.

WAITE, P.B. (1975) *Macdonald, His Life and World.* Toronto: McGraw-Hill Ryerson Limited.

WATERFRONTORONTO (2003) *AnnualReport: 02-03.*
Toronto: Waterfrontoronto.
(2011) *Management Report,* 2010-2011. Toronto: Waterfrontoronto.

WINKS, R.W. (1997) *The Blacks in Canada: a long history,* 2nd Edition, Montreal & Kingston Carleton Library Series 192: McGill-Queen's University Press.

WRIGHT, J.V. (1981) *La préhistoire de l'Ontario.* Ottawa : Musée national de l'Homme.

WRIGHT, J. & Darrell, B.(2009) *We know what you're thinking: From Dollars to Donuts-Canada's premiere pollsters reveal what Canadians think and why.* Toronto: Harper Collins.

YOUNG, P. (2005) *Canadian Obsessions: A Century of National Preoccupations, as Seen by Maclean's.* Vancouver: Douglas & McIntyre Ltd.

PUBLICATIONS CITED

Bloomberg Business Week
Cityspace
Courrier International
Expansion
Financial times
Foreign Affairs
India Abroad
La presse
Le Droit
Le Métropolitain
Le Monde
Le Point
Les Affaires
Maclean Magazine
Revue du Nouvel Ontario
The Economist
The Globe and Mail
The Magazine of the Rotman School of Management
The National Post
The New York Times
Toronto Star
University of Toronto Quaterly
Wall Street Journal